Globalizing Education Policy

In what ways have the processes of globalization reshaped the educational policy terrain?

How might we analyse education policies located within this new terrain, which is at once local, national, regional and global?

Over the past two decades, educational systems throughout the world have undergone significant changes as systems continue to interpret and respond to the ever-changing economic, social and political contexts within which education takes place. Educational policies have been deeply affected by these developments, as national governments have sought to realign their educational priorities to what they perceive to be the imperatives of globalization.

In *Globalizing Education Policy*, the authors explore the key global drivers of policy change in education and suggest that these do not operate in the same way in all nation-states. They examine the transformative effects of globalization on the discursive terrain within which educational policies are developed and enacted, arguing that this terrain is increasingly informed by a range of neo-liberal precepts which have fundamentally changed the ways in which we think about educational governance. They also suggest that whilst in some countries these precepts are resisted, to some extent, they have nonetheless become hegemonic. The book provides an overview of some critical issues in educational policy to which this hegemonic view of globalization has given rise, including:

- devolution and decentralization
- new forms of governance
- the balance between public and private funding of education
- access and equity and the education of girls
- curriculum particularly with respect to the teaching of English language and technology
- pedagogies and high-stakes testing
- the global trade in education.

These issues are explored within the context of the major shifts in global processes and ideological discourses currently being negotiated by all countries. The book also outlines an approach to education policy analysis in an age of globalization and will be of interest to those studying globalization and education policy across the social sciences.

Fazal Rizvi is a Professor in the Department of Educational Policy Studies, University of Illinois at Urbana-Champaign, USA.

Bob Lingard is a Professorial Research Fellow in the School of Education, University of Queensland, Australia.

Globalizing Education Policy

Fazal Rizvi and Bob Lingard

LONDON AND NEW YORK

First published 2010
by Routledge
2 Park Square, Milton Park, Abingdon, Oxon OX14 4RN

Simultaneously published in the USA and Canada
by Routledge
270 Madison Avenue, New York, NY 10016

Reprinted 2010 (twice)

Routledge is an imprint of the Taylor & Francis Group, an informa business

Typeset in Garamond by Saxon Graphics Ltd, Derby
Printed and bound in Great Britain by
CPI Antony Rowe, Chippenham, Wiltshire

British Library Cataloguing in Publication Data
A catalogue record for this book is available from the British Library

Library of Congress Cataloging in Publication Data
Rizvi, Fazal, 1950-
Globalizing education policy / Fazal Rizvi and Bob Lingard.
p. cm.
Includes bibliographical references and index.
1. Education and state. 2. Education and globalization. I. Lingard, Bob.
II. Title.
LC71.R59 2009
379—dc22 2009016869

ISBN 10: 0-415-41625-6 (hbk)
ISBN 13: 978-0-415-41625-2 (hbk)

ISBN 10: 0-415-41627-2 (pbk)
ISBN 13: 978-0-415-41627-6 (pbk)

ISBN 10: 0-203-86739-4 (ebk)
ISBN 13: 978-0-203-86739-6 (ebk)

For Patricia Rizvi and Carolynn Lingard

Contents

Acknowledgements

We view this book as a sequel to a book we wrote more than 12 years ago, with Miriam Henry and Sandra Taylor. And although Miriam and Sandra have not collaborated on this book, it would not have been possible without the ringing in our ears of their voices and wisdom. This book has benefited greatly from the comments of our students at the University of Illinois at Urbana-Champaign in the United States, the University of Edinburgh in Scotland, the University of Sheffield in England and the University of Queensland in Australia. Fazal would like to thank his students in the Illinois programme in Global Studies in Education, particularly Jason Sparks, Laura Engel, David Rutkowski, Viviana Pitton, Rodrigo Britez, Esther Kim, Gabriela Walker, Ergin Balut, Daniel Taseema, Rushika Patel, James Thayer and Shivali Tukdeo. He would also like to acknowledge the support and wise counsel he has received from his Illinois colleagues: Michael Peters, Tina Besley, Nick Burbules, Linda Tabb, Nicole Lamers, Garret Gietzen, James Anderson, Walter Feinberg, Bill Cope, Mary Kalantzis, Jan Nedeveen Pieterse and Cameron McCarthy. Bob would like to thank the students in his policy classes at the Universities of Sheffield, Edinburgh and Queensland, as well as his recent doctoral students, especially Georgina Webb, Kentry Jn Pierre, Shaun Rawolle, Ian Hardy, Hazri bin Jamil, Farah Shaik and Sajid Ali and his colleagues at those universities. In particular, he would like to thank Shereen Benjamin, Sotiria Grek, Martin Lawn, Pamela Munn, Jenny Ozga, Lindsay Paterson, David Raffe, Sheila Riddell, Lyn Tett and Gaby Weiner at the University of Edinburgh, Wilf Carr, Jennifer Lavia, Jackie Marsh, Jon Nixon and Pat Sikes at Sheffield University and Martin Mills and Peter Renshaw at the University of Queensland. Our gratitude also goes to our friends at Routledge: Anna Clarkson, who unfailingly supported this project, even as we asked for extensions, and also Catherine Oakley, for her editorial support. Sincere thanks also to Glenda McGregor, who proofread various versions of the text, to Stephen Heimans who proofread the penultimate version of the book, to Ian Hextall who read the entire manuscript and commented on it, to Holly Chen and Minglin Li, who helped with the reference list, and to Rebecca Donohue who assisted with formatting. Finally this book is dedicated to Patricia Rizvi and Carolynn Lingard, who have tolerated and supported our lives as globally mobile academics.

Preface

In 1997, together with Miriam Henry and Sandra Taylor, we published a book on education policy studies called *Educational Policy and the Politics of Change*. The book was designed to examine the ways in which education policies are developed and can be analysed, within the broader context of the politics of change. We explored the ways in which particular interests were served by public policies in education, and suggested that educational policy analysis was an inherently political activity. We argued that through public policies the state laid out a framework which guided educational practices but did not wholly determine them. Education policies were articulated at various levels of specificities; some were merely symbolic, while others had more material consequences, such as the redistribution of resources or allocation of authority structures and value positions. Through public policies, the state expressed its value preferences, either as an expression of democratic choices of a community or in steering that community's expectations. But we insisted that just as policies embody particular values, so does their analysis.

Policy analysis, we maintained, served numerous purposes, from providing an environmental scan for the development of policy options to evaluating the effectiveness of particular policies. Much depends on the reasons for undertaking policy research, and on the terms of reference set. Sometimes a distinction is made between analysis *for* policy, which contributes to actual policy production, and analysis *of* policy, which is a more academic and critical activity. Academic research into the political processes of policy development, analysis *of* policy, is likely to differ markedly, for example, from consultancy work conducted to determine policy options or to hold particular institutions accountable, or from research conducted by policymakers located inside the educational bureaucracy, analysis *for* policy. The tasks allocated to policy analysts thus determine, to a significant extent, how the context in which the policy was developed is interpreted, the theoretical and methodological resources that are used, and the recommendations that are articulated. The location of the policy analyst is significant. Analysis conducted by the lone academic researcher, positioned within a university, is likely to adopt a different approach from someone working with a team of evaluators within an organization, such as a large bureaucracy. This is not to say that there are no general standards for assessing the quality of policy research, but simply to note that the nature of the analytical task undertaken, the location of the analysts and the perspective they bring to the task are not irrelevant to policy analysis. The question of positionality in policy analysis is thus of utmost importance.

In this book, we explore many of these issues in more depth. Our aim is to provide a new account of educational policy studies based on our experiences working with, and teaching about, educational policies over the past two decades, as well as the insights we have developed from our various research projects designed to examine the dramatic changes brought about by the processes of globalization and how they require rethinking education policy. In our previous book we included a chapter on globalization, and argued then that globalization had the potential to shift the broader context within which educational policies were developed and would therefore need to be analysed and taken account of in future educational policy studies. We noted that globalization has reconfigured the state and its authority in developing public policies, and that national and local policies are now linked to globalized educational policy discourses, pressures from international organizations and global policy networks, and globalization effects more generally. Ten years on, we now have a much better grasp of the global transformations, and how they demand new ways of conducting policy research in education. In this book, then, global processes lie at the centre of our attempts at providing a new introduction to the field of educational policy studies.

This introduction is informed not only by our scholarly engagement with the recent literature on globalization and educational policy, but also by our personal experiences of policy processes. In the mid-1990s both of us worked at the University of Queensland in Australia, while our colleagues Sandra Taylor and Miriam Henry taught educational policy at Queensland University of Technology. Given our experiences, the examples we used to discuss policy issues in education in our earlier book were mostly derived from Australia, even if we sought to generalize from them. Much has changed since that time. While both Sandra and Miriam have now left academic jobs, our careers have taken us to various parts of the world. This has helped us to 'internationalize' our understanding of policy processes, as we have had to engage with global processes on the one hand and historically embedded differences in policy practices on the other. We have come to realize that globalization cannot be viewed as a generalized phenomenon, but rather needs to be seen as a dynamic phenomenon expressed in particular histories and political configurations. Thus, while there are today global policy pressures and globalized policy discourses, these always manifest in vernacular ways, reflecting the varying cultures, histories and politics within different nations. We have also come to appreciate the importance of agency in the interpretation and negotiation of policy processes, and in policy effects.

The account of public policy in education we present in this book is therefore based on insights we have developed through the opportunities we both have had in working in different organizations in a number of countries. In the mid-1990s, Fazal was a member of Australia Council for the Arts, where he chaired a committee responsible for developing a policy on Arts for Multicultural Australia. This position enabled him to recognize how the development of national policies could not overlook policy developments taking place around the world; how globalization was producing intricate demographic profiles through immigration and the global mobility of cultural workers, which produced new policy challenges and opportunities for the arts; and that educational policies could not be easily separated from other policy domains such as those relating to economic and cultural matters. He began to see in new ways how global processes affected the cultural field in which education is located.

Towards the end of the 1990s, Fazal took up a position at RMIT University in Melbourne, Australia as a Pro-Vice-Chancellor, responsible for coordinating the vast array of international activities in which that university was involved. This gave him an opportunity not only to become familiar with the higher education policies of various Asian countries from which RMIT drew most of its 15,000 international students, but also to understand how globalization was placing new demands on universities, requiring them to work in an emerging global education market for their economic sustainability. This required them to renew their curriculum and pedagogy, in response to their changing demography and to the demands of transnational corporations for new kinds of global worker. In 2001, Fazal moved to the United States to take up an academic appointment at the University of Illinois at Urbana-Champaign, where he now directs its programme in Global Studies in Education. Living and working in the United States after September 11, he has come to realize that globalization does not represent a spatially and temporally static phenomenon, but that it can be transformed as a result of major world events, as well as by particular policy dictates of powerful nations such as the United States.

In the 1990s, Bob had the opportunity to work closely with the Department of Education in Queensland, where he directed a major research project designed to investigate how policies affected educational practice, and how they could be better articulated to ensure significant improvement in educational outcomes. The project produced a major report, proposing the concept of 'productive pedagogies', in order to challenge the dichotomy between state-mandated and locally-initiated educational reform. Later, Bob also chaired the Queensland Studies Authority, a statutory authority with responsibility for curriculum and assessment across all schools in the state of Queensland. These positions gave him an acute sense of the important social and cultural changes that are taking place in Queensland, as they are elsewhere – the policy responses to which require not only empirically grounded research to garner a better sense of how policy imperatives are interpreted and translated into practice, but also a normative commitment to use policy to steer education policy in the direction of democracy and justice. He is now convinced that empirical and normative aspects of educational policy cannot be easily separated because education is ultimately about a better moral order. Educational policy always sits at the intersection of the past, present and future, with the latter often expressed in policy texts as an imagined desired future.

Over the past few years, like Fazal, Bob too has worked outside Australia, first at the University of Sheffield in England and then at the University of Edinburgh in Scotland. At Sheffield, he directed an offshore doctoral programme in the Caribbean, working with students employed in a range of teaching, administrative, union and policymaking positions. This gave him a deeper appreciation of the ways in which globalization is interpreted and negotiated to develop and implement educational policies in developing countries; how policy processes operate in an uneven and unequal geo-political space, creating conditions that often extend global inequalities; and how historical traces of colonialism are not easily erased and are rearticulated in various post-colonial ways within the new configurations of a globalizing world. At Edinburgh, Bob's attention was drawn to issues surrounding an emergent European educational space, and how the European Commission represents a new transnational policy actor in Scottish education, with the capacity to steer policy priorities in education. His policy research has reaffirmed his conviction about the important role that transnational organizations such as the EU, OECD and UNESCO now play in forging educational policy at the level of national systems, and holding them accountable against international indicators and benchmarks of various kinds.

The insights we have developed as a result of our experiences, both as policy actors and researchers, and as a result of our engagement with the scholarly literature, are thus fundamental to the arguments developed in this book. We have drawn heavily on examples of policy processes in education from both of these sources of information and understanding. Our argument is that public policy in education is still largely made by national governments, but that the nature of the state is now rapidly changing. The state now represents a site increasingly influenced not only by transnational institutions, but also by global ideologies that constantly seek to steer the social imaginaries of policy actors everywhere, but in ways that are mediated by national traditions and local politics.

This book is intended as a general introduction to education policy studies, but from a particular perspective. It seeks to show how educational policy is becoming increasingly 'globalized' and how this requires new ways of analysing policies in ways that are 'deparochialized' – that is, they take seriously their global, postnational dimensions without ignoring the realities of the state. This requires developments in theoretical and methodological approaches to studying and researching education policy in an age of globalization dominated by a neoliberal social imaginary. During 2008 and into 2009, the global neoliberal order has been challenged in a number of ways, especially against the realization of its role in creating the global financial crisis that is now affecting all policy areas, education systems and nations. This crisis has given rise to the urgent task of negotiating a new social imaginary that not only deals with the economic and social consequences of the failures of neoliberalism, but begins also to consider new ways of conceiving education policy and practice.

Fazal Rizvi and Bob Lingard
January 2009

1 Conceptions of education policy

Introduction

Policy studies is a relatively recent field of academic endeavour. It emerged during the 1950s in mainly liberal democratic countries, where governments sought the resources of the social sciences to develop public policies, replacing earlier approaches that were largely intuitive and *ad hoc*. Fifty years later, policy studies has become an established field of study, central to the ways in which societies are now governed. Governments now employ a large number of policy experts to help them think through social problems, develop programmes and assess their effectiveness. Policy experts are also used to justify and promote political decisions, helping to steer social formations in particular directions. In this sense, policy studies as a field is inextricably linked to the processes of change. Especially in its more technical and bureaucratic forms, it has even come to replace politics, sidelining debates about values, shifting attention instead to matters of administrative dictates and directions.

In the early stages of its development, policy studies was grounded mostly in 'policy sciences', an approach developed by political scientists to enquire into the ways in which public policies were best developed, implemented and evaluated (de Leon and Danielle 2007). Policy studies thus largely addressed the needs of the state, helping it to develop its priorities and programmes and determine ways of ensuring their efficiency and effectiveness. Governments believed that the intractable problems they faced could only be solved through the rigorous application of research knowledge and techniques developed by social scientists. There thus emerged a so-called 'rationalist' approach to policy processes, which prescribed a number of determinate steps, from an analysis of the policy context and the elucidation of a range of policy options to the processes of policy selection, production, implementation and evaluation (Wagner 2007). In addition to providing information helpful to policy-makers, academic policy researchers were also interested in what governments did: how they negotiated various political interests, and more generally managed policy processes.

The rationalist approach to policy studies in liberal democratic countries was developed during a period when it was widely believed that government intervention was both desirable and necessary for solving social problems. It was widely assumed that increased expenditure on social programmes would not only enhance national economic performance, but would also ensure greater equality of opportunities, especially through various redistributive measures. This state activity, however, required reliable information and advice upon which to base decisions and create programmes. Governments thus turned to policy scientists to help them both create and promote policies and programmes. In response, political groups outside the state also began to embrace this approach, marshalling information to argue for particular policy preferences. This inevitably blurred the dividing line between policy analysts inside and outside government – between policy development and advocacy. As sources of policy advice multiplied, lobby and pressure groups came into existence, professing technical expertise that often masked their particular interests (Knoepfel *et al.* 2007).

During the 1980s, however, the rationalist approach to policy studies began to lose popularity for a number of reasons (Wagner 2007). First, it was believed that the approach did not produce the reliable, generalizable and predictable policy knowledge it had promised. Secondly, the positivist view of (social) science upon which the rationalist approach was based was increasingly discredited or at least challenged within the social sciences. Thirdly, a range of new theoretical developments such as critical theory, feminism, post-structuralism and post-colonialism undermined rationalist approaches and claims to knowledge, and their alleged value neutrality. Fourthly, the Keynesian economic theories upon which many policy interventions were based lost popular support, especially following the ideological assault on them by the Thatcher and Reagan governments. Market ideologies framed by neoliberalism became ascendant around the world. And finally, and perhaps most significantly, the emerging processes of globalization transformed the political and economic contexts in which public policies were developed (Kennett 2008). More than anything, the fall of the Berlin Wall in 1989 signified a fundamental shift in policy thinking around the world, both resulting from and giving rise to the globalization of capitalism and the emergence of a 'neoliberal' ideology, reshaping the ways in which policies are now forged, implemented and evaluated.

Public policies were once exclusively developed within a national setting, but now are also located within a global 'system'. While national governments continue to have the ultimate authority to develop their own policies, the nature of this authority is no longer the same, affected significantly by imperatives of the global economy, shifts in global political relations and changing patterns of global communication that are transforming people's sense of identity and belonging. In the early 1990s, these epochal shifts led some scholars such as Francis Fukuyama (1992) to even speak of the 'end of history', suggesting that liberal democracy and market ideologies had now become 'globalized' and that this was the endpoint of ideological struggle.

These shifts have inevitably affected education policy. With the rejection of the ideas associated with the Keynesian welfare state, governments have increasingly preached a minimalist role for the state in education, with a greater reliance on market mechanisms. As educational systems around the world have become larger and more complex, governments have been either unable or unwilling to pay for educational expansion, and have therefore looked to market solutions. This has led to an almost universal shift from social democratic to neoliberal orientations in thinking about educational purposes and governance, resulting in policies of corporatization, privatization and commercialization on the one hand, and on a greater demand for accountability on the other (Lipman 2004). At the same time, educational purposes have been redefined in terms of a narrower set of concerns about human capital development, and the role education must play to meet the needs of the global economy and to ensure the competitiveness of the national economy.

Over the past two decades, then, a new global policy paradigm seems to have emerged. Yet while similarities in policy shifts occurring in a wide variety of nations are clearly evident, it is also the case that these changes are mediated at the national and local levels by particular historical, political and cultural dynamics (see, for example, Mok and Tan 2004). An understanding of the nature of this mediation suggests that there is nothing inevitable about these changes. The concept of globalization does not have a single uniform meaning, and its various expressions are as dynamic as they are context-specific. If this is so, it is important to try to elucidate the reasons for the global dominance of the neoliberal policy paradigm: how it might be unravelling in the current global economic crisis, and how it might be possible to resist its negative effects and forge a different, more just and democratic globalization that implies a broader conception of education's purposes.

This book is largely concerned with an examination of the ways in which global processes are transforming education policy around the world, in a range of complicated, complex, commensurate and contradictory ways. It seeks to provide a new introduction to policy studies in education, informed by our recent experiences in policymaking and evaluation, and with our scholarly engagement with the literature designed to understand processes of globalization. It is based on our conviction that some of the older theoretical and methodological resources are no longer sufficient, and that new tools are needed to understand policy processes in a world that is increasingly networked and shaped by a range of transnational forces and connections, demanding a new global imagination. We want to argue that while some of the older accounts of policy processes might still hold to some extent at least, the processes that now frame education policy are often constituted globally and beyond the nation-state, even if they are still articulated in nationally specific terms. Using insights from a range of theoretical and methodological traditions, including critical theory, post-structuralism, post-colonialism and critical discourse analysis, we provide a somewhat eclectic view of critical education policy analysis, which attempts to show how education policies represent a particular configuration of values whose authority is allocated at the intersection of global, national and local processes. Our focus is on both new policy content and processes; the new production rules for education policy associated with globalization; and the related need for new approaches to education policy analysis.

What is policy?

Let us begin with a discussion of the question: 'what is policy?' Over the years, a wide variety of definitions has been suggested, indicating that policy is a highly contested notion. The simplest of all definitions has been provided by Dye (1992), who argues that policy is 'whatever governments choose to do or not to do'. Two points might be made about this statement. First, Dye is concerned here about public policy – that is, policy developed by governments. Other institutions such as intergovernmental organizations (IGOs) and corporations also make policy. Our focus in this book is largely on public policy. It needs to be noted, however, that in the contemporary context, a range of public/private partnerships are becoming common, resulting in more private sector involvement in policy processes (Ball 2007). Secondly, sometimes non-decision-making is as much an expression of policy as are the actual decisions made. Significant manifestations of policy and power are often evident when things stay the same or when issues are not discussed or are deliberately suppressed. In this way, policy can be expressed in silences, either deliberate or unplanned.

More than 20 years ago, Hogwood and Gunn (1984: 13–19) suggested a number of meanings for the concept of policy. The concept of policy, they argued, is variously used to describe a 'label for a field of activity', for example education policy or health policy; as 'an expression of general purpose'; as 'specific proposals'; as 'decisions of government'; as 'formal authorization'; as a 'programme'; and as both 'output' and 'outcome', with the former referring to what has actually been delivered by a specific policy, and outcomes referring to broader effects of policy goals. Wedel and colleagues (2005: 35) more recently have offered a similar account of the meaning of policy, suggesting it refers to a field of activity (e.g. education policy), a specific proposal, government legislation, a general programme or 'desired state of affairs', and what governments achieve. Public policy, then, refers to the actions and positions taken by the state, which consists of a range of institutions that share the essential characteristics of authority and collectivity. While policy is often synonymous with decisions, an individual decision in isolation does not constitute policy. A policy expresses patterns of decisions in the context of other decisions taken by political actors on behalf of state institutions from positions of authority. Public policies are thus normative, expressing both ends and means designed to steer the actions and behaviour of people. Finally, policy refers to things that can in principle be achieved, to matters over which authority can be exercised.

Policies are often assumed to exist in texts, a written document of some kind. However, a policy can also be viewed as a 'process' involved in the production of an actual text, once the policy issue has been put on the political agenda. Policy processes thus include agenda setting, as well as work on the production of policy texts. They also refer to implementation processes, which are never straightforward, and sometimes also to the evaluation of policy. In this sense, then, policy may refer to both texts and processes. In Stephen Ball's (1994: 10) terms, 'Policy is both text and action, words and deeds, it is what is enacted as well as what is intended.' This observation recognizes that policy purposes and goals are not always achieved in practice. This is because policies as they are implemented always encounter complex organizational arrangements and already-existing practices. For policy is not the only factor in 'determining' practices. In recognition of this policy/practice gap, Ball notes, 'Policies are always incomplete in so far as they relate to or map onto the "wild profusion of local practice"' (Ball 1994: 10). In our earlier book on education policy studies (Taylor *et al.* 1997: 24–25), we summarized this distinction in the following way:

> ... policy is much more than a specific policy document or text. Rather, policy is both process and product. In such a conceptualization, policy involves the production of the text, the text itself, ongoing modifications to the text and processes of implementation into practice.

Writing from an anthropological perspective, Wedel *et al.* (2005: 35) suggest that although the question 'What is policy?' is important, a more important question might be, 'What do people do in the name of policy?'

Policy is about change (Weimer and Vining 2004). It is through policy that governments seek to reform educational systems, for example. Policy desires or imagines change – it offers an imagined future state of affairs, but in articulating desired change always offers an account somewhat more simplified than the actual realities of practice. In many ways policies eschew complexity. Given the level of generality, policies could be seen to be more like a recipe than a blueprint (Considine 1994). They are designed to provide a general overview, leaving a great deal of room for interpretation. To use another metaphor, a policy is designed to steer understanding and action without ever being sure of the practices it might produce.

Policy texts often take the form of a legal document, but not always. Other kinds of text, such as speeches and press releases by a Government minister and papers by senior policymakers, can express policy intentions and have real effects. Here we are in agreement with Jenny Ozga (2000: 33), who works with a very broad and ecumenical definition of policy. She observes that a policy text is any 'vehicle or medium for carrying and transmitting a policy message'. Further, in terms of the trajectory across the production of the policy text and its implementation into practice, practitioners can also be regarded 'as policy makers or potential makers of policy, and not just the passive receptacles of policy' (ibid.: 7). In the context of schooling systems, policy is also mediated by the leadership practices within the school, as well as by the ways teachers interpret that policy and translate it into practice (Bell and Stevenson 2006). This process of translation is fundamental to understanding how policies play a role in producing and shaping change.

It is possible to conceptualize policy processes in terms of what has been called the 'policy cycle' (Ball 1994). This view rejects a one-way, linear account of relationships between the setting of policy agendas, the production of the policy text and its implementation into practice. Instead, the notion of a policy cycle points to the messy, often contested and non-linear relationships that exist between aspects and stages of policy processes. Ball (ibid.) has written instructively about the various contexts of the policy cycle, namely the context of influence, the context of policy text production and the context of policy practice or implementation, to capture the interactive, synergistic set of relationships between these contexts.

There is often contestation within and across these contexts. In the production of policy texts, for example, there are attempts to appease, manage and accommodate competing interests. Jane Kenway (1990: 59) has argued that policies (here read policy as the actual text) represent 'the temporary settlements between diverse, competing, and unequal forces within civil society, within the state itself, and between associated discursive regimes'. Drawing from theories within literary criticism, then, we can see most policy texts as being heteroglossic in character; that is, policy texts often seek to suture together and over competing interests and values. At the same time, policies usually seek to represent their desired or imagined future as being in the public interest, representing the public good. As a result they often mask whose interests they actually represent. Thus, contestation occurs right from the moment of appearance of an issue on the policy agenda, through initiation of action, to the inevitable trade-offs involved in formulation and implementation.

Policies are also often assembled as responses to perceived problems in a field such as education. Here, however, we again have to be aware of the discursive work that policies do in constructing problems in certain ways, perhaps differently from what the best research-based empirical and theoretical analyses might suggest. The nature of the problems is never self-evident, but is always represented in a specific manner, from a particular point of view (Dery 1984). Policies thus proffer solutions to the problem as constructed by the policy itself (Yeatman 1990). McLaughlin (2006: 210), in an extensive review of the US policy implementation literature in education, speaks of the 'problem of the problem' – of the manner in which the problem is constructed in order to give a policy proposal its legitimacy. Nor is the idea of policy context objectively given, but it is similarly constructed (Seddon 1994), designed to present issues in a particular light. The description of the context, so constructed, may include the historical backdrop to the policy. The constructed nature of such history is intended to give legitimacy to the policy's intentions.

An example might be helpful here. In recent years, many countries have instituted new policies on literacy education. These policies have been based on an understanding of the broader context, over the representation of which there has been much argument. On the one hand, there are those who have characterized the context in terms of what they regard as the declining levels of literacy. They have demanded the re-institution of the traditional policy emphasis on phonics, grammar and canonical texts (see Snyder 2008). The critics of this view, on the other hand, deny such a crisis, and represent the context instead in terms of the changing nature of society which is increasingly multicultural, and in which new forms of media literacy have become essential, thus necessitating, for example, a focus on 'multiliteracies' (Cope and Kalantzis 2000). It is not hard to see how the competing policy proposals are grounded in differing representations of the context, historical narratives of what has worked or has not, and the contemporary problems that need to be solved through policy.

In another useful discussion of education policy, Luke and Hogan (2006: 171) have emphasized policymaking as opposed to policy as text: 'We define educational policy making as the prescriptive regulation of flows of human resources, discourse and capital across educational systems towards normative social, economic and cultural ends.'

In their use of 'prescriptive regulation', they stress the authoritative, mandating aspects of policy – that is, policy tries to change the behaviours and practices of others so as to steer change in a particular direction. Luke and Hogan's definition also suggests that the idea of policy involves allocation of resources of various kinds, namely human, economic and ideological. Policies have discursive effects, often changing the language through which practitioners engage with policy in practice. Further, their definition also recognizes the normative nature of education policy, emphasizing the goals or purposes of education. They suggest that education policy is about having effects in the broader social, cultural and economic domains or what could be seen as policy outcomes. Considine (1994: 4) has similarly observed that 'A public policy is an action which employs governmental authority to commit resources in support of a preferred value.' Values are either implicit or explicit in any given policy.

The issue of values is thus central to policy. In an early definition of policy, the American political scientist David Easton (1953: 129–130) argued that:

> The essence of policy lies in the fact that through it certain things are denied to some people and made accessible to others. A policy, in other words, whether for a society, for a narrow association, or for any other group, consists of a web of decisions that allocates values.

This definition was encapsulated in Easton's well-known statement that policy involves 'the authoritative allocation of values', to a discussion of which we shall return later in this chapter. But suffice to say at this stage that the authoritative allocation of values is often evident in terms of the funding for certain things and denial of funding for others. It is also evident in the ways in which policy problems are framed and contexts represented. It is evident in the discourses within which policies are located.

The distinction between policy as text and policy as discourse demands further clarification. Stephen Ball (2006) argues that policy texts are framed by broader discourses. The text here refers to the actual words on paper, the use of certain language to signify certain meanings. Thus, for example, policies are often written in the first person plural, with the heavy use of 'we' and 'our' seeking to reflect and constitute a putative consensus about the concerns of the policy and its prescribed direction of change, between the creators of the policy and the readers of it. It is Ball's contention that such policy texts are located within and framed by broader discourses, more comprehensive ways of conceptualizing the world. As he puts it: 'Discourses are about what can be said, and thought, but also about who can speak, when, where, and with what authority' (Ball 2006: 48).

Ball's concept of discourse is derived from Foucault (1977), and is designed to suggest that policies are located in a collection of interrelated policies – a 'policy ensemble'. Ball (2006: 48) notes, 'we need to appreciate the way in which policy ensembles, collections of related policies, exercise power through a production of "truth" and "knowledge", as discourses'. Discourses help to position us – they speak us rather than us speaking them. Policy texts and policy ensembles, then, are framed by discourses that we need to understand in order to better grasp the actual policy text. The concept of a policy ensemble also implies 'intertextuality' between policies that constitute the ensemble. Intertextuality refers to the specific and explicit cross-referencing to other policy texts, but also to implicit referencing to other texts in the echoing usage of words, phrases and concepts. In this book, we use the notion of 'social imaginary' to suggest that policies are not only located within discourses, but also in imaginaries that shape thinking about how things might be 'otherwise' – different from the way they are now. It is in this way that policies direct or steer practice towards a particular normative state of affairs.

Purposes and types of policy

Why do we need public policies? As we have already noted, policies involve the authoritative allocation of values. But values can be allocated in a number of ways and for a variety of purposes. Most frequently, policies are designed to steer actions and behaviour, to guide institutions and professionals in a certain direction. Sometimes this is done simply for symbolic purposes, while on other occasions policies have more material consequences with respect, for example, to the allocation of resources, such as the distribution or redistribution of funds. Some policies are sanctioned and the failure to pursue them can lead to all kinds of penalties, while others are forged in order to build consensus around certain ideas. But above all, policies are designed to ensure consistency in the application of authorized norms and values across various groups and communities: they are designed to build consent, and may also have an educative purpose.

Different purposes, then, shape the ways policies are articulated and promoted. This much can be shown, for example, by pointing to the differentiation between symbolic and material policies. Symbolic policies are often political responses to pressures for policy. They usually carry little or no commitment to actual implementation and usually do not have substantial funding attached. Rein (1983) has argued that there are three factors which significantly affect the likelihood of the implementation of policy: the clarity of the goals of the policy and their potential for effective operationalization; the complexity of the envisaged implementation strategy; and the commitment or otherwise to funding the policy and its implementation. Such commitment and funding are usually absent in the case of symbolic policies. They also tend to have vague, ambiguous and abstract goals statements and lack well thought-through implementation strategies. Now this is not to say that they have no effects. Rein (ibid.: 131) suggests that their very existence can have strategic functions in terms of legitimating particular political views and also of altering the climate in which some issues are discussed and dealt with. Further, in respect of highly contested policy domains, for example gender equity, the existence of a symbolic policy might be the perceived first step in a longer-term strategy by policymakers working inside the state. It might also offer some policy legitimacy to the work of the activists (Lingard 1995). A material policy, in stark contrast, is strongly committed to implementation. It is accompanied by funding, and sometimes effective evaluation mechanisms to ensure the achievement of its goals. The symbolic/material distinction then turns on issues of resourcing and commitment to implementation, and in some cases strong sanctions. Today, symbolic policies are often associated with 'media spin' created around a policy (Gewirtz *et al.* 2004).

A distinction is often also drawn between incremental and rational policies. This refers to the way the policy text is produced. Incrementalism recognizes that policies are usually built on or developed out of previous policies. In this way policy development and change are seen to be small step by small step, rather than through large steps or disregard for policies that have preceded the emergence of new ones. In political terms, policymakers usually want to stress the extent to which *their* policies are different from those that have gone before. In some ways there are always some incremental aspects to policymaking, given the continuity of state structures and policy history.

Rational policies are pointedly prescriptive; that is, they are directed to policymakers inside the state and are prescriptive about the steps that need to be followed in their development. This involves a number of distinct and quite linear phases through policy development, text formulation and implementation. Usually these phases include: problem definition; clarification of values, goals and objectives; identification of options to achieve goals and objectives in line with values; assessing options including, sometimes, cost-benefit analyses; selecting a course of action; developing an implementation strategy; evaluation of the policy as implemented; modifications to the program in light of the evaluation. Sometimes this rational approach to policy production is referred to as the 'stage heuristic' (Weaver-Hightower 2008: 153), given its focus on assisting governments to develop actual policy that is technically sound. These steps or stages might be a useful 'guide' to those in bureaucracies, but in reality most actual policy development occurs in a less rational, more disjointed fashion with more politics and trade-offs involved.

In providing an account of a rational approach to policymaking, one of the major rational theorists of public policy from an earlier era, Carley (1980), suggested that there are three elements to policy and its development: first, political decisions about the values to be allocated through a given policy; secondly, rational determination through the phases listed above; and finally the impact of the bureaucratic organizational arrangement upon the actual policy. Carley argued that values and organizational realities mediate and have effects, even when the policy production processes are highly rational. Recognizing the political character of actual policymaking and commenting specifically on the evaluation phase of the rational model, Hudson and Lowe (2004: 228) observe that 'decision makers are rarely inclined to conduct policy making according to the rational, evidence rich, scientific approach that forms the classic model'.

In a similar vain, Rein (1983: 135) saw policy processes as attempts by the state to 'resolve conflicts among authoritative, rational and consensual imperatives'. What this suggests is that state policymaking processes are never totally rational, and involve political negotiations of various kinds, both within and outside the state. Claus Offe (1975: 135) has noted a symbiotic relationship between the state, its bureaucratic structures and policy processes:

> ... it is not only true that the emergence of a social problem puts into motion the procedural dynamics of policy formation, program design, and implementation, but also, conversely, the institutionalized formal mode of political institutions determines what potential issues are, how they are defined, what solutions are proposed, and so on.

The state, then, is crucially involved in the political organization of policy processes in all phases of the policy cycle, including the politics of implementation. Furthermore, the ways in which its own structures are defined have implications for the actual focus and content of policies, as well as in relation to the discourses that frame them.

For example, when the bureaucratic state in most western countries was reconstituted in the 1980s under what has been called 'new public management' (Clarke and Newman 1997) or 'corporate managerialism' (Yeatman 1990), policy discourses changed significantly to meet the new demands for faster policymaking and implementation. The restructured state utilizes new policy discourses surrounding such concepts as choice, markets, and steering through measuring policy outputs. What is clear, then, is that changes in the structures and modalities of the state almost invariably imply new production rules for education policy in relation to both its content and its processes.

Policies may also be said to be either distributive or redistributive. Distributive policies, as the term implies, simply distribute resources, human and otherwise, while redistributive policies seek to intervene against disadvantage through positive discrimination, usually but not always in relation to funding. Redistributive policies in education were quite common in most liberal democratic societies during the 1960s and 1970s. In Australia, for instance, there was a disadvantaged schools programme (Connell *et al.* 1991), which sought to redistribute funding to schools enrolling disadvantaged students in an attempt to open up opportunities for them. More recently, focus has shifted to distributive policies with an attempt to produce self-sufficient individuals. *No Child Left Behind* in the US, for example, is a largely distributive policy, the focus of which is funding allocated on the basis of various accountability measures and performance against targets, rather than on redistribution to achieve greater equality of opportunity.

The distinctions between symbolic and material, rational and incremental, and distributive and redistributive public policies discussed above are useful in understanding the various purposes of policies – from the allocation of resources to the use of policy as an instrument for containing political demands, steering public opinion and affirming the symbolic importance of certain values. Of course, useful as these distinctions are, they are never absolute. Many public policies serve multiple purposes. They reflect both the shifting nature of the state and the ways in which the state relates to outside agencies, in the allocation of values, produced through complex processes of negotiation and compromise, both within and outside the state.

Public policy and state authority

Our discussion in this chapter has revolved around a most succinct but durable definition of policy proposed more than 50 years ago by David Easton (1953) – as the 'authoritative allocation of values'. Policies, he argued, are normative: they either articulate or presuppose certain values, and direct people towards action, but in a way that is authoritative. Their legitimacy is thus derived from an authority, be it a government or a corporation or a social institution such as a school system. Easton's use of the concept of authority is deliberate, and is designed to mark a distinction from the idea of power. Following Weber (1948), Easton regards authority as legitimate power. A policy is designed to ensure that power is exercised legitimately. This legitimacy is achieved through various institutional norms and practices.

The distinction between power and authority assumed by Easton is not always clear-cut, however. The claim to authority can sometimes mask aspects of power for which no community consent is ever secured. The unsaid, the unspoken can be the clearest manifestation of hegemonic power, where 'common sense' goes unchallenged. Despite a lack of clarity about the ways in which policies embody authority, Easton's definition is useful just the same, not least because it underlines the importance of understanding how policy is translated into practice with an assumption of legitimacy. For policy researchers, both those working within the positivist and rationalist traditions as well as those inclined towards interpretivist and critical approaches, issues of authority are thus central to their accounts of policy processes.

Stephen Ball (1994), for example, regards an exploration of the nature and scope of authority to be one of the central tasks of policy research. Policy research, he argues, involves an examination of three key aspects of policy: texts, discourses and effects. Policies, he suggests, are always contested, value-laden and dynamic, and are a product of various compromises. They are encoded in representations of what is mandated and what ought to be done. They are often expressed in a textual form, but within the framework of a broader discourse that assumes authority. Policy analysis thus involves the decoding of texts, in relation both to the context in which they are embedded and the context they construct, and to the effects they have on practice, linked to broader social effects, sometimes called 'policy outcomes'. If the idea of authority is central to interpreting and analysing policies, where does the authority underpinning a policy come from, and how is it exercised or allocated? Who has the authority to develop policy, to ensure consent to policy prescriptions and to steer practice?

As far as public policies are concerned, it is the nation-state that has traditionally been assumed to have this authority. Without this authority, it is believed, public policies can neither be supported with resources nor have the symbolic value to guide action. Indeed, the state uses its authority to justify policies, and in turn uses policies to legitimate its authority. It is through these dynamics that it seeks to manage community expectations and to develop subjects/citizens who are sufficiently vested in its political priorities. It utilizes various professional organizations, institutional arrangements and the media to ensure that its policies are implemented in the desired manner. As Foucault (1991) has pointed out, in contemporary society the state thus plays a major role in creating 'self-governing individuals', a process he refers to as 'governmentality'.

Expressed in these terms, while the idea of authority is central to the notion of policy, few policy researchers address it explicitly. So, for example, while Ball's discussion of the idea of policy highlights the complexities of the various ways in which a policy is constructed and interpreted, it does not *problematize* issues surrounding the nature of the authority underpinning that policy. In his earlier work, Ball assumed this authority to be located within the structures of the nation-state, from where policy texts and discourses got their purchase. This is not surprising, because public policies in education have traditionally emanated from a national (or sub-national) government and its agencies, designed to deliver educational provision in a most effective and efficient, and sometimes equitable, manner. Understandably, therefore, most policy researchers assume state authority to be sovereign. This assumption is based on a *Westphalian* understanding of the nature of political authority (Krasner 2000), which includes the contentions that authority can only be exercised by a state over a defined geographical territory, that each state has the autonomy to develop its own policies, and that no external actor can direct that state's priorities.

Modern nation-states are thus assumed to hold ultimate territorial jurisdiction, organized around a specific set of administrative functions. This assumption of territoriality can be found in the work of most twentieth-century social theorists and policy researchers alike. Indeed, it has been considered a fundamental feature of modernity, upon which the political architecture of the modern state system is based (Mann 1997). The modern nation-state is represented as a kind of container that separates an 'inside' of domestic political interactions from an 'outside' of international or interstate relations (Brenner *et al.* 2003: 2). The state is thus given an authoritative monopoly over the subjects and institutions located within its territory, allocated through a system of international relations.

This conception of authority, based on the institutional, territorial and centralized nature of the state, cannot however be sustained without popular consent. It requires a social imaginary, a collective conception that people have about the nature and scope of political authority. It demands people's consent to view national formations as inevitable, timeless and natural, territorially bounded and entirely legitimate. This view is in line with Anderson's contention (1991) that nations are 'imagined communities' that were brought into existence in early modernization processes initially by intellectuals, artists, political leaders and others, and which only later became infiltrated into the whole society, through mass literacy and mass schooling systems, myths, stories, songs and the like. Processes of formal schooling played a major role in developing and sustaining national imaginaries. The nation-state came to be widely accepted as having the authority to enforce its will, sometimes even through the exercise of violence. As Weber (1991: 23) argues, for example, the state has the legitimate right to exercise violence (e.g. imprison and punish people, go to war), but this right is exercised mostly through the inculcation of a social imaginary that cannot even conceive of how things could be otherwise. Bourdieu (1998b) refers to this as 'symbolic violence'. Most policy research in education continues to operate within this *Westphalian* framework, which takes the authority of the nation-state as given and assumes that policies are developed within its boundaries.

While the concept of the nation-state has been much debated over the years, there is a general agreement that 'nation' in the construction 'nation-state' refers to cultures and histories of a people within a bounded space, while 'state' refers to the bureaucratic administrative structure inside that bounded space. As we have already noted, traditionally it has been assumed that the legitimacy a public policy has is derived from the authority a nation-state has over its citizens, and that this authority is exercised through a wide variety of state structures and processes. In this book, we will show how globalization has destabilized this assumption, and has created conditions for the reconstitution of both nation and state. In what follows in this chapter we present, in a very general way, a set of observations of how, under the conditions of globalization, public policy processes are changing; how education policy is now framed, produced, disseminated and implemented differently; and how there have been significant shifts in the manner in which education policy relates to other domains of public policy. These observations are then elaborated in subsequent chapters, with examples that seek to show how education policy is becoming globalized, and therefore requires a new approach to education policy studies.

Shifts in education policy processes

As we have already observed, *policy is more than the policy document or the legislation, that is, the text* (Taylor *et al.* 1997). Processes of policy production and implementation are also significant. These processes refer to the chronology of an issue coming onto the policy agenda, the construction of a policy text, its implementation and sometimes evaluation. This is not to suggest that the words contained within a policy text are not important; on the contrary, they are often carefully crafted, and hide the contestation and compromises involved in the actual construction of the text itself. The words of the policy text are today often 'mediatized' (Fairclough 2000), with final drafts finessed by journalists working in the education bureaucracy or the policymaker's office, with an intended readership of the public rather the professionals who will implement the given policy. This suggests that text is always affected by the context of its production, which has in recent years been increasingly shaped by the discourses of globalization and globalized discourses.

The discourses that frame policy texts are no longer located simply in the national space but increasingly emanate from international and supranational organizations such as the Organization for Economic Cooperation and Development (OECD), the World Bank and the European Union (EU) (Henry *et al.* 2001; Lawn and Lingard 2002; Dale 2006; Kallo and Rinne 2006). However, texts and indeed discourses do not exist in material vacuums. Rather, they are located in specific material realities and cultural formations. These include the nation-state, but increasingly also what we might call, after Appadurai (1996), post-national spaces. Lingard *et al.* (2005) have described an emergent global education policy field. They have pointed out that in recent years the scalar framing of policy discourses and texts has extended beyond the nation; the context of policy texts is now multilayered in scalar terms across the local, national and global, leading to what Robertson *et al.* (2006a) refer to as the 'rescaling of contemporary politics'.

What this suggests is that *policy is multidimensional and multilayered and occurs at multiple sites*. Globalized discourses and agenda-setting and policy pressures now emerge from beyond the nation. The relationships between the various sites of policy production and implementation have been extended in many instances. But even in considering a national policy and its implementation at a school level, for example, we can see the different positioning of the different policy players; those involved in policy text production compared with those involved in policy implementation or practice will often have different and competing interests. Both sets of players are also located within different logics of practice and differential power relations (Bourdieu 1998b; Rawolle and Lingard 2008). Consider, for example, a policy emanating from an international organization and its take-up within a nation of the Global South through to implementation: here we see a stretching and dispersing of the multilayering and multidimensionality of contemporary policy processes in education.

Spatial thinking now appears essential in understanding education policy texts as well as the processes of their production and implementation (see Gulson and Symes 2007). Massey has written about the deep imbrication of the local and the global, noting how each helps constitute the other. Speaking about daily life, she observes (Massey 2005: 184):

> The lived reality of our daily lives is utterly dispersed, unlocalised in its sources, and in its repercussions. The degree of dispersion, the stretching, may vary dramatically between social groups, but the point is that the geography will not be simply territorial.'

This observation applies equally well to considerations of policy production and practice in education and to the extended multilayering of policy, recognizing the simultaneous plays of the local, national and global as spatial relations in the education policy cycle. The geography of policy discourses and processes is today not simply territorial.

Yet *policies exist in context:* they have a prior history, linked to earlier policies, particular individuals and agencies. In the past the policy context was largely viewed in national terms. In recent years, however, new scalar considerations have become important, requiring us to rescale our lenses from the national to also include the global. What Mahony and her colleagues (2004) call the 'policy creation community' in education has been extended and stretched to include policy agents and agencies beyond the nation. Global agents and agencies, both public and private, are now often involved in the gestation and establishment of education policy agendas. The involvement of new actors in policy processes is affected by the changing public/private relationships in relation to education policies. Here, Mahony *et al.* (2004) speak of the 'privatization of policy'. The context of education policy production is thus changing, and involves a complex rescaling across the local, regional, national and the global. There is also a new context for education policy production in terms of the spatial location of their rationale, often expressed today in terms of global competitiveness and other global imperatives. This extended context has implications for analysing and understanding policy ecologies (Weaver-Hightower 2008).

This suggests that *policy is value-laden*. Values pervade policy processes and policy content. Traditionally these values articulated national interests. However, in the past two decades, as will be discussed in greater detail in Chapter 4, global considerations now enter the articulation of values as never before, transforming the balance between economic efficiency and the social equity goals of education. This shift can be observed in the discursive policy frames of an international organization such as the OECD (Rizvi and Lingard 2006), where market efficiency concerns now seem to override equity ones. This economistic reframing of education policy has led to an emphasis on policies of education as the production of human capital to ensure the competitiveness of the national economy in the global context. In most countries now, economic restructuring has become the metapolicy framing proposals for education policy reform. This focus on instrumental values has been strengthened with talk today of education's role in the creation of a *knowledge economy*, whose dominant discourse has a decidedly global character.

Yet, *public policy remains a state activity* and is produced in the bureaucratic structure of the education state. The state, however, is a complex structural arrangement with complex relationships existing between its various component parts, say Treasury and the Education Ministry, and between the state and civil society and the private sector in the economy. Today, however, education policymakers within the state are also networked with policymakers in agencies beyond the nation, including international organizations such as the OECD, UNESCO and supranational organizations such as the EU, resulting in the creation of an emergent global education policy community. There are also looser policy networks that work in new scalar and cellular ways. This has extended and reconstituted the frame of reference of the state in education policy production.

So far from becoming obsolete in the face of global pressures, as some theorists have suggested, the state now works differently in education policy production. It is now positioned in particular ways in relation to a range of organizations which sit outside or beyond the nation, for example the OECD, the World Bank, UNESCO, the EU. These relationships are asymmetrical, with different nations being positioned in different ways. For example, a developing country relates differently to an organization such as the World Bank than does the United States. In his late work, Bourdieu (2003) argued that 'national capital' mediated global effects upon the state and nation. This suggests that an understanding of policy processes now requires a 'global analysis of contemporary states', rather than an acceptance of a 'stateless globe' (Therborn 2007: 91). In considering a global analysis of contemporary state activities and relations, we need to take account of history (e.g. colonialism), political aspirations (e.g. post-colonialism) and the state's geopolitical location within a changing world order.

The emergence of what Cerny (1990) has called the 'competition state', that is, the restructured managerialist state, has also affected its workings and both the content and production of education policy. The state has traditionally been associated with public sector activities. Under new managerialism, public/private sector relationships have been reconstituted through privatization, through the creation of quasi-markets in the public sector and through a range of public–private partnerships (Ball 2007). However, these policy agendas are played out in different ways in different nations. As Appadurai (1996) has pointed out, the flows of global ideologies always come up against local and national histories, cultures and politics; in a word, such global flows are 'vernacularized' in the context of specific nations as they meet local cultures and politics. This is clearly the case in respect of the privatization agenda in education, which is articulated in India and Britain, for example, in radically different ways.

Given the flows of people (migrants, refugees) associated with contemporary globalization, Appadurai (1996) has argued that the relationship between nation (ethnic composition and national identities) and state (political and administrative structure) has become somewhat attenuated, with each now the project of the other. Education policy is linked to the construction of the imagined community of the nation (Anderson 1991) and to issues of difference and national identities. While globalization has seen an enhanced number of scapes and flows crossing national borders (Appadurai 1996), September 11 and subsequent events have witnessed some interruption to such flows and more state intervention around them, an attempt at strengthening national borders. Education policy is tied in to these state activities (Rizvi 2004) and the enhanced fear of difference, which has resulted from state policies in the so-called age of terrorism (Gilroy 2004). Such developments have not gone unchallenged, so that there is simultaneously some policy talk about the need for education to produce global, cosmopolitan citizens able to value and work with difference.

The new state formation, new managerialism and new public/private sector relations have been described as ushering in a transition from government to governance (Rhodes 1997). This is a move away from a state-centric approach to policy production and implementation, to the utilization of multiple agencies and agents across the public/private divide, which is no longer a discrete binary. This form of governance works through the discursive production of self-responsibilizing individuals (Rose 1999), including policymakers and implementers, and involves networks and partnerships of various kinds that cut across older hierarchies. This shift from government to governance is more developed in some nations than in others, but the 'polycentric state' (Jessop 1998) associated with it has begun to emerge in many nations and has reconstituted public/private relationships. In a sense, we see horizontal networked governance forms operating simultaneously with hierarchical government forms, in a way similar to the simultaneous workings of both Westphalian and post-Westphalian relations. The argument about a transition from government to governance is also used to depict the significance of post-national realities in governmental processes.

Education policies interact with policies in other fields. Today, in the context of globalization, education (as we have observed) is seen as the best economic policy, necessary to ensure the competitiveness of the national economy. Here, education is regarded as the producer of the required human capital. This economizing of education policy has also seen a push for valid and reliable comparative measures of educational outcomes, so that a nation can see where it sits within a global field of comparison to give it a measure of its potential global economic competitiveness. Since our earlier thoughts on education policy (Taylor *et al.* 1997), such international comparisons and educational indicators have become more influential, constituting an emergent global policy field. OECD's Program for International Student Assessment (PISA) has become very influential in this way.

The 2006 PISA involved 57 countries, almost twice as many as the actual number of OECD member nations. Involvement by some nations of the Global South in PISA is sometimes a requirement of World Bank funding. The OECD's World Education Indicators are also another component of the emergence of a global field of comparative education performance, covering many of the nations of the Global South. The OECD's annual publication *Education at a Glance* is yet another manifestation of such a field. For members of the EU, a range of performance indicators also work as an above-the-nation field of comparison (Grek *et al.* 2009). So the interactive aspect of education policy today includes its intimate relationship to economic policy as well as a stretching to a global field of performance comparison. Most national educational bureaucracies today have their international divisions, which deal with global educational indicators and comparative performance measures.

Policies in education such as a focus on citizenship are at times linked to a post-September 11 concern about strengthening the nation and are also related to new requirements about citizenship and migration. Anti-racism and multiculturalism, under some pressure since September 11, can also be seen as linked to a whole range of other social policies. Education policy is often closely aligned with science policy and so on. Indeed, governments today attempt to achieve what they call 'joined-up government', building policy coherence with a particular policy ensemble across portfolios so as, they would contend, to better address social issues.

There is too a way today in which policies produced in other parts of the state bureaucracy also have an educational focus. This reflects, perhaps, what Bernstein (2001a, 2001b) has referred to as the 'totally pedagogized society' or what Thomson (2006) calls the 'pedagogization of everyday life'. These descriptors pick up on the ways in which aspects of most public policies today have pedagogical or educational components; think, for example, of health policy and preventative measures; think of culture, heritage and museum policy and its pedagogical functions; think of welfare policies and some of their training requirements. So there are important ways in which education policy today is also produced in ministries and bureaucracies of state other than the specific education one. Young (1998) has spoken of the 'de-differentiation' of educational institutions to encapsulate these broader social changes that carry implications, we suggest, for the study of education policy. There are substantial openings here for education policy analysis.

Policy implementation is never straightforward. The idea of policy as edict from on high was always a crude measure to achieve effective change. This is particularly so when more effort is put into the production of the actual policy text than to a thought-out implementation strategy involving, amongst other things, adequate funding and support for professional development. We demonstrated the complex contestation, resistances and refractions at play between policy text production and practice. Policy is palimpsest in the move from production to practice and sometimes back again. We mentioned above the issue of positionality and differing logics of practices framing the work of policymakers and those who actually implement the policy. We also noted in our earlier book how, if we are considering schools, the principal or head is a very important mediator between these two sites of practice, a topic which is the focus of Bell and Stevenson's (2006) book on education policy.

The number of steps in the policy process from text to practice is another factor complicating the implementation process in education. And, of course, when professionals implement a policy they demand a degree of autonomy and space for professional judgement in the practice of the policy. Indeed, it is the latter understanding which has seen education policy in England attempt to tighten state control of teacher practices, with the resultant resistances and strife and lowered morale of the profession. The culture of change in the institutions of policy production and practice is also a factor affecting policy implementation. Globalization has also sometimes witnessed policy 'requirements' coming from agencies above the nation, for example a request to a school to participate in the national PISA sample.

Policy has also become more 'mediatized' (Lingard and Rawolle 2004) since we wrote our earlier policy book. This has seen the policy text itself often being more of a public relations, glossy document, constructed to put a positive 'spin' on the actual policy, trying to 'sell' the policy. Often aphorisms, catchy titles, alliterations in the actual policy text reflect the mediatization of the policy's production. Policy releases today in some ways can be seen as synonymous with media releases. The spinning of policy is perhaps most advanced in England (Gewirtz *et al.* 2004), but there are aspects of this in most education policy production in the nations of the Global North today (see Rawolle (2005) and Blackmore and Thorpe (2003) for two Australian examples). This mediatization of the policy text has significant implications for implementation, as its implied readership is often the public, the electorate, rather than the professionals who will be involved in its actual implementation.

Policies result in unintended as well as intended consequences. In our earlier book we commented: 'Policy making is a precarious business, the consequences of which are unpredictable given the complex interrelationship of contextual factors, different and sometimes opposing interests, linguistic ambiguities and the variety of key players involved in policy processes' (Taylor *et al.* 1997: 17). This observation about the often unintended consequences of policy, resulting from the complexity of factors, individuals and interests involved, holds equally true today. Perhaps the expanded scalar framing of education policy production and the global flows of education policy discourses and rationales have made the policy cycle even more complex, a contributing factor in producing unintended consequences from policy implementation.

Recognition of these refractions in the policy cycle has seen some education systems attempt to put in place tighter accountability frameworks to ensure achievement of policy goals. Such legislated conformity can often result in a situation where the goals of one policy are achieved, but the resulting conformity inhibits the achievement of other goals. Think, for example, of the tension in the Singapore system between the focus of good academic outcomes set against the desire for more creativity in schools (Koh 2004). In England, there has been strong usage of performance data linked to academic and other outcomes to measure school performance, ensure accountability and steer school and professional practices. However, such a policy regime appears to inhibit the achievement of the policy goal of producing creative, proactive individuals (Hartley 2003).

The policy as numbers approach has seen the development of an expansive infrastructure of measurement and a culture of performativity (Lyotard 1984) pervade the schools and education system. New computer systems have expedited this development. Accountability and performance measures for teachers also contribute to this culture, which is associated with the new managerialism in state practices. This is as much about being seen to perform as actually performing. It has also technicized pedagogies and encouraged teaching to the test and concentration on those pupils who are close to the desired achievement levels to the neglect of others, who are often the focus of a range of other policies to do with social inclusion (Gillborn and Youdell 2000). Further, the sorts of pedagogy necessary to the achievement of the types of entrepreneurial individual thought necessary for the emerging knowledge economy are not produced by such policies and accountability demands (Hartley 2003; Ranson 2003; Lingard 2007). Stephen Ball (2004) has extensively documented the unintended and dysfunctional effects of this culture of performativity within English education, while Ranson (ibid.) has shown the profound effects of the new frameworks of accountability on the practices of teachers and the resultant thinning out of pedagogies and educational goals.

The paradox in one sense is the tension between mandating required policy change, which implicitly denies the extent of professional autonomy in policy practice necessary to achieve the articulated policy goals. In the period of the last 20 years or so when education policy has become almost synonymous with educational change and linked to what we might call fast policymaking, education professionals have become more sceptical of reform agendas and thus less committed to fidelity in policy implementation, often resulting in unintended consequences. Ball (2007: 3) speaks of a 'confusing interplay of trust/distrust' inside the discourses of contemporary public sector reform that reconstitute education systems. There is sometimes talk of 'reform fatigue', regarded as a form of resistance by those implementing top-down policy and as a form of intransigence by those wanting the policy implemented, an example of the significance of positionality to policy stances.

To this point we have spoken generically about policy and policy processes in education. We would stress again, however, the need to take account of the specificities of particular national education systems and national cultures, politics and histories. This much is evident in considering, for example, the relationship between education policy and legislation. In some nation-states, education policies flow from legislation that creates laws which then result in the production of education policies. This tends to be the case, for example, in the USA, particularly at the federal level, for example in relation to affirmative action policies. It also tends to be the case in contemporary China. In the UK and Australia, in contrast, there is not necessarily a specific legislative framework for education policy. Thus we need to recognize the complex interplay between legislation and policy and the way this works its way out in different nations.

The overarching point, though, is that globalization and the emergence of a post-Westphalian reality mean that both policy content and policy production processes have been affected, requiring us to rethink our approaches to policy studies in education. The general move from Westphalian assumptions to post-Westphalian considerations lies at the heart of our attempt to rethink education policy studies. We are interested in showing how post-Westphalian considerations require us to examine not only the shifting character of the activities of the nation-state, but also the ways in which global networks and imaginaries have become more relevant than ever before in both policy content and policy production processes. We would also make the point that policy has become even more important in the working of education systems in the context of globalization. Policy at times is an expression of the specific effects of globalization, but can also be seen as the way the state and policymakers seek to manage and rearticulate global pressures, balanced against competing national and local pressures and interests.

2 Perspectives on globalization

Introduction

In the previous chapter we suggested that over the past two decades there have been major shifts in the ways in which education polices are developed, implemented and evaluated. We indicated that the values that national systems of education now promote through policy are no longer determined wholly by policy actors within the nation-state, but are forged through a range of complex processes that occur in transnational and globally networked spaces. As a result, we have witnessed the reconfiguration of the state's authority structures, altered by new patterns of communication, competition, cooperation and coercion across national boundaries. Not only has the authority of the state been transformed, so have the processes through which states now allocate their policies so that citizens regard them as legitimate. Indeed, one of the main tasks of public policy now is the creation of subjects predisposed towards the values it embodies. In this respect, the media play a more significant role than ever before.

These shifts in public policy processes are historically significant. They have resulted in a particular conception of education becoming dominant. The so-called neoliberal view of education is widely promoted by most intergovernmental and many non-governmental organizations and is readily embraced by national systems. International organizations such as the World Bank and the OECD have now become major policy players, determined to influence national education policies and their evaluation. International practices of benchmarking and regional coordination of policies and programmes have now, for example, become common. Policy circulation and comparison across national boundaries occur on a regular basis. In this chapter we want to examine how contemporary processes of globalization influence these historical shifts, and how these shifts demand new ways of interpreting and analysing education policy.

Globalization, we will suggest, is a highly contested notion. It refers not only to shifts in patterns of transnational economic activities, especially with respect to the movement of capital and finance, but also to the ways in which contemporary political and cultural configurations have been reshaped by major advances in information technologies. It is a concept that is used not only to describe a set of empirical changes, but also to prescribe desired interpretations of and responses to these changes. Within this mix, globalization affects the ways in which we both interpret and imagine the possibilities of our lives. In this way, the idea of globalization represents both an ideological formation and a social imaginary that now shapes the discourses of education policy. We describe some of the processes through which a neoliberal global imaginary has become dominant. We argue, however, that there is nothing inevitable about this social imaginary of globalization and that alternatives are not only possible, but also necessary. This much became evident in 2008, with the global financial crisis further illustrating the ideological character of neoliberal globalization, pointing to the pressing need to imagine another form of globalization.

Debates about globalization

It is now widely noted that contemporary processes of globalization are reshaping most aspects of our sociality. In his book *Globalization and Everyday Life*, Larry Ray (2007) goes so far as to suggest that globalization has reconstituted the concept of the *social* itself. It has transformed economic, political and cultural institutions, and even the manner in which we think about ourselves and imagine our futures. Pervasive as its reach is, the idea of globalization does not, however, admit any simple definition. Debates about globalization relate not only to its definition, but also to its origins and consequences. These debates focus on such questions as: how globalization should be measured; what is its chronology; what are its causes; how might we explain the ways in which globalization contributes to various economic, social and cultural transformations; and, more relevantly, what are its implications for public policy.

In their highly influential analysis, Held and McGrew (2005) argue that while there are no definitive or fixed lines of contestation surrounding the globalization debate, at least three contrasting positions can nonetheless be identified. The *globalists*, they argue, view globalization as a real and significant historical development that has fundamentally altered all aspects of our lives. The *sceptics* deny this claim, and view globalization as a primarily ideological social construction that has limited explanatory value. Global enthusiasts such as Giddens (1990) argue that globalization involves a significant reconfiguration of the organizing principles of social life and world order. By eroding the constraints of time and space on patterns of social interaction, globalists maintain, globalization creates the possibility of new modes of transnational social organization. In contrast, sceptics believe that the claims about globalization are based on various myths, and that the changes that are described are largely exaggerated, and indeed there is nothing new about global changes, which have been occurring at least since the 1880s (Hirst and Thompson 1996).

While the debate between *globalists* and *sceptics* is indeed intense, it needs to be recognized that these categories are *ideal-types*, constructed as heuristic devices that are helpful in understanding the principal lines of disagreement. No one completely denies the significance of recent global changes that have been caused by the revolutionary developments in information and communication technologies. Nor does anyone suggest that everything has changed, and that we live in a world that is unrecognizably different. Much of the debate centres instead on the degree to which we are witnessing the 'transformation of dominant patterns of socio-economic organization, of territorial principles and of power' (Held and McGrew 2000: 7). Held and McGrew take a middle position between the globalists and sceptics, which they refer to as *transformationalist*, a perspective that suggests that globalization has an undeniably material form insofar as it describes shifts resulting from growing flows of trade, capital and people as well as ideas, images and ideologies. Globalization, they argue, has produced entrenched and enduring patterns of worldwide interconnectedness – the stretching of social relations and activities across national spaces and regions, resulting in almost all communities becoming enmeshed in worldwide systems and networks of interaction.

It is recognized, however, that these shifting patterns of global interaction do not affect all communities in the same manner. Globalization is an outcome of various structural processes that manifest in different ways in the economy, politics and culture (Glenn 2007). The globalized world is fundamentally heterogeneous, unequal and conflictive, rather than integrated and seamless. It is experienced differently by different communities, and even individuals, and is sustained and created by people and institutions with widely different histories and political interests. If this is so, how should we describe its various forms? We want to suggest that it is possible to understand globalization in at least three different ways: as an empirical fact that describes the profound shifts that are currently taking place in the world; as an ideology that masks various expression of power and a range of political interests; and as a social imaginary that expresses the sense people have of their own identity and how it relates to the rest of the world, and how it implicitly shapes their aspirations and expectations.

Of course, these three ways of understanding globalization are not mutually exclusive, but describe different aspects of the same phenomenon. Much of the confusion surrounding the idea of globalization, including the debates between *globalists* and *sceptics*, stems from the failure to recognize it as a discourse that is descriptive and normative simultaneously. As an idea that has clearly become ubiquitous, used widely around the world in policy and popular discourses alike, globalization does not only describe how the scale of human interaction has linked distant communities with each other, but also often suggests a value orientation towards these changes. But beyond these aspects of globalization, it represents a social imaginary, an awareness of growing interconnectedness that has the potential for international understanding and cooperation on the one hand and reactionary politics and xenophobia on the other (see Appadurai 2006).

At the level of description, the idea of globalization is used to understand the various ways in which the world is becoming increasingly interconnected and interdependent. It refers to a set of social processes that imply the 'inexorable integration of markets, nation-states and technologies to a degree never witnessed before – in a way that is enabling individuals, corporations and nation-states to reach round the world farther, faster, deeper and cheaper than ever before' (Friedman 1999: 7). Globalization has enabled people in disparate locations to experience events simultaneously. Increasing instantaneity has 'created a complex range of social interactions governed by the speed of communication, thereby creating a partial collapse of boundaries within national, cultural and political spaces' (Ray 2007: 1). Such global integration is far from complete and, as we have already noted, clearly benefits some communities and people more than others. This suggests also that global processes are dynamic, constantly changing in light of new economic and political, as well as technological, developments.

It is thus impossible to periodize globalization because its different forms are spatially and temporally specific. Historically, it can be argued that the contemporary expressions of globalization grew out of a range of colonial practices (Rizvi 2007), built upon the patterns of global inequalities produced by colonial conquest. Indeed, colonialism sought to bring communities across vast distances into a singular political space, controlled and coordinated from a centre. In this way, globalization is not entirely a new phenomenon. Scholte (2000) has suggested that an incipient globalization was already evident in the second half of the 19th century, with the development of capitalism, along with the emergence of more consistent and coordinated practices of colonialism. Under colonial regimes, globally integrated markets and financial systems were forged, as it became possible to transport goods across vast distances, and as people were able to remain in touch with each other using new communication technologies such as the telegraph. International brand names like Campbell's® Soup, Coca-Cola® and Heinz® Foods all emerged in the 1880s and, in less than 20 years, became household names in many parts of the world. Also during this period, new international organizations and civil society bodies were formed to regulate the market and to promote political causes such as women's suffrage and the campaign against slavery.

Globalization's more recent forms are associated with even more extensive and profound technological developments in transport, communications and data processing, which have altered concepts of time and space. In earlier eras space was understood largely in terms of concrete localities. Mobility was limited, and for most individuals it was safer to stay in the same place. Horse-drawn coaches or ships travelled at no more than ten miles per hour, while jetliners today can go from Singapore to New York in less than 15 hours. Similarly, it took time for ideas to travel from one place to another. Today, it is possible to send a message around the world instantaneously, giving rise to globalized media. It has thus become possible to lift cultural meanings out of their original social context and transplant them in a radically different community.

Recent developments in information and communications technology, especially the satellite technologies, have revolutionized the circulation of ideas and information. It is now possible to transfer a large amount of money across national boundaries with the click of a computer key, and hold a meeting of the representatives of a transnational corporation from every continent without ever having them leave their offices. These developments have transformed the nature of economic activity, changing the modes of production and consumption. As Harvey (1989: 7) points out, in the age of globalization, time and space have become compressed in a number of ways, through better communication, virtual contact, cheaper travel and digitization. Capitalism has clearly taken advantage of these possibilities, stretching the reach of markets and bringing the whole globe into its sphere of influence.

Improved systems of communication and information flows, and rationalization in the techniques of distribution, have enabled capital and commodities to be moved through the global market with greater speed. At the same time, there has been a shift away from an emphasis on goods to greater trade in services, not only in business, educational and health services, but also in entertainment and lifestyle products. The rigidities of Fordism, which emphasized standardization, mass production and predictable supply and demand chains, have been replaced by a new organizational ethos that celebrates flexibility as its foundational value, expressed most explicitly in ideas of subcontracting, outsourcing, vertically integrated forms of administration, just-in-time delivery systems and the like, producing niche products for a highly differentiated market.

Harvey (1989) uses the term 'flexible accumulation' to characterize the radical shift in economic activity that has taken place in the past three decades. National boundaries no longer act as tight containers of production processes, with fewer and fewer industries oriented towards local, regional or even national markets. At the human level, Harvey argues, this has resulted in increased worker insecurity, unpredictable quality and increased pace of life. The new global economy 'emphasizes the fleeting, the ephemeral, the fugitive and the contingent' (Ibid.: 171). An 'intense period of time-space compression', Harvey insists, has produced 'a disorientating and disruptive impact on political-economic practices, the balance of class power, as well as upon cultural and social life'.

Recent developments in information and communication technologies have not only resulted in new transnational modes of production, but have also helped create a new kind of economy that is knowledge-based, post-industrial and service-oriented. As Manuel Castells (1996) argues, globalization not only embeds national production and financial and commercial activity within worldwide networks of economic organization, through the existence of global markets, manifested most obviously in round-the-clock trading across world's financial centres; but also involves more rapid flows of information than ever before. He suggests that the global space of flows is facilitated by the hardware of microelectronics, telecommunications and the like, the nodes and hubs where the information is stored, exchanged and distributed, and by the spatial organization of the social actors who participate in information flows across national spaces. He speaks of an 'informational mode of development' through which global financial and informational linkages are accelerated. The new economy, he maintains, is thus 'organized around global networks of capital, management, and information, whose access to technological know-how is at the roots of productivity and competitiveness' (ibid.: 23).

The ideas of a 'flexible regime of accumulation', an 'informational mode of development' and 'network society' focus our attention on the changing nature of work. The global economy is not only informational, but also implies a shift from manufacturing to service jobs. In 1950, services accounted for almost 50% of the jobs in the United States; they now represent more than 75% (Dicken 2003: 525). Leisure and services industries, with low-paid low-skills jobs, have been the fastest growing areas of employment. At the other end, high-skills jobs have emerged in technology and financial services, creating a major differentiation between not only income levels but also the skill sets required. At both ends of the occupational structure, jobs have increasingly become casualized and insecure. George Ritzer (2004) suggests that the global services economy has been successful because it has maximized the market and profitability potential provided by four operating principles: efficiency, calculability, predictability and control through technology. But this success has largely benefited corporations and the global elite, creating increased levels of insecurity for workers (Sassen 1998). In European and North American countries, labour insecurity has been intensified by the decline of union power to negotiate conditions, and also by the experiences of growing competition from the Newly Industrialized Countries (NICs) in Asia in particular (Lee 2002).

As global capitalism has become fragmentary, time and space have been rearranged by the dictates of multinational capital. Acquiring a new form, capitalism has extended its reach, and now potentially shapes all aspects of human life and relations. Traditionally, nation-states defined the social and economic conditions under which people worked, but they are no longer the sole arbiter of these conditions. Increasingly, global capital in the form of transnational corporations (TNCs) has become equally if not more important. In an era of flexible accumulation, TNCs are able to exercise an enormous amount of power and influence, especially in the least developed countries. Controlling economic activity in two or more countries, TNCs benefit from globalization by maximizing the comparative advantage between countries, profiting from differences in wage rates, market conditions and related political and fiscal regimes. They have geographical flexibility and are hence able to shift resources and operations between different locations on a global scale. They are also the carriers of a global political ideology that stresses such notions as a diminished role for the state, free trade, privatization, and individualism and consumerism (Cohen and Kennedy 2007: 176). Together, these ideas constitute what is now widely referred to as 'neoliberalism' (Harvey 2005).

According to Dicken (2003), TNCs are the single most powerful force in creating global shifts in economic activity. By definition, TNCs are spatially dispersed and therefore have employees in many countries. The degree to which they invest, and the proportion of employees they have in countries other than the country in which their headquarters are located, have indeed become indexes of the extent to which they have decentralized their operations and have become globalized. Yet their freedom to operate around the world is greatly dependent on both favourable international trade regimes such as those supported by the World Trade Organization (WTO) and supportive national governments with taxation, infrastructure and other policies sympathetic to capital accumulation on a global scale. Such policies include favourable education policies that TNCs often demand from national governments in order to meet their human resource and skills needs. In order to attract foreign direct investment from TNCs, national governments are happy enough to oblige, creating 'export processing zones' (EPZs) within their national borders, offering special tax privileges, duty-free imports, the promise of cheap labour, limited safety and environmental regulations and perhaps free infrastructure. EPZs effectively become transnational economic spaces, where TNCs can exercise a great deal of power without national responsibility.

Cultural and political shifts

This brief discussion of globalization of economic activity shows that capitalism requires the help of national governments to sustain its accumulation strategies, and that it needs to create social subjects sufficiently invested in its operations, as well as cultural practices predisposed towards its products and services. What this also indicates is that far from the state becoming redundant in a globalized economy, it is now required to play a crucial role in developing public policies favourable to the processes of global capital accumulation. In this way, global economic shifts are dialectically related to contemporary political and cultural shifts. The changing architecture of the state may thus be viewed as both an expression of and a response to global economic processes, and the cultural changes we are now experiencing are partly a product of the consumerism promoted by the global economy.

Over most of the 1990s, many social theorists argued that the exclusive link between the state and political authority was broken. They maintained that sovereign states could no longer claim exclusive authority over their citizens and their territory, and that recent changes in the structure of the global economy, as well as international law, regional political associations and institutional formations, had altered the fundamental constitution of the state system. In her highly influential book, *The Retreat of the State*, Strange (1996: 13) went so far as to argue that governments had lost much of their authority: 'the impersonal forces of a world market, integrated over the postwar period more by private enterprise in finance, industry and trade than by cooperative decisions of governments, are now more powerful than states'.

Over the past decade, and especially since September 11, however, these claims about the imminent demise of nation-states (Ohmae 1990) appear grossly exaggerated (Rizvi 2004). Indeed, against a new discourse of security, it has become clear that many powerful states, such as the United States, have reasserted their authority; and that national policy authority is indispensable in coordinating and controlling global mobility, interactions and institutions. It has become equally clear that this new discourse of security is linked inextricably to the imperatives of global capitalism. Evidently, without global security, the structures of global capitalism cannot be sustained. But if capitalist and security imperatives now work off each other, they need, more than ever before, a system of nation-states. As Wood (2003: 152) has argued, 'the more universal capitalism has become, the more it has needed an equally universal system of reliable local states'.

The need for the state can also be demonstrated by looking at the recent US rhetoric of the 'war on terrorism' (Buck-Morss 2006). It has been suggested that the 'war on terrorism' is a war without borders, because the terrorists work across national boundaries. However, as we have seen, the main targets of this war are nation-states, albeit 'weak' ones such as Afghanistan and Pakistan. This is so because it is argued that it is the weak states that inevitably harbour terrorists. Stronger states, on the other hand, can more readily control the movement and actions of their citizens. Global capitalism thus requires strong, reliable nation-states, which do not pose great risks to global economic activity but can influence and coordinate the behaviour of their citizens. In the supposed interests of security, nation-states are able to exercise considerable coercive power in order to produce the social conditions necessary for capital accumulation, including greater educational provision and individual dispositions favourable to market activity.

Wood (2003: 140) maintains that 'globalization has certainly been marked by a withdrawal of the state from its social welfare and ameliorative functions; and, for many observers, this has more than anything else created an impression of the state's decline'. But this is misleading, for it is impossible for global capitalism and organizations to dispense with many of the social functions performed by the state, such as security, social stability and infrastructural provisions, that have proven essential for economic success. Global capitalism depends more than ever on 'a system of multiple and more or less sovereign states'. Wood (ibid.: 141) insists:

> The very fact that 'globalization' has extended capital's purely economic powers far beyond the range of any single nation state means that global capital

> requires many nation states to perform the administrative and coercive functions that sustain the system of property and provide the kind of day-to-day regularity, predictability, and legal order that capitalism needs more than any other social form.

This suggests that issues of economic and political globalization are inextricably linked, and that public policy, including education, is now increasingly required to serve the interests of global capitalism.

Within the system of modern nation-states, considerable cultural importance was always attached to education. Educational systems carried the narratives of the nation. As Gellner (1983) points out, it was mass educational systems that provided a common framework of understanding, enhancing the processes of modernization. Through diffusion of ideas, meanings, myths and rituals, citizens were able to 'imagine' the nation, and filter conceptions of their 'other'. While education continues to serve this function, many globalization theorists (for example Steger (2003)) suggest that the nation-state faces a more difficult task in performing it. This is so because the lives of its citizens are now inextricably linked to cultural formations that are produced in faraway places, and the dispersion of people implies multiple senses of belonging and loyalty.

Under the conditions of globalization, the assumption of discrete national cultural formations can no longer be taken for granted, as there is now an ever-increasing level of cultural interactions across national and ethnic communities. With the sheer scale, intensity, speed and volume of global cultural communication, the traditional link between territory and social identity is now much more complicated; people now more readily choose to detach their identities from particular times, places and traditions. Not only the global media, but also greater transnational mobility of people, have had a 'pluralizing' impact on identity formation, producing a variety of hyphenated identities which are less 'fixed or unified' and which are hybrid in character. This has led to the emergence of a 'global consciousness' which may represent the cultural basis of an 'incipient civil society' (Hall 1996: 332).

Among the many factors that have contributed to the development of this global consciousness, the increased movement of people across national boundaries has played an important role. Characterized by a new international division of labour, the activities of transnational corporations, the effects of liberal trade and capital flow policies, together with better communication and cheaper transport, a globalizing economy means that a greater number of people inevitably cross national borders (Cohen 1997: 157). The movement of people – for family visits, business, international education, intermittent stays abroad and sojourning – has given rise to new global sensibilities and imaginations, leading to cultural practices based on what Tomlinson (2000) refers to as 'complex interconnectivity'.

Increasing levels of mobility and the intensification of economic, political and cultural interconnectivity have created conditions for the development of 'global cities', 'whose significance resides more in their global, rather than in their national role' (Cohen 1997: 157). However, as the scale of mobility from the developing to developed countries has become a major problem for global cities such as London and New York, it is only the nation-state that has the capacity to control the volume of flows of people through policies that encourage the mobility of global capital and the cosmopolitanization of city spaces, on the one hand, but to discourage the unfettered movement of people, especially unskilled workers and refugees, on the other (Sassen 1998).

What this discussion shows is that we are not so much experiencing the demise of the system of nation-states as witnessing its transformation. What is challenged is the traditional conception of the state as the fundamental unit of world order, a unitary phenomenon characterized by its relative homogeneity with a set of singular purposes. A fragmented policy arena, permeated by transnational networks as well as domestic agencies and forces, has replaced this system. As Held and McGrew (2005: 11) argue: 'the contemporary era has witnessed layers of governance spreading within and across political boundaries', transforming state sovereignty into a shared exercise of power. With the emergence of new patterns of political interconnectedness, 'the scope of policy choices available to individual governments and the effectiveness of many traditional policy instruments tends to decline' (ibid.: 13). The transformed state is now increasingly located within various webs of global and regional networks that not only challenge the traditional authority of the state, but also require the state to perform new functions of policy coordination and the development and delivery of programmes. Recent shifts in education policy are arguably located within this changing architecture of the state and cultural practices, responding to the demands of global capitalism, promoting a particular ideology consistent with its political interests.

Globalization as an ideology

Globalization represents a range of loosely connected ideas designed to describe new forms of political-economic governance based on the extension of market relationships globally. It replaces an earlier view of governance that implied the provision of goods and services as a way of ensuring social well-being of a national population. In contrast, the dominant view of globalization – widely referred to as 'neo-liberal' – is associated with a preference for the minimalist state, concerned to promote the instrumental values of competition, economic efficiency and choice, to deregulate and privatize state functions. As Peck and Tickle (2002: 394) maintain, as a constellation of ideas, neoliberal globalization promotes and normalizes a 'growth-first approach' to policy, relegating social welfare concerns as secondary. It rests on a pervasive naturalization of market logics, justifying them on the grounds of efficiency and even 'fairness'. It emphasizes the notion of choice, and privileges 'lean' government, privatization, deregulation and competitive regimes of resource allocation over the notions of a centralized state. It stresses global regimes of 'free trade', applying to both goods and services, even to services such as health and education that were traditionally marked by their highly national character.

In much of the recent literature, neoliberal globalization is presented as simply a description of global processes, as an objective set of social processes, implying their historical inevitability. But arguably neoliberalism is but one way of interpreting globalization, designed to steer a particular formation of the subjective or phenomenological awareness of people. It not only encourages a particular 'reading' of recent changes in global economy and culture – a specific way of interpreting the 'facts' of global interconnectivity and interdependence – but arguably presupposes a set of values attached to that 'reading', which directs us towards a consciousness of the world as a single space in which our problems are said to be interconnected; requiring a cosmopolitanism that demands us to recognize our interdependence, but from a particular point of view. Cohen and Kennedy (2000) refer to this phenomenon as 'globalism', which they contrast with globalization which 'mainly refers to a series of objective changes in the world that are partly outside us'. Globalism, on the other hand, suggests a set of value preferences – 'changes associated with globalization so that they are now incorporated into our emotions and our ways of thinking about everyday life' (ibid.: 58).

This distinction between objective and subjective interpretations of globalization is helpful, but perhaps too simplistic, because the norms with which we interpret the world necessarily affect the ways in which we describe that world. These objective and subjective dimensions are therefore inseparable. In this way, many popular discourses on globalization found in both corporate and academic literatures can be viewed as highly ideological. One of the main problems with these discourses is that they treat globalization as 'a pre-given thing, existing outside of thought' (Smith 2000: 21) with its own developmental logic. In so doing, Smith argues, they privilege economic over political and cultural processes. But this mode of analysis pays scant attention to the subjectivities of people, how these are formed, and how communities develop a sense of global interconnectivity and interdependence. In this manner, these discourses lack an effective theory of political agency, or any other kind of agency. They do not view global processes as ever-changing products of human practices, but interpret them instead as expressions of the deeper logic of economic imperatives, failing to come to terms with their 'situatedness' in the world of people, communities and nations alike. Time-space compression, for example, does not occur independently of the ways people experience their social location and relations, and this is not simply a product of some deeper structural imperatives.

Neoliberal discourses on globalization, and indeed some of the accounts critical of them, run the risk of treating global processes as historically inevitable, as a kind of juggernaut, which people and nations simply have to come to terms with and negotiate as best they can. These discourses are based on a politics of meaning that appear to seek to accommodate people and nations to a certain taken-for-grantedness about the ways the global economy operates and the manner in which culture, crises, resources and power formations must be filtered through their universal logic. They thus 'ontologize' the global market logic, creating global subjects who are asked to consider policy options through its presupposed conceptual prism, which revolves around such market principles as free trade; the production of profits through greater productivity; a minimalist role for the state; a deregulated labour market; and flexible forms of governance. In this way, the term 'globalization' is deeply ideological, implying certain power relations, practices and technologies, playing a 'hegemonic role in organizing and decoding the meaning of the world' (Schirato and Webb 2003: 1). This is what Bourdieu (2003) has referred to as a performative usage of the concept of globalization – one taken to mean neoliberal globalization, which elides other more critical accounts of recent global transformations.

An ideology is a highly contested theoretical construct. In popular parlance, it refers to a set of ideas to which one is totally committed, even if those ideas have no basis in fact or empirical reality. It is a system of widely shared beliefs, guiding norms and values, and ideals accepted as truth by a group of people. The dominant account of globalization contains an unmistakable ideological dimension filled with a range of norms, values, claims, beliefs and narratives which, while they are not always grounded in truth and are often inconsistent, are nonetheless sufficiently plausible to suggest historical accuracy. The debate about whether globalization is good or bad arguably takes place within the arena of ideology. It has become a strong ideological discourse, so much so that it is, as Steger (2003: 96) points out, 'notoriously difficult to resist and repel because it has on its side powerful social forces that have already pre-selected what counts as "real", and that it therefore shapes the world accordingly'. It suggests that globalization of the economy in particular is inevitable and irreversible. It implies moreover that nobody is in charge of globalization; and that it benefits everyone. Now it is possible to contest each of these claims, but as ideological assertions they are often assumed, rather than put forward as claims to be tested or debated.

The social imaginary of globalization

If many of the recent claims about globalization and its implications for practice are ideological, the question remains as to how it is that people internalize them. How do these claims become a part of their world view, shaping the ways in which they think about their social relations and forge conceptions of their future? In short, how is ideology translated into actual material practices steering our sense of possibilities and conceptions of the future? In what follows, we make a distinction between ideology and a social imaginary to understand this process of translation. This is not an absolute distinction, but is nonetheless useful for understanding how the ideology of globalization is reshaping people's social imaginary, in ways that lead to the development of a heightened sense of what Robertson (1992) calls a 'global consciousness'. Globalization has produced not only material economic shifts, but also a changing sense of identities and belonging. It has done this, we argue, through the development of a social imaginary about how the world is becoming interconnected and interdependent, an imaginary that now guides and shapes people's sense of the options for organizing their conduct.

According to the Canadian philosopher, Charles Taylor, the idea of a social imaginary involves a complex, unstructured and contingent mix of the empirical and the affective; not a 'fully articulated understanding of our whole situation within which particular features of our world become evident' (Taylor 2004: 21). In this sense, the idea of social imaginary is akin to Pierre Bourdieu's notion of 'habitus' (1986), or Raymond Williams's idea of 'structures of feeling' (1977). A social imaginary is a way of thinking shared in a society by ordinary people, the common understandings that make everyday practices possible, giving them sense and legitimacy. It is largely implicit, embedded in ideas and practices, carrying within it deeper normative notions and images, constitutive of a society. It involves (Taylor 2004: 23):

> ... something much broader and deeper than the intellectual schemes people may entertain when they think about social reality in a disengaged mode. I am thinking, rather, of the ways in which people imagine their social existence, how they fit together with others, how things go on between them and their fellows, the expectations that are normally met, and the deeper normative notions and images that underlie these expectations.

A social imaginary is thus carried in images, myths, parables, stories, legends and other narratives and most significantly, in the contemporary era, the mass media, as well as popular culture. It is through this shared social imaginary that relations and sociability among strangers within and across societies become possible.

Taylor maintains, however, that a social imaginary is embedded not only in everyday notions and images, but also in theories and ideologies and, by implication, in policies. For Taylor, the distinction between social theory and social imaginary is highly significant. Theories are often in possession of a relatively few people, while a social imaginary is more broadly accepted, rendering possible a widely shared sense of legitimacy, without which people might not be able to work collectively towards common goals. Theories emerge out of an established social imaginary, even if they suggest an alternative way of interpreting the world. While they might start off as theories held by a small group of people, to be successful, theories must infiltrate the wider community and then the whole society, creating a new sense of imaginary. For a theory to become part of a social imaginary, it must evolve into a kind of common understanding that enables us to carry out our everyday social practices: that is, 'a sense of how things usually go, but (this is) interwoven with an idea of how they ought to go, of what missteps would invalidate the practice' (Taylor 2004: 24).

It is important to stress, then, that a social imaginary is not simply inherited and already determined for us, it is rather in a constant state of flux. It is thus an enabling concept that describes the ways people act as world-making collective agents within a given symbolic matrix that refuses an 'ontology of determinism' (Castoriadis 1987). It is a creative force in the making of social-historical worlds, a force that has to be attentive to the 'signs of the time' and interpret all those particular, rather uneven and emotionally charged, events that make up everyday life (Maffesoli 1993). A social imaginary thus involves a collective social force that is not only specific to time and space, but is also always multiple and highly contested within and across particular communities. It is through the collective sense of imagination that a society is created, given coherence and identity, but is also subjected to social change, both mundane and radical.

Taylor's analysis suggests that neoliberal discourses of globalization are embedded within a social imaginary; and that their transformation requires the exercise of collective political agency, in imagining them differently. Significantly, then, a social imaginary exists in a double sense. It exists in ideological representations of existing discursive and material practices, but it is also the means by which individuals and communities are able to understand their identities and their place in the world differently, able to suggest transformations of the prevailing social order. The transformation of a social imaginary is of course never easy to achieve, requiring a whole range of formal and informal strategies to shift the popular images that people associate with discourse and practices that are sometimes expressed explicitly, but mostly not (Steger 2008).

Arjun Appadurai (1996) has analysed the role of a social imaginary in the formation of subjectivities within the globalizing context in which we now live, a context that is characterized by diffusion of social images, ideas and ideologies across communities around the world. This diffusion is facilitated by electronic media, mass migration and the mobility of capital and labour, creating conditions through which most societies around the world are becoming culturally diverse and hybrid, and cannot therefore avoid, in a fundamental sense, engaging with social relations transnationally. As Appadurai (ibid.: 14) puts it, the 'system of nation-states is no longer the only game in town', not only insofar as international governance and transnational economic and political traffic are concerned, but also with respect to cultural formations and identities. Any attempt to rethink the role of policy in the era of globalization can no longer overlook how our social imaginary is being reshaped simultaneously by both global and local processes, and how we might critically engage with these processes in order to develop alternatives to their hegemonic expressions.

In the global era, we live amid a multiplicity of social imaginaries. We live in a world in which ideas and ideologies, people and capital and images and messages are constantly in motion, transforming the vectors of our social imaginaries. We have access to many social imaginaries, in addition to those that are nationally prescribed. Each has a different point of origin, different axis, and travels through different routes and is constituted by different relationships to institutional structures in different communities and nations. Like Taylor, Appadurai (2001: 6) maintains that imagination as a collective social fact in the era of globalization has a split character: 'On the one hand, it is in and through the imagination that modern citizens are disciplined and controlled – by states, markets and other powerful interests. But it is also the faculty through which collective patterns of dissent and new designs for collective life emerge.'

Thus, competing social imaginaries now exist side by side in a constant state of political struggle. There are thus different and competing ways of interpreting the realities of global interconnectivity and interdependence, and of deriving education policy implications from them. Richard Falk (1993), for example, has pointed to a distinction between 'globalization from above' and 'globalization from below', that is, the distinction between neoliberal globalization advocated by the transnational corporate elite and that proffered by a whole range of social movements committed to global justice and democracy. But these competing imaginaries do not exist in a neutral space, but in a context that is produced not only by the residual forces of colonialism, but also by contemporary global dynamics of power relations through which a particular imaginary has become dominant. Over the past three decades, as we have already noted, neoliberalism has become ascendant, in the terms of which most recent accounts of globalization and their implications for public policy appear to be couched. These accounts are expressed in a language that is increasingly magisterial, demanding the implicit consent of national governments and ordinary people alike.

On the one hand, the neoliberal social imaginary of globalization is designed to forge a shared implicit understanding of the problems to which policies are presented as solutions, seeking a sense of political legitimacy. On the other hand, it is designed to discipline people and is aimed at guiding and shaping their conduct. The French philosopher Michel Foucault (1991) refers to this as *bio-power*. Foucault argues that governments are now less interested in imposing laws and more in engaging in tactics and strategies to ensure consent through policies, both symbolic and material. He argues that governments are deeply concerned with the *art of government* … with securing the fragile link between ruler and ruled, through the 'art of manipulating relations of power' (ibid.: 90). In terms of Easton's definition of policy as the 'authoritative allocation of values', governments secure their authority by allocating values through attempts to forge people's subjectivities in terms of a dominant social imaginary. In this way, the processes of allocation – the tactics and strategies designed to secure popular legitimacy for public policies – become just as important as the values articulated in the policy text.

Processes of policy allocation

So, how has the neoliberal social imaginary become globally dominant in the development and promotion of public policies? To answer this question, we need to point first to the strategies and tactics governments have employed. These have included the highly ideological claim that there is no longer any choice but to pursue neoliberal policies, an idea captured in the acronym TINA (There Is No Alternative). Furthermore, most government reports, not only in the countries of the Global North but also of the South, now begin with a customary framing discourse of the 'global imperatives', of how best to meet the challenges of globalization, or take advantage of the opportunities it offers (Spring 1998). This discourse has been particularly salient in accounts of education systems – the problems they confront and policy reforms that are needed to solve them.

It is not possible, however, to explain the emergence of the neoliberal social imaginary by pointing to the strategies and tactics of governments alone. A range of complicated global processes has also been involved, resulting from the new networks of transnational communication and interactions. Indeed, it can be argued that these processes have largely shaped national strategies of public policy allocation. Each of these processes has involved a different pattern of political activity, and each has had varied consequences for educational systems, but together they help to explain how a neoliberal social imaginary of globalization has become globally normalized, informing education policy deliberations around the world, helping to steer them in a particular direction.

The neoliberal imaginary of globalization has not emerged in a political vacuum, but in a context of the global flows of policy ideas. With revolutionary developments in transport, communication and information technologies, these flows have never been greater, mediated by the global mobility of people. People move for a wide variety of reasons, from tourism and immigration to education, trade and business, creating new diasporas. The elite among these diasporas are no longer reluctant to intervene in the policy processes of countries that they have left to settle elsewhere. New technologies enable them to remain connected. In relation to this, Appadurai (1996) talks of a postnational or diasporic public sphere. An inevitable consequence of this mobility is an increased circulation of ideas, images and ideologies across national spaces, and the emergence of transnational policy networks around a particular set of policy ideas. These ideas are reproduced in business schools that an increasingly large number of international students now attend and that produce corporate leaders. As Waters (1995: 82) points out, these ideas are embedded in Master of Business Administration programmes, form the basis of research on organizational and commercial questions, and are 'written up as easily digestible popular books that can be peddled to managers as manuals for organizational transformation'. These are thus located within what Thrift (2005) refers to as the 'cultural circuit' of global capitalism.

In the formation and promotion of the neoliberal social imaginary, global media have also played a major role. The media have become centrally important in the processes of policy production. The production of policy texts inside the state has become increasingly 'mediatized' as an element of what Fairclough (2000) calls the 'mediatization' of politics and policy. More journalists are involved in the finessing of policy documents to place the appropriate spin on them to ensure positive renditions in the media of policy development. This has seen a 'glossification' of policy texts. Fairclough (ibid.: 157) suggests that language is central to the practices of government, but the involvement of journalists in policy text production brings another logic of practice to bear on the texts produced (Bourdieu 1996).

At the global level, Appadurai (1996) has spoken of *ideoscapes,* which are constituted as 'concatenations of images' which circulate throughout the world in a profoundly political manner. While it is of course possible for both neoliberal ideologies and ideologies opposed to them to circulate freely through global media spaces, education policies have globally converged towards a particular concatenation of neoliberal ideas, despite some opposition from many sources. This concatenation is evident in the processes of policy borrowing, modelling, transfer, diffusion, appropriation and copying that occur across the boundaries of nation-states and which lead to universalizing tendencies in thinking about educational reform responsive to the challenges of globalization (Phillips and Ochs 2004).

These tendencies are strengthened by the work of intergovernmental organizations (IGOs), whose policy deliberation and evaluation are increasingly couched in neoliberal terms. We (Rizvi and Lingard 2006) have shown how the Organization for Economic Cooperation and Development (OECD), traditionally a site for the free exchange of educational ideas, has now become a policy player in its own right, influencing, cajoling and directing member states towards a predetermined social imaginary. The OECD (1985: 3) once viewed itself not 'as a supranational organization but a place where policy-makers and decision-makers can discuss their problems, where governments can compare their points of view'. But in more recent years it has evolved as an instrument of policy advocacy, promoting a range of neoliberal ideas about the global economy and its implications for public policy. It has worked hard to promote a particular view about how best to restructure the public sector to meet the requirements of the global economy. It has argued that:

> The common agenda that has developed encompasses efforts to make governments at all levels more efficient and cost-effective, to increase the quality of public services, to enable the public sector to respond flexibly and more strategically to external changes, and to support and foster national economic performance.

The OECD's advocacy for the policies of deregulation and privatization has been based squarely on its ideological beliefs about the role of the state, free trade and individual enterprise. It would be a mistake, however, to assume that the OECD's audiences throughout the world receive, interpret and experience its policy ideas in the same way. Indeed, the processes of reception have always been much more complicated than this. As Bourdieu (1999: 221) has noted:

> The fact that texts circulate without their context, that – to use my terms – they don't bring with them the field of production of which they are a product, and the fact that recipients, who are themselves in a different field of production, re-interpret the texts in accordance with the structure of the field of reception, are facts that generate some formidable misunderstandings and that can have good or bad consequences.

Nevertheless, the policy proposals the OECD has circulated are largely couched within the neoliberal social imaginary, as indeed are the ideas promoted by other major international organizations concerned with education policy such as the World Bank and, increasingly, also UNESCO, which once promoted a contrasting perspective but which has now joined forces with IGOs created specifically to address economic issues.

It needs to be noted that the circulation of policy ideas often takes place against the backdrop of a range of international and regional settlements, both formal and informal. These settlements are expressed in terms of consensus and conventions, and involve agreements and commitments that expose national policy practices to external dictates and scrutiny. They reduce the policy autonomy that nation-states possess to set their own policy priorities. Examples of conventions include agreements on human rights, democratic elections and social benefits and educational opportunities. While conventions are supposedly entered into voluntarily, there is often a great deal of pressure on countries to conform to particular ideologies. In recent years, almost all conventions have been framed in ways that make them consistent with market principles located within the social imaginary of neoliberalism.

Perhaps the best example of a consensus that promoted a neoliberal view of the economic and social order is the Washington Consensus. The term 'Washington Consensus' was coined by John Williamson in 1990 to refer to 'the lowest common denominator of policy advice being addressed by the Washington-based institutions to Latin American countries' (Williamson 1990: 1). Williamson viewed the Washington Consensus as an example of an 'intellectual convergence' towards a set of beliefs about the need for and content of economic reform. George Soros (1998) refers to these beliefs as 'market fundamentalism' and suggests that their worldwide popularity represents their success in the battle of policy ideas. These policy ideas, accepted by most Washington-based development agencies, include the values of macroeconomic discipline, trade openness and market-friendly microeconomic policies. In the field of education, this has implied fiscal discipline about educational funding, and a redirection of public expenditure policies towards fields offering both high economic returns and the potential to improve income distribution, such as primary education, as well as privatization and deregulation.

Through most of the 1990s, the Washington Consensus was used by development agencies in the Global North to persuade debt-ridden countries of the Global South that they had no other choice but to follow its dictates. Already captured by a social imaginary, most Western-trained economists in the Global South had no difficulty embracing policy proposals that assumed that poverty reduction and economic redistribution were impossible without trade openness and the deregulation of economic activity. And despite doubts expressed by many non-government organizations (NGOs) and some governments, the Washington Consensus reigned supreme in the field of development. It served to institutionalize everywhere the neoliberal notion that governments were highly inefficient in promoting growth, and even in addressing the problems of social inequalities. It promoted the ideology that only markets could solve the intractable problems facing societies. Markets thus defined the limits of national politics, by exerting an unprecedented amount of influence in shaping policies and in allocating funds for social and educational programmes. The policy role of nation-states was thus redefined as a facilitator of markets rather than an instrument that steered them or mediated their effects.

The Washington Consensus, of course, never delivered the kind of benefits it had promised. Towards the end of the 1990s, many policy experts, organizations and governments began to view the Washington Consensus as a relative failure. Williamson (2000) himself spoke of the need to develop a new discourse of a Post-Washington Consensus (PWC), which admitted some of the limitations of the Structural Adjustment Programs to which the Washington Consensus had given rise, and through which national governments in the Global South were forced to deregulate their economies, leaving them open to the exploitative practices of global capitalism. However, so entrenched is the neoliberal imaginary that the formulation of a PWC remained tied to the same ideological assumptions. As Jayasuriya (2001: 1) maintains, the PWC 'should be more properly viewed as an attempt to develop a political institutional framework to embed the structural adjustment policies of the Washington Consensus'. This discussion shows that conventions that governments sign are never neutral with respect to differing interests, but are located within a social imaginary that seeks to divorce its key assumptions from the murky terrains of political contestation, rendering them beyond critical scrutiny and challenge.

The neoliberal social imaginary has not, however, remained uncontested. The 2001 Porto Alegre Declaration, signed by Iberian and Latin American activist groups, for example, is radically opposed to its tenets (Gret and Sintomer 2005). The Declaration objects, for example, to deregulation policies in education, citing fears that these might lead to the removal of legal, political, fiscal and educational quality controls, and to national governments abandoning their social responsibilities for combating social inequalities. It maintains, furthermore, that deregulation policies serve only to weaken national sovereignty and erode some of the cultural values that define and sustain communities. Also, it suggests that in the field of education, deregulation benefits only those who already possess the resources to access education. In the battle over competing social imaginaries, however, the Porto Alegre Declaration has largely been sidelined by national governments facing greater pressure from IGOs. Even the Brazilian government has been unable to resist this pressure, developing educational policies that are mostly in line with the dictates of neoliberalism.

In the countries of the Global South, these policies have led to the consolidation of ideological power that has a transparently global character, based on a common set of ideological beliefs about the capitalist path of accumulation and appropriation of new resources and new labour power. This can be shown by pointing to the politics of international aid. To policymakers in poorer countries, the offer of aid and grants represents a major dilemma. On the one hand, it is almost impossible for the countries in severe economic difficulties to reject the offer of help, and yet this often means having to accept alienating and exploitative policies that have perhaps little chance of success in the longer term. Ultimately, these policies require nation-states to concede some of their autonomy, and to pass legislation designed more to create conditions conducive to investment of international capital than to the improvement of social conditions and educational opportunities.

It is not only the international lending agencies that demand neoliberal restructuring of educational systems as a condition of loans to developing countries; the transnational corporations (TNC) offering to invest in them do so as well. The relationship between TNCs and governments is a complex one, involving dynamics of both conflict and cooperation. Dicken (2003) argues that sometimes governments and TNCs may be rivals, but they may also collude with one another. In a global economy, governments need TNCs to help them in the process of material wealth creation, while TNCs require nation-states to 'provide the necessary supportive infrastructures, both physical and institutional, on the basis of which they can pursue their strategic objectives' (ibid.: 276). TNCs and governments are often involved in a bargaining process as each tries to get maximum advantage from the other. As Dicken (ibid.: 276) observes, 'states have become increasingly locked into a cut-throat competitive bidding process for investments; a process which provides TNCs with the opportunity to play off one bidder against another'. Some of this bargaining involves the demand by TNCs that education be restructured, with policies conducive to creating a human resource pool they need as low-cost labour.

Conclusion

What this discussion indicates is that there is no single process that has resulted in neoliberalism becoming a dominant social imaginary of globalization, but that this has occurred through a range of historically specific and interrelated processes which include: the global circulation of ideas and ideologies; international conventions and consensus that steer educational policies in a particular direction; cooperation and competition inherent, for example, in the practices of international trade in education; formal bilateral and multilateral contracts between systems which often involve a high degree of coercion. The circulation of ideas and ideologies through social and policy networks has become a noted feature of the global community. Conventions involve agreements in which educational systems expose their own policy practices to external scrutiny, agreeing to subscribe to an ideological consensus forged multilaterally. In a globally interconnected order, both cooperation and competition can generate similarities in educational policies, which different systems might pursue to achieve market advantage. A contract is an agreement between two or more parties to pursue policies that have been negotiated bilaterally or multilaterally. And finally, coercion involves an imposition of policies upon a weaker system under threat of sanctions. Each of these global processes not only plays a significant role in driving national systems of education towards a similar policy outlook, but also has served to institutionalize the neoliberal imaginary of education.

It needs to be said again, however, that these global processes do not affect all educational systems in the same way. They are filtered through particular national political and cultural traditions, as well as the specific ways in which policymakers engage with global pressures. If this is so, policies are still made by national governments, but in ways that cannot overlook global processes. We have noted in this chapter that globalization has spawned a highly contested debate, but a particular social imaginary of globalization has become dominant. While this is so, we have also pointed to the risks associated with naturalizing the concept of globalization. Our view is thus consistent with that of Ball (2007: 6), who argues that a transitive meaning of globalization helps in overcoming the temptation to reify globalization as the explanation for certain contemporary education policy developments and pushes us instead to seek for the organizational and individual sources of emergent policy discourses on a global scale. Dale's (1999) attempt to document the mechanisms of globalization stems from a similar motivation to avoid reifying globalization as the 'cause' of education policy developments.

It is clear that technology has facilitated the formation of extended policy networks and communities, which now sit within and across new spatial relations (rescaling) of the local, national, regional and global and facilitate relations between national and provincial arms of the state, as well with international organizations of various kinds. These networks and communities are more than just a policy-generating community, which has also been broadened through the networking of policymakers around the globe; they include participants in all aspects of the politics of policy processes. We have noted that international and supranational agencies such as the OECD, the World Bank, UNESCO and the EU now play an enhanced role in policy processes, and have often been central to the development of the emergent global education policy field. While all policies self-construct their own contexts, the involvement of more international agencies has seen context constructed as global. Indeed, competitiveness within the global economy is articulated as a central rationale for education policy changes. As noted earlier, to facilitate an understanding of this policy field we also need a global analysis of contemporary states and their location geopolitically, as well as of their specific histories.

An examination of the ways in which education policies have been reshaped in neoliberal terms, demands new ways of carrying out education policy analysis, linked not only to local and national considerations, but also to global forces, connections and imaginaries (Burawoy *et al.* 2000). This raises a range of new theoretical and methodological issues about education policy analysis. It is to a discussion of these issues that we now turn in Chapter 3.

3 Globalizing education policy analysis

Introduction

Working with an ecumenical definition of policy as the 'authoritative allocation of values', we have argued that an awareness of the processes of globalization demands paying attention to the effects these processes have upon the location of political authority, practices of allocation via a reconstituted state at the national level, and the framing of policy by discourses which, while they often have their gestation in various global networks, are negotiated and rearticulated at regional, national, provincial and local levels. These changes have been referred to as the rescaling of politics (Paul 2005). Such rescaling, we have noted, has affected both policy content and the processes of policy production. There have emerged new globally networked education policy communities. Changes associated with the processes of globalization raise a range of new political, theoretical and methodological issues, demanding a reconsideration of how we ought to carry out education policy analysis.

We have noted, however, the danger of reification, which often lurks in considerations of globalization in education policy studies; that is, a temptation to explain policy shifts simply as a causal outcome of global processes. It is mistaken, we have argued, to focus resolutely on the structural transformations that globalization represents, without recognizing the role that political agencies play in the creation of discursive and material practices associated with education policy. We have suggested instead that changing histories of global relations in education policy need to be understood in their specific cultural and political contexts, with a focus on the institutions, organizations and individuals who are the bearers of globalized education policy discourses. Good education policy analysis thus involves an understanding of how globalization effects actually work, rather than reifying globalization as the blanket cause of specific policy developments (Dale 1999, 2006). In this chapter we explore some of the major characteristics of such 'good policy analysis' in education, as a backdrop for a discussion in subsequent chapters of recent shifts in education policy thinking in a number of areas in a range of different locations. Our approach to policy analysis departs from traditional rationalist and interpretivist approaches and uses instead resources from critical, post-structural and post-colonial theories to suggest ways of globalizing studies of education policy.

Purposes and positionalities

We begin this exploration with the recognition that there is no recipe for carrying out policy analysis in education (Ozga 2000). In part, the appropriate approach to adopt will depend on the nature of the policy being analysed. Here one could contrast the articulated policies in education of governments with strong reform agendas with policies produced within a school concerning, for example, student dress and behaviour; or compare both with an education policy of the World Bank and its effects in the education systems and on professional practices within nations of the Global South. Policy analysis depends on the site of production of the policy as well as on the nature of the policy in question.

The purposes of policy analysis are equally important for the theoretical and methodological approaches to be adopted. In the traditional policy literature a distinction is made between what is called *analysis of* and *analysis for* policy (Gordon *et al.* 1977). The former is the more academic exercise, conducted by academic researchers, seeking to understand why a particular policy was developed at a particular time, what its analytical assumptions are and what effects it might have. The latter, *analysis for* policy, refers to research conducted for actual policy development, often commissioned by policymakers inside the bureaucracy within which the policy will be developed, and *ipso facto* is more constrained as to theoretical framework and methodology and most often has a shorter temporal frame. Analysis of policy sets its own research agenda; it does not take for granted the policy construction of the problem which a new policy seeks to address. Indeed, the first step in policy analysis might very well be a critical deconstruction of the problem as constructed by the policy, and of the context and history assumed by the policy. In contrast, analysis for policy takes as given the research problem as constructed by those framing policy, and thus often lacks a critical orientation.

We would not want to overstate this binary, however. Perhaps it might be better to see the two sitting at various points on an academic/applied education policy studies continuum (Cibulka 1994). Academic policy research, nonetheless, also has policy and political effects. Some policymakers inside educational organizations are knowledgeable about such research and utilize it in their work. Carol Weiss's (1979) classic documentation of research utilization in public policy, however, suggested that the most common mode of effect was indirect through 'percolation' or 'enlightenment', as social science research changed the way policymakers thought about things, including policy problems. Policy activists, located inside the policy bureaucracy as well as outside (Yeatman 1998), often have a more explicit awareness of academic policy research. In some policy domains in education, for example in gender policies, feminist policymakers have worked with short- and long-term strategies towards gender justice and could be seen as inside policy activists. The same is the case with indigenous policy activists inside government bureaucracies in Australia. In this way, even what might be seen as symbolic policy, that is, one constructed in response to pressures of various kinds but with little material commitment to implementation, might be important as a first policy step towards more progressive material policies. Research for policy also need not be of an instrumental and narrow kind. Additionally, sometimes research for policy can provide grounds for *not* pursuing a particular policy.

The analysis of/for binary also implies different relationships between these two forms of policy research and actual policy, which we might see as an activist relationship geared to enhancing understanding or 'enlightenment', as opposed to a more instrumental, 'engineering' relationship geared to problem solving and sometimes legitimation (Trowler 2003). Implicit here are the purposes of policy research. All of this goes to broader considerations of how research, in this instance education policy analysis, reaches policymakers and practitioners and has effects. There are multiple, multifarious and mediated ways in which policy research reaches policymakers and practitioners (Whitty 2006; Pawson 2006).

The focus of policy research can vary from the analysis of: the context of policy; the construction of the problem which the policy addresses; values articulated by the policy content; policy production processes; the information needed for policymaking; the policy actors and processes of advocacy; policy allocation, dissemination and implementation; to policy evaluation and review. (See Figure 3.1 for a more elaborated listing of possible questions for education policy analysis across contextual, textual and implementation considerations.) Given the multiple foci of policy analysis, we need to consider issues relating to the positionality of the policy researcher and the significance of such positionality to policy analysis. The questions of who is doing the policy analysis and for what purposes, and within what context, are clearly relevant in determining the approach to be taken to policy analysis. Purposes may stretch from the more utilitarian through the legitimating towards more critical approaches aimed at understanding or enlightenment.

Positionality here has at least three meanings, perhaps four. The first relates to the actual location of the policy researcher in respect of the focus of analysis. For example, we can contrast the positionings of the academic researcher, the doctoral student, the policy bureaucrat, the commissioned researcher, the freelance analyst for hire, the consultant researcher, the policy entrepreneur; and consider how such positioning frames the type of policy analysis conducted. The second meaning of positionality links to the theoretical and political stance adopted by the policy researcher, which has implications for the intellectual resources brought to bear on the research topic, including theory and methodology. Theoretical and methodological considerations also include matters of ontology (what we believe the nature of reality to be) and epistemology (how we justify knowledge claims).

Here one could contrast positivist and interpretivist accounts of social reality and positivist and post-positivist and critical accounts of knowledge claims. In very general terms, the positivist view justifies knowledge in terms of observable, generalizable and predictable data, while interpretivism emphasizes the social construction of reality and seeks to provide explanations of human behaviour in terms of intentionality. Post-positivist perspectives, in contrast, focus on the processes involved in meaning-making, while critical approaches underline the importance of power in the construction and justification of knowledge claims. One of these critical approaches is critical race theory, which many researchers in the United States in particular (for example Ladson-Billings 2004; Sleeter 2005) have used to consider the ways in which policy authority is exercised through racial configurations.

In contrast, commissioned policy research – that is, research for policy – usually demands methodologies that often assume a kind of rationalist 'engineering' model, involving a series of steps, from the specification of policy goals, an examination of the possible implementation strategies, a determination of the resources available for implementation, the selection of the most efficient strategies to realize the specified policy goals, to actual implementation. In this approach ends and means are resolutely separated, while the operational values of efficiency and effectiveness are considered paramount. The emphasis is on evidence and calculations of performance. In recent years this approach, which represents policy realities through numbers, has become globally popular among IGOs and governments alike. Rose (1999) has used the phrase 'policy as numbers' to refer to the ways in which the new public management associated with the restructuring of the state in the face of globalization has constituted policies in relation to certain outcome accountabilities, often framed through sets of key performance indicators. These indicators are part of what Power (1997) has called the 'audit state'. The emergence of this audit culture clearly has implications for analysis for policy, and certainly for policy evaluation.

There is at least a third meaning of positionality in respect of policy research that is intimately linked to the features of globalization. Here, positionality is taken to refer to the spatial location of the researcher, specifically national location and the positioning of that nation in respect of global geopolitics, including location within the Global North/Global South divide, and we recognize the danger of essentializing these categories. As noted in Chapters 1 and 2, issues of spatiality have become new foci of contemporary social theory and research in the context of the apparent time/space compression associated with globalization, affected through new communication technologies. Tikly (2001) has observed that the problem with much theorising about globalization and education – and we would add education policy – is that it fails to recognize the different positionings of different nations vis-à-vis IGOs such as the World Bank, UNESCO and the OECD. In developing their educational policy, the countries of the Global South are, for example, much more constrained than those of the Global North. This differentiation is further underlined by the fact that social theories produced in the high-status universities of the metropolises of the Global North (Appadurai 2001; Connell 2007) often sideline other voices, treating the nations of the Global South simply as sites of empirical research and the application of theories developed elsewhere. Connell (ibid.: vii–viii) has examined how 'modern social science embeds the viewpoints, perspectives and problems of metropolitan society, while presenting itself as universal knowledge'. This situation is being challenged, however, with calls for a stronger form of internationalization of academic theorizing, what Appadurai (ibid.) has referred to as the need to 'deparochialize' research, and methodological developments. Connell (ibid.) has also emphasized the usefulness of 'Southern theory'.

It is important to recognize that positionality may also refer to the national location of the policy researcher, which has implications for the nature of the analysis done and the theoretical and methodological options available. Working with doctoral students from various nations of the Global South has made us aware of this meaning of positionality in education policy analysis. Indeed, we have realized that in many nations of the Global South the only extant education policy analysis is research commissioned by donor agencies such as the World Bank or the UK Department for International Development (DfID), with all the implications that result in relation to problem setting, theoretical frameworks and methodologies. It would not be inaccurate to describe some of this research as 'quick and dirty', reflecting positionality and purposes of the research.

This discussion underlines the importance of taking an historical approach to understanding how globalization might affect policy processes (Rizvi 2007). This point is well exemplified in respect of the postcolonial aspirations of many nations of the Global South and the role that education policy is expected to play in achieving those aspirations. Neglecting the history of their education systems – what Gregory (2004) calls the 'colonial present' – will necessarily reduce the veracity and quality of the education policy analysis we carry out. Colonial histories are necessary to an understanding of the education policy effects of globalization. In this way, the temporal location of the education policy analyst is another fourth aspect of positionality, which is important in the chronological consideration of what policies have preceded any given policy, and the extent to which the policy represents an incremental or a radical change.

Contemporary accounts of research methodologies in the social sciences stress the significance of reflexivity to quality research. Reflexivity demands transparent articulation of researcher positionality and the significance of this to data collection and analysis. Bourdieu (Bourdieu *et al.* 1999), for instance, has spoken of the need to reject 'epistemological innocence', a stance which can be compared with Appadurai's (2001) call for 'epistemological diffidence' and Smith's (1999) talk of the need for 'epistemological openness'. Such a rejection of epistemological innocence demands that researchers articulate their positioning within the research, in terms of their value stances, their problem choice, and their theoretical and methodological frames. Bourdieu (2004: 94) thus sees the necessity of researchers 'objectivating' themselves in order to deconstruct their 'taken for granted' assumptions. Bourdieu's argument, with which we agree, is that doing this is necessary to arrive at more trustworthy and justifiable accounts of the data. Positionality, in the multiple meanings of the concept considered above, then affects the form of analysis taken, but also demands that all policy analysis practises reflexivity.

It is perhaps important here to make a distinction between how policy analysis is actually conducted in various ways and how we would suggest it ought to be conducted. Some times the analyst does not have much degree of choice. We are thinking of the academic policy analyst commissioned by the state to conduct policy analysis. Here the researcher is most often constrained by the research problem, which is taken from its bureaucratic construction and which is taken as given, and often restricted as to theoretical and methodological approaches. However, this is not always so. For example, one of us (Lingard) conducted a large commissioned research project for a State Department of Education in Australia, which through a number of political contingencies, including the politics of the commissioning of the research and a change of government, granted the researchers considerable space theoretically and methodologically and in respect of publishing from the research. On the other hand, we have also been involved in policy research in relation to issues of racism and boys' education, where there was much tighter control of the research and policy analysis proffered, from problem setting through research design, data collection, analysis, write-up and policy recommendations.

In recent years, there has been much talk of the need for evidence-based policy and professional practice in the public sector, a focus on 'what works' as the basis for public policy. This rise of evidence-based policy is linked to the new public management and pressures for efficiency and effectiveness in the delivery of public policy (Head 2008) and perhaps could be seen as the contemporary version of the rational approach to policymaking. This evidence-based movement is another example of how the purposes of policy analysis and the positioning of the policy researcher are important factors in framing the type of analysis conducted. Its emphasis assumes a direct instrumental relationship between policy research and policymaking, also often providing legitimation of the given policy. However, because of the contested nature of theory and research methodologies within the social sciences, some 'evidence', derived from certain research, gets utilized, while other 'evidence', derived from different research and theoretical and methodological frameworks, is neglected.

Given our acceptance of a definition of policy as the authoritative allocation of values, we would suggest that in reality evidence (research- and practice-based) can only ever be one contributing factor to policy development in education. As Head (2008: 9) has demonstrated, policies in the public sector are 'inherently marked by the interplay of facts, norms and desired actions', reflecting three knowledge bases: those of political judgement and professional practice in addition to (social) scientific research. We prefer the descriptor, evidence-informed policy. We would hope that such evidence would also include evidence that is critical of extant policies. (See also Pawson 2006.) We should also note that contemporary education policy associated with the restructured state and new public management has also been concerned with supporting certain types of education research and rejecting other types. Indeed, in both the UK and the USA there has been a politics around education research generally, attempting to legitimate certain kinds of research and denying other kinds, with support for more traditional experimental design and dismissive attitudes to more critical and qualitative approaches (Ozga *et al.* 2006).

To sum up our discussion in this section, we have argued that there is no straightforward recipe for policy analysis in education, and that the approach adopted will be affected by the nature of the policy being analysed and the site of production of the policy. The positionality of the researcher is another important factor, as are the purposes of the policy analysis: whether the analysis is *of* or *for* policy, whether it is conducted as a stage in the policy development or policy review, or for the purposes of political advocacy or a general academic exploration. Important, therefore, is the positionality of the policy analyst and relationship to the realpolitik of actual policymaking, theoretical and methodological stance, national location in global politics and temporal position. In other words, policy analysis not only explores the workings of political power and authority, but is also embedded within relations of power. As Foucault (1980) has suggested, every relation of power has an associated knowledge and every form of knowledge exists within relations of power. This is an important insight in relation to policymaking and analysis. Issues of power are thus centrally involved: in whose interests are the policy made and the analysis conducted?

Questions for policy analysis

Our own interest in policy analysis is concerned with understanding policy content, its related processes and its effects in order to contribute to making things better in educational practice, contributing to progressive social change. Our theoretical approach is located within what Jenny Ozga (1987) has called 'policy sociology'. Policy sociology is 'rooted in the social science tradition, historically informed and drawing on qualitative and illuminative techniques' (ibid.: 144). We have already shown how historical understanding is important to policy analysis, but argue that policy sociology is affected in a number of ways by globalization. For example, globalization affects an elision of a simple homology between society and nation in relation to what we call the *social*. As Massey (1994) has noted, globalization is social relations stretched out. Thus, for example, such 'stretching out' challenges ethnography as a research methodology, given the focus of such a methodology on the local and the specific, which is now imbricated in the global and vice versa. How we define the local has become deeply problematic.

Burawoy and colleagues (2000) have investigated methodological issues arising from global shifts, particularly in relation to ethnography. They have suggested that there are three axes of globalization, namely 'global forces', which refer to the large structural developments in respect of global capitalism and so on, 'global connections', which refer to the connections between local and global flows of people, and a 'global imagination' to encapsulate how these structural changes and connections provoke the mobilization of meaning about globalization and the changes it has effected. In a sense, these axes of globalization provide a specific contemporary account of how the central problem of social theory, namely the recursive relationships between structure and agency, might be reconceptualized and interrogated in the context of globalization.

Methodologically, much of the recent research conducted in the name of policy sociology has been 'qualitative and illuminative'. We, however, would deny an absolute bifurcation between qualitative and quantitative approaches, for many policy problems empirical quantitative methods can also be appropriate, given specific needs. What we would note, however, is the need for reflexivity in the usage of such methodologies. As Gale (2001: 382) has noted, 'quantitative data can also prove illuminating, particularly when it is subjected to the methodological assumptions of critical social science. To dismiss such data entirely is to curtail "our ability to raise and answer critical questions about the large scale effects"'. We thus accept the point made by Fitz *et al.* (2006: 3) that the difficulties and complexities associated with quantitative methods ought not to mean the abandonment of such methods, nor do such approaches have to be non-critical. What we would stress is the need to achieve an appropriate fit between research problem and methods adopted, together with an historically informed reflexivity. The type and site of the policy, and the focus and purpose of analysis, are all important considerations to find the methodological fit. Ball (2008) has used the metaphor of a pragmatic toolbox to suggest that methodologies should not determine the approach to education policy analysis, but that methodology should be framed in terms of research purpose and researcher positionality.

Policy sociology has multiple purposes, not only descriptive and analytical but also normative and imaginative. In our view, policy sociology should not only describe relations of power and processes through which policies are developed and allocated, but should also point to strategies for progressive change which might challenge oppressive structures and practices. In the contemporary era, considerations of progressive change are, however, more complex than they once might have appeared. The construction of a progressive politics is now affected by and must take account of globalization. Progressive social change relates to issues of what Nancy Fraser (1997) has called a politics of redistribution, seeking to achieve a more equal society, and to a politics of recognition, which works with a politics of respect for difference, as well as a politics of representation which enables marginalized voices to be heard. The first politics is concerned with equality and issues of poverty and social class, the second with matters of identity, while the third relates to global structures of power and democratic participation.

Our view of policy sociology is based on a set of normative principles, which encourages equality, respect for difference and democratic participation in both the content of policy and the manner in which policies are constructed and implemented. We thus reject the contention that policy analysis can be value-neutral, involving a set of rational-instrumental techniques, as much of the traditional policy sciences sought to assert. These rational-instrumental techniques take the status quo for granted, as a given, as well as a policy's definition of the problem for which the policy is the intended solution. This type of policy analysis is circumscribed and does not confront larger questions relating to the changing structure and functioning of the state and whose interests are represented in both decision-making and non-decision-making in policy processes. The traditional policy sciences, then, were only concerned with how best to solve problems and determine the best course of action to take to realize given ends. In contrast, we maintain not only that policies embody a particular set of values, but that analysis of policy is an inherently political activity. We are thus interested in considering who are the winners and losers with regard to any given policy and whose interests the policy serves. The articulation of our normative stance here is thus central to the reflexivity endemic to our approach to education policy studies and analysis.

This approach to education policy analysis, then, is at one level ecumenical, but at another it explicitly specifies the normative position we adopt in analysing texts which have policy effects. This position affects 'how' we research and how we interpret 'what we find', and how we suggest alternatives. Drawing on Kenway (1990) and our earlier work (Taylor *et al.* 1997), we suggest that policy sociology, as analysis of policy, involves a range of questions in respect of any given policy, situated against reflexive consideration of the positionality of the policy researcher. Critical social science theories and methodologies offer ways to research these questions. These questions are elaborated in Figure 3.1 under a number of categories that suggest differing foci. We have framed these questions in Figure 3.1 around Contextual Issues, Policy and Textual Issues, and Implementation and Outcomes Issues, drawing on our earlier framework for policy analysis of context, text and consequences (ibid.). We have then located questions against these issues and also attempted to suggest the need for a deparochialized disposition and global outlook in asking and answering these questions. As a multifarious activity, policy analysis need not, of course, address all of these questions at once, but may focus on a selected set: much depends on both the purpose of analysis and the position of the analyst. For example, research might focus on the 'origins' of policy, textual analysis of a policy or policy outcomes through implementation. Trajectory and ecological approaches to education policy (Weaver-Hightower 2008) are also concerned with policy across this cycle and its location in the broader context. In this way they can be contrasted with rational approaches, which narrow and contain the focus of policy development (Hudson and Lowe 2004).

Within the broad spectrum of questions that can be asked in analysis of policy as illustrated in Figure 3.1, various approaches have emerged, each defined by its focus. It is possible to focus exclusively, for example, on implementation (Implementation and Outcomes Issues in Figure 3.1). Implementation studies in education have been highly influential, particularly in the USA (Honig 2006). These studies are either top-down or bottom-up, with a 'backward mapping' approach being a component of the latter type of studies (Elmore 1979/1980). Backward mapping as a normative policy production approach looks at the site of practice which the policy wants to change, and then strategizes backwards to create the policy, structures, culture and implementation strategy necessary to achieve such change. Top-down implementation studies are usually concerned with refractions, failures or deficits in policy implementation, while the bottom-up studies recognize the inevitability of mediations by professionals. When professionals implement policies they inevitably take the specificities of the context into account, seeking to align policy directives to the local conditions. A useful distinction here might be to see the policy as 'strategy' and its implementation as 'tactic', using the distinction developed by de Certeau (1984).

Another common approach to policy analysis is concerned with the critical analysis of actual policy texts, including analysing and documenting the discourses within which the texts are located (Taylor 2004). (Figure 3.1 outlines some of the questions that might be addressed when taking a textual focus.) This approach recognizes that policies are often as much about language as anything else (Fairclough 2001) and that policies are often positioned within what Bourdieu and Passeron (1977) called 'magisterial discourse', that is, language which is unidirectional and which commands and instructs. Such discourse attempts to constrain the possibilities for interpretation. Rizvi and Kemmis (1987) view policy implementation as 'interpretation of interpretations', a situation which the magisterial nature of discourse seeks to limit.

An attempt to understand the problem to which a given policy is a putative solution represents yet another approach to policy analysis. This requires an appreciation of the problem, rather than simply taking the policy construction of the problem as a given. As Gil (1989: 69) suggests, the first task of policy analysis is 'to gain understanding of the issues that constitute the focus of the specific social policy which is being analysed or developed. This involves exploration of the nature, scope and distribution of these issues, and of causal theories concerning underlying dynamics.' Similarly, McLaughlin (2006: 210) points out that 'assumptions about the nature of the policy problem determine the policy solutions pursued and the logic of action advanced by a policy. And notions about preferred solutions also determine

Figure 3.1 Policy analysis, analysis of policy: Key questions (Framed by reflexive consideration of the 'positionality' of the policy analyst)

Policy issues:	*Questions for analysis:*
Contextual Issues	
Issues of historical, political and bureaucratic origins	Where did this policy originate, including consideration of any relevant global factors/institutions?
	Why was this policy adopted?
	Why was it adopted now?
	Does this policy have incremental links to earlier policy/policies?
	Is the policy part of a policy ensemble?
	Who were the 'players' (groups, interests, individuals) involved in establishing the policy agenda and the policy?
Policy and Textual Issues	
Discursive formation of policy and policy problem	What discourses frame the policy text? Are these globalized discourses?
	To which 'problem' is the policy constructed as a solution?
	How is the policy problem conceptualized?
	What alternative problem constructions have been rejected/ neglected?
	How has the policy constructed its context and/or history?
	Will the policy as constructed 'solve' the problem to which it is a response?
	What complementary policies are required (in education and elsewhere) to ensure the achievement of the policy's goals?
Textual considerations	How has the policy text been constructed linguistically?
	How does the policy 'work' as a text?
	Has the policy text been 'mediatized'?
	How have any competing interests been sutured together in the text?
	What is the implied readership of the policy?
	What is the 'intertextuality' of the policy; that is, how does it sit in relation to other policies or a 'policy ensemble'?
Interests involved and underpinning the policy	Who has advocated and promoted the policy and why?
	Where are the advocates located (inside/outside the state bureaucracy and policy processes, inside and outside the nation)?
	How have competing interests been negotiated in relation to the policy agenda and in relation to the production of the specific policy text?

Figure 3.1 (continued)

Policy issues:	*Questions for analysis:*
	What policy communities and/or policy networks have been involved in the processes of policy production?
Policy structuration	What have been the effects of national/provincial state structures on the policy processes?
	What role have international agencies played in its promotion?
	Have globalization and associated changes been invoked as a rationale for the policy?
	Has the policy been 'borrowed' from a 'reference society'?
	Is the policy driven more by ideology than by research evidence?
Resource issues	How have empirical research and policy precedents been used in support/justification/production of the policy?
	What resources (intellectual, empirical, research, human, material) are mobilized by the policy?
Implementation and Outcomes Issues	
Implementation strategies	How is the policy 'allocated' and disseminated to its target population?
	What are the strategies for implementation? Will these strategies achieve the policy's goals?
	Is this a material or symbolic policy?
	Is this a distributive or redistributive policy?
	Are adequate resources and professional development mobilized by the policy?
	Is there an evaluation strategy for the policy and its implementation? If so, is there an 'appropriate' time-frame for evaluation? Who will conduct the evaluation?
	Does the implementation time-frame fit within the temporality of politics or that of professional practice?
	Have indicators been constructed for measuring policy effects and accountability? Are these relevant and appropriate?
	What is the reception given to the policy at the site of implementation practice?
	How does the policy fit with the dominant logics of professional practice?
	What is the implied 'ideal professional practitioner' in the policy?
	How does the policy fit with other policies at the implementation site?
Policy outcomes	What are the consequences of the policy, both short term and long term?
	What is the relationship between policy outputs and policy outcomes?

Figure 3.1 (continued)

Policy issues:	*Questions for analysis:*
	Does the policy have unintended consequences?
Policy outcomes *continued…*	In whose interests does the policy actually work?
	Is this a significant material or symbolic policy in terms of outcomes?
	Has the policy had material effects or largely discursive ones?
	How does this policy fit with other cognate policies within education and across government?
	Will the policy achieve its goals and objectives? (Policy evaluated against its own goals and framework)
	What are the social justice effects of the policy? (Policy evaluated against some articulated ideal)

how policies are formulated – the policy target, nature of policy implements, level of support and regulatory structures, for example.'

Traditionally, most policy problems and solutions were constructed within the nation-state. In recent decades, however, policy gestation, especially for national, state-centric, top-down policies, can now increasingly be traced to international organizations and globalized education policy discourses. While there has always been policy borrowing and policy lending across nations (Steiner-Khamsi 2004), these processes today have been speeded up with the emergence of a global field of education policy production, even if local factors remain important for many nations. But even for these nations, measures of comparative educational performance on an international scale have become important. They take the measures of quality and equity outcomes in education on the OECD's PISA, for example, as a point of comparison, thus locating the national system within a global system. As Nóvoa and Yariv-Mashal (2003) suggest, the global eye works together with the national eye today in both education policy and governance.

To reiterate, then, in recent decades the space of policy processes has changed significantly. While national structures remain important to policy production, their character and ways they work have changed. If this is so, it has implications for the ways in which policy research is conducted, in an attempt to answer the analysis questions listed above and adumbrated in Figure 3.1. We note here as well how the recognition of the economic significance of education has seen restructuring of education policy production processes within nations as national/provincial/local relationships have been restructured, with national governments seeking enhanced policy roles, even in federal political structures such as in Australia, the USA, Canada and Germany.

Research and policy analysis

In theoretical and methodological terms, education policy research has been framed differently in different intellectual contexts. So one can compare, for example, policy analysis in education in the UK with that in the USA. The dominant approaches in the UK come out of critical sociological traditions, while those in the USA fit more within traditional instrumentalist perspectives, tending towards positivist and functionalist methodologies. Policy analysis in the USA is more conscious of policy's legal framing and consequences than is the case in the UK, where educational bureaucracies have much more sway. Policymakers in the USA are highly conscious of the possibilities of legal challenges that often reach all the way to the Supreme Court, while policy analysts have to consider how policies were developed within the legal requirements of the American Constitution. Even critical studies of education policies in the USA have been linked to legal considerations, as in, for example, critical race theory.

In the UK, the policy sociology approach first came into prominence during the 1980s when, under the Thatcher government, sociology of education as a field of study was politically attacked in a sustained fashion, leading many sociologists of education to switch focus to policy as a major topic of analysis. Since that time policy sociology has also been affected by various critical developments in the social sciences including (pro)feminism, post-structuralism, post-colonialism and postmodernism, as well as accounts that suggest the need to take account of globalization. Extending the tradition of policy sociology, Gale (2001) has spoken of policy historiography, policy genealogy and policy archaeology as approaches to education policy analysis, while a number of education policy scholars such as Peters (2002) have developed an approach to policy analysis based on Foucault's (1991) concept of governmentality. Olssen *et al.* (2004) have also provided a Foucauldian approach to the analysis of education policy in the context of globalization.

In the US context, following Lasswell's 'policy sciences' approach developed after the Second World War (see Peters and Pierre 2006), education policy analysis has remained largely within a politics of education framework, informed by positivism and functionalism. Critical work of the kind found in the UK and Australia has been resisted. These differing intellectual/national traditions are reflected in the content carried in the two major journals in the field, notably the *Journal of Education Policy* from the UK and the American Educational Research Association (AERA) journal, *Educational Evaluation and Policy Analysis*, which focuses on educational evaluation, educational policy analysis and the relationship between the two. Yet while these differences are significant, globalization has speeded up the flows of ideas and academics across the globe as part of the global 'cultural circuits' of capitalism (Thrift 2005), such that even with these differences it is now possible to speak of an emergent global intellectual field of education policy studies. This field in some ways parallels the emergent global education policy field. (See Simons *et al.* (2009) for an extensive contemporary coverage of the education policy field.)

In 1990, commenting in a UK context, Stephen Ball had observed that critical education policy analysis then had the character of commentary and critique, which was not often supported by empirical evidence. We would suggest that this situation has changed somewhat over the past almost two decades. There have been two sets of pressures here: the first relates to the theoretical developments within the social sciences generally, while the second concerns the framing of policy research by government policies, which is located within the broader move to new public management and a desire for evidence-based policy. Research paradigms in education have become the focus of government policy, directly and indirectly (through funding priorities, output and impact emphases, encouragement of policy-relevant research), and have sought to valorize certain theoretical and methodological frames over others (Ozga and Lingard 2007: 77–79). This has seen an eclecticism in education policy analysis (critical and functionalist, qualitative and quantitative), but also a greater concern with theoretical and methodological issues.

Maguire and Ball (1994) classified qualitative approaches to education policy analysis into three kinds: elite studies ('situated studies of policy formation'), trajectory studies and implementation studies. To this categorization we would add policy text analysis. Elite studies usually involve interviews with the major policy players as a way of understanding policy texts and policy processes across the policy cycle, with a particular focus on the politics of policy text production. Such studies recognize the politics of relationships between politicians and policymakers and the politics involved inside the actual site of policy production itself. Elite studies can also be linked to policy histories, focusing on changing policies over time. For example, Lingard *et al.* (1995) drew on interviews with senior policymakers, educational advisers and ministers for education over a ten-year period as of way of understanding developments nationally in education policy in Australia and their mediation by federal/state relations during the period of Labor governments (1983–1996). This study was thus concerned with structures and agency, with field and practice in policy processes. Indeed, it was these elite interviews that suggested the emergence of a global education policy field and the significance of the OECD to education policymaking in Australia.

There is a range of methodological issues which are raised by the elite studies approach, because such research utilizes interviews with elite policy players and thus requires access to them. Such access is usually easier for seasoned academic researchers than emerging researchers, with the power relations between the researcher and the interviewees becoming highly problematic. Interview processes are often also gendered and racialized. Sometimes methodological issues of access can also provide important research evidence. For example, as senior researchers interviewing many senior policymakers in relation to the creation in Australia in 1987 of the *National Policy for the Education of Girls in Australian Schools*, we were granted ready access, yet our doctoral students had much more difficulty in respect of access to these same policymakers, reflecting their different academic status but also, importantly, a different policy climate. Ten years on, these policymakers were much more considered and careful in the things they said and were much more careful about checking interview transcripts and the like for accuracy etc, seeking to ensure that they had not said anything which would create political or work problems for them. The vastly different policy research data collection context also tells us a lot about the substantive policies which were the foci of each research study – in 1987, concerned with gender equity in its broadest sense and, ten years later, with a focus on boys' issues within a reactionary or recuperative men's politics framework (Lingard *et al.* 2009).

Trajectory studies deal with policy across the stages of the policy cycle, beginning with elite interviews, concerned with the gestation of a policy and the often internecine politics involved in the production of the actual policy text through to implementation and the reception and effects of the policy in practice. Figure 3.1 lists the extensive questions which would underpin such a trajectory study. Similar to trajectory studies, policy ecology studies offer another way of locating policy in its broader ecological contexts (Weaver-Hightower 2008). Weaver-Hightower (ibid.: 155) suggests that 'a policy ecology consists of the policy itself along with all the other texts, histories, people, places, groups, traditions, economic and political conditions, institutions, and relationships that affect it or are affected by it'. While trajectory studies trace policy across the policy cycle, policy ecology does this, but also locates the text and policy processes in a much broader context, as signified by the metaphor of 'ecology' (ibid.: 155). A policy ecology approach would look at all the questions outlined in Figure 3.1 and locate them within an extended timeframe and broader ecology. An anthropology of public policy takes a somewhat similar approach to that of policy ecology from within a different disciplinary framework (Wedel *et al.* 2005).

Implementation studies deal with the context of policy practice and use a variety of research methods including interviews, observations, document analysis and sometimes ethnographic case study work. In trajectory studies there has been opposition to separating out policy production from policy implementation (Gale 1999; Vidovich 2001), with Cibulka (1994: 111) noting that 'implementors have an explicit policy role, not merely a technical one'. Those who use backward mapping for policy production acknowledge that reality. Nonetheless, implementation studies have been a particularly strong focus of educational policy analysis in the USA with a cognate literature in this field, stretching from McLaughlin's (1987) earlier influential essay on changes in foci of implementation studies in the USA through Elmore and McLaughlin's (1988) Rand Corporation study and talk of 'backward mapping' to the more recent collection edited by Honig (2006). In the USA a more policy-relevant version of implementation studies is policy evaluation, usually commissioned by governments or state bureaucracies and more limited in scope and responsive to the demands of those who commission such research.

Evaluation studies take the policy problem as a given, as well as the time frame for measuring effects as established by the bureaucracy and those who commission the research. This latter type of work – analysis for policy – is often published in the USA in the journal *Educational Evaluation and Policy Analysis.* Traditionally, evaluation studies have fitted within a rational approach (Hudson and Lowe 2004: 223ff.) and have been framed by a positivist epistemology (Bate and Robert 2003).

Analysis of policy texts is another common approach to policy analysis. These studies often take a critical discourse analysis (CDA) approach to text analysis. These studies are located in the contention that the contemporary world of consumer capitalism and new global media has become text saturated and that text and language have become central to contemporary politics and policymaking. In this context, Luke (2002: 98) has spoken of 'semiotic economies' in which 'language, text and discourse become the principal modes of social relations, civics and political life, economic behaviour and activity'. Regarding such economies, Fairclough (2000) has written at some length about the politics of the language used by the Blair Labour government in the UK. Focused analyses of specific policy texts usually emphasize either the linguistic features of the policy text or work with Foucauldian (and post-structuralist) inspired accounts of texts in context, including discursive context. Fairclough's (2003) approach to CDA works across these two categories and is becoming more influential in this approach to policy analysis (e.g. Taylor 2004; Mulderrig 2008; Adie 2008). CDA recognizes what Yeatman (1990) has referred to as the 'politics of discourse' associated with policy texts, but is also concerned with texts in context.

Taylor (2004) has made a strong, illustrated case for the usage of such a critical discourse analysis approach to policy analysis, analysing an important metapolicy in Queensland education, *Queensland State Education 2010*. In her work, she also recognizes the material effects of discourses and the way discourses position players across the policy cycle. This is not the place to document the fine detailed types of analysis taken by CDA approaches, but suffice to say that Fairclough (2001: 241–242) has suggested the following as features of texts which should be the focus of analysis: 'whole text organization (structure, e.g. narrative, argumentative, etc.), clause combination, grammatical and semantic features (transitivity, action, voice, mood, modality), and words (e.g. vocabulary, collocations, use of metaphors, etc.)'. So, for example, there have been analyses of the use of 'we' in policy texts in education. Adie (2008), in a CDA analysis of *Queensland Smart State* policies, for example, shows how 'we' is used in the texts to mean both the government and the people, with slippages between the two. Fairclough's (2000) analysis of Blair's political language in the UK has also argued similarly with respect to usage of 'we' and these dual and blended meanings. Sennett (2004) has noted that 'we' is a dangerous pronoun, excluding at the same time as it includes. 'Our' is another first person collective pronoun which can do interesting discursive work in a policy text.

Such textual analysis might also make us aware of what Fairclough (1992) called 'overwording', the repetitive usage of certain words and types of word, for example 'new', in attempts to justify the need for a policy. We would note here as well the significance of the silences of a policy text; just as a politics of non-decision-making can be important in relation to policy, so too can silences in policy texts tell us a lot about power. The post-colonial critic Edward Said (1983) speaks of reading (literary) texts contrapuntally, that is, reading into them their silences – the unsaid. This is equally necessary to policy analysis of a specific text. Said has also talked about how spoken language carries its context with it, while this is not the case for a written text. To fully understand the written text the policy analyst has to 'world' the text, situate it in its context. Fine-grained textual analyses of policies can thus produce many insights into the politics of policy production and policy processes and provide insights into likely policy effects.

Honan (2004) has established an approach to the analysis of policy texts derived from the work of Deleuze and Guattari on rhizomes, which connote the complex relationships and connections between texts and their effects. She refers to her approach as 'rhizo-textual analysis of policy texts'. Here the text is understood as a rhizome with connections into various 'semiotic chains', while she understands the relationship between the reader of the policy text (for example a teacher) and a particular education policy as rhizomatic.

Bourdieu's work is also helpful to an analysis of policy texts and particularly those which circulate globally. Talking about the global circulation of texts, Bourdieu (2003) argues that policy and other texts are taken from their context of production and read in a different context of reception. This leads to multiple slippages across national borders and between sites of policy production and policy implementation, and can also be seen to work in relation to subnational policy texts implemented in schools. Using Bourdieu's notion of fields, it can be argued that the context of the field of text production has particular logics which are often different from those of the field of policy reception, school and classroom practices, which have different logics and which thus ensure policy as 'palimpsest', literally a new text written over a partly erased older text. Policy in practice is palimpsest, as policy gets reread, rewritten as it moves from text to practice, from the field of policy production to the field of pedagogical practice.

The concept of social fields was one of the last additions to Bourdieu's theorizing, when he suggested that the social arrangement consists of multiple quasi-autonomous fields with their own logics of practice, overarched by a field of power linked to the economic field and a field of gender relations. Bourdieu's use of social field appears to refer to studies of social institutions, but rather than speak of politics he talks of 'the field of politics', instead of the media 'the journalistic field', in place of literature and the arts 'the field of cultural production' and so on. Thus, instead of policy, Bourdieu would talk of the policy field and we suggest that, in the context of globalization, in addition to the national education policy field we also need to recognize an emergent global education policy field (Lingard *et al.* 2005). These fields encourage certain dispositions or habitus amongst agents and involve contestation over various resources or capitals which are valued in various ways within the field. The nature of relationships between fields or cross-field effects (Lingard and Rawolle 2004), here for example the global and national education policy fields, then becomes an important task for contemporary education policy analysis.

Also important to explore in our media age are the ways in which policy texts are distributed – how their authority is allocated. Here the work of Fairclough (2000) is useful. In his analysis, Fairclough speaks of the 'mediatization' of policy and politics. In some ways this refers simply to the enhanced role of the media in contemporary politics. However, it can have an even more specific meaning in relation to education policy production, with implications for policy analysis. As Rawolle (2005) has demonstrated, today many policy texts are mediatized, that is, the logics of practice of journalism affect policy production processes. This sometimes involves journalists in the production of the actual policy text and the implied readership of the policy (the imagined policy community) becomes the public, rather than the professional community which will actually implement the policy in question, with implications for implementation. The media logic, including the proclivity to aphorism, alliteration, metaphor and catchy phrases, seeps into the wording of the policy and renders it less professionally relevant.

In this sense, today a policy release in education might be simply synonymous with a media release and the release of the glossy policy document whose production has been mediatized. In the UK, for example, Gewirtz *et al.* (2004) comment on the mediatization of education policy, and show how the Blair government sought to 'policy spin' both the development and launch of its policy on Education Action Zones (EAZs), using a set of promotional words in policy documents. Thus close discourse analysis of policy texts needs to be alert to the possibility of the mediatization of the policy text, which the analyst might become aware of through interviews with those involved in the policy process.

Trevor Gale (2001) has used Foucault's concepts of archaeology and genealogy to also stress the important of discourse analysis. He argues that if *critical* policy sociology is to work towards progressive social change, it needs to understand how policy problems are historically constituted from a wide variety of perspectives, requiring different modes of analysis of the ways in which discourses acquire authority. Gale constructs three approaches or methodologies for critical policy analysis. The first is 'policy historiography', which focuses on 'the substantive issues of policy at particular hegemonic moments' (ibid.: 385). The second is 'policy archaeology', which is concerned with the conditions that regulate policy formations at a specific moment and the actions of policy players in relation to them. And finally, the third is 'policy genealogy', which is concerned with the engagement of policy actors with policy.

Gale suggests some important questions related to each approach to analysis. Policy historiography asks three broad questions: 'what were the "public issues" and "private troubles" within a particular policy domain during some previous period and how were they addressed?; what are they now?; and what is the nature of the change from the first to the second?' (Gale 2001: 385). To these, necessitated by the criticality of this approach, he adds the following two questions: 'what are the complexities in these coherent accounts of policy? And what do they reveal about who is advantaged and who is disadvantaged by these arrangements?' (ibid.: 385). The latter question is a measure of policy outcomes set against an articulated ideal of social justice, what Ball (1994) calls second-order policy outcomes. These questions are: 'what are the conditions that make the emergence of a particular policy agenda possible?; what are the rules or regularities that determine what is (and is not) a policy problem?; how do these rules and regularities shape policy choices? And how is policy analysis similarly regulated?' (Gale 2001: 387). The last question is an expression of reflexivity in policy analysis and research. While policy archaeology is concerned with framing policy settlements, policy genealogy is concerned with specific realizations of policy (ibid.: 389). Such genealogy is interested in the development of policies over time, interested in policy continuities and discontinuities.

Mark Olssen and his colleagues (2004: 56–58) are critical of Gale's take on Foucault, particularly in relation to his distinction between policy historiography and policy genealogy. They argue that Foucault's methodological approach to history is a genealogical one which subsumes what Gale calls historiography. They argue that genealogy as a methodology traces backwards from the present (policy) through a line of descent and forwards to understand emergence (of policy). In this way, it implies the need to combine such a genealogy with recognition of policy texts framed within broader policy discourses and social practices that are not only aligned to various political ideologies, but are also embedded in dominant social imaginaries. Critical discourse analysis is helpful in providing an account of how political ideologies are authorized through policies by locating them in the dominant popular imaginaries so that they are interpreted as emerging from a commonly agreed set of values.

Globalizing education policy analysis

Our arguments in this chapter so far have thus emphasized an approach to policy analysis that requires close and fine-grained analysis of texts, analysis of their framing discursive practices (text production, distribution and consumption) and social conditions and social practices. These have been necessary attributes for understanding processes of education policy development and implementation within the context of nation-states. However, globalization demands at least a set of new dispositions: the rejection of epistemological innocence. We now live and work in a globalized space, which implies the need to challenge taken-for-granted assumptions of a society/nation homology in policy research. Today society is in some ways simultaneously local, national, regional and global in terms of experience, politics, effects and imaginaries. Further, these spaces are overlapped with unequal power relations, which reflect both contemporary geopolitics and past political struggles. Residual, dominant, emergent and contested geographies of power, including those of the colonial past and post-colonial present, are at play across these global spaces and manifest in vernacular ways in the local, national and regional. Fisher and Mosquera (2004: 5) have noted that Western 'metaculture' relates to geographies of power, which include academic theories, epistemologies and research methodologies. Recognition of the researcher's positionality within western universities and their relationships to these geographies of power is a central beginning for challenging the silent valorization of Western epistemologies in research of all kinds, including education policy research (Connell 2007).

Such a challenge is central to what Arjun Appadurai (2001) calls the 'deparochialization' of research and a strong internationalization of the western academy, in the light of enhanced global flows of students and academics as part of the mobilities and networks of globalization. He argued for the need to deconstruct, in both an anthropological and a pragmatic sense, the 'taken for granted' assumptions of contemporary systems of research. In the context of increased flows of capital, people, ideas, images and technologies and disjunctions and related asymmetries of power, he specifically calls for a 'deparochialization of the research ethic' (ibid.: 15). He suggests a number of ways in which the research ethic might be challenged, including a reconnection with earlier pre-research paradigm thinking premised on a strong moral position; the promotion of the style of argumentation of public intellectuals; and paying greater attention to research linked to policymaking and state functions in a range of nations, particularly those in the developing world.

Appadurai postulates that 'epistemological diffidence' is necessary to the project of deparochialization of research, the need to move beyond the epistemological certainty of dominant forms of modernization theory of the 1950s and 1960s and its effects, particularly in the so-called 'Third World'. That theory accepted without question that theory and research were metropolitan, modern and western, while the rest of the world was simply a research site to test and confirm such theory. Here, relations of researcher and researched paralleled relations of colonizer and colonized, even within decolonizing and post-colonial politics and aspirations. Linda Tuhiwai Smith (1999) similarly calls for *Decolonizing Methodologies*. In her study of the relationships between research and indigenous peoples and knowledges in New Zealand, she suggests that the term 'research' is inextricably linked to European imperialism and colonialism. Raewyn Connell (2007) calls for acknowledgement of, and respect for, 'Southern theory'. We need to recognize, then, that relations of power and politics in both macro and individual relations senses distort even the most arcane theories to some extent.

In rejecting an epistemological innocence characteristic of the dominant forms of social research, Appadurai, Smith and Connell call for an 'epistemological openness'. Such a project, according to Appadurai, needs to be aligned with 'grassroots globalization' or 'globalization from below'. We need to ask: 'whose globalization?' and in doing so, issue a challenge to globalization from above as driven by leading international organizations and the global cultural industries (Klein 2001). In his book, *Modernity at Large*, Appadurai (1996) speaks of 'vernacular globalization' to refer to the ways in which local sites and their histories, cultures, politics and pedagogies mediate to greater or lesser extents the effects of top-down globalization. This is an outcome of relations and tensions between the context-productive and context-generative effects of globalization; some local sites are more able to be context-generative and mediate global effects. The idea of globalization from below seeks to extend and strengthen this mediation and enhance global connections that resist globalization from above, read simply as neoliberal economics, what Bourdieu (2003) calls the performative construction of globalization. Policy is now increasingly located within this struggle.

Appadurai emphasizes the need for research to examine its own rhetoric and practices of 'systematicity, prior citational contexts, and specialized modes of inquiry', replicability, and 'an imagined world of specialized professional readers and researchers' (2001: 12), which taken together work to inhibit the deparochialization of research, its theories and methodologies. Prior citational contexts and an imagined world of specialized readers ensure the reproduction of more 'parochial', western or northern-dominated theories. The argument here is that a particular post-colonial politics is a useful starting point for a rereading, re-examination, re-imagining, indeed deparochializing of research in the globalized context that is dominated by US and western scholarship, a situation which is often glossed over in talk about globalization.

As we have noted, the reality of trans- and supranational processes labelled as globalization has challenged contemporary social theory. In sociology, Urry (2000, 2002) has argued the need to refocus from the social as society to the social as mobilities, indicating the weakened connectivity between society and nation-state and the stretching of networks across the globe. We consider the matter of mobilities associated with globalization in some detail in Chapter 8 of this book. The spatial turn in social theory has been another response to the rescaling of experience. Massey (1994: 2) has noted that the 'spatial is social relations stretched out'. The important spatial turn in social theory, exploring these relations between space and place as social constructions, reflects the new scalar politics. Brennan (2006: 136) has suggested that the centrality of space and place in contemporary globalization theory manifests the apparent 'overcoming of temporality', with this new theoretical optic ushering in a transition from 'tempo to scale', from 'the chronometric to the cartographic'.

The anthropologist Auge (1995: 77) has written about non-places, and suggests that while places are 'relational, historical and concerned with identity', non-places do not have these features. He suggests the contemporary world has witnessed a growth in non-places, with airports and supermarkets as archetypal non-places. Brennan (2006: 136) makes a similar distinction between space and place, suggesting '"space" is more abstract and ubiquitous: it connotes capital, history, and activity, and gestures towards the meaninglessness of distance in a world of instantaneous communication and virtuality'. 'Place' in contrast, he notes, connotes 'the kernel or centre of one's memory and experience – a dwelling, a familiar park or city street, one's family or community'. The research disposition we are arguing for acknowledges this space/place distinction in relation to the conduct of education policy analysis. It is interesting to contemplate the significance of a conceptualization of the *space* of policy production and the *place* of policy implementation in relation to Brennan's argument, and their differing logics.

Recognizing the mobilities associated with globalization, Castells (2000) argues that today power is located in flows, while most people still live in the space of places; this disjunction, he suggests, results in political schizophrenia. Other theorists have demonstrated the implicit national space of much social theory and a complementary 'methodological nationalism' (Beck 2000). Bourdieu, for example, has observed how '[i]ntellectual life, like all other social spaces, is a home to nationalism and imperialism' (1999: 220) and that 'a truly scientific internationalism' requires a concerted political project; this is another way of expressing the project in which Appadurai invites us to participate, namely the deparochialization of research and theory.

Bourdieu's theoretical stance and methodological disposition allow a way beyond such spatial and national constraints, a necessary position for analysing and understanding global effects in contemporary educational policy and the emergence of a global policy field in education. Globalization has resulted in the compression of time and space, which has had the phenomenological effect of enhanced awareness amongst (privileged) peoples across the globe of the world as one place, evidenced in, for example, talk of the 'world economy', 'world recession', 'global financial crisis', 'global warming', 'world heritage sites', 'world policy', 'global educational indicators', 'global higher education market' and so on. Castells (2000) speaks of the flows and networks across the globe, which render national boundaries more porous. He argues, somewhat like Appadurai (1996), that society is now organized around flows, namely 'flows of capital, flows of information, flows of technology, flows of organizational interaction, flows of images, sounds and symbols' (Castells 2000: 442), with technology facilitating these flows via nubs and nodes located across the globe that are dominated by elites of various kinds. While the post-national accounts proffered by Castells and others perhaps overstate the 'porousness' of national boundaries (Gregory

2004), particularly post-9/11, the suggestion that the world is become increasingly interconnected is now beyond doubt. This implies that the local and the national are now nested within regional, international, transnational and global spaces. It also implies the need to see the social relations of educational policy production as stretched out. It becomes the task of policy analysis to determine how, and with what effects. The policy cycle needs to be globalized.

Such a task involves a refusal to reify the concept of globalization, a failure to historicize it and to recognize its hegemonic role. It needs to determine the asymmetries of power between nations, and attend to their colonial and neo-colonial histories and post-colonial aspirations. Also important is the need to calibrate the differential national effects of neoliberal globalization. Bourdieu offers a way beyond such reification of globalization and allows for an empirically grounded account of the constitution of a global policy field in education – an example of globalization from above – and an account of global effects in national policy fields – globalization from below. In his later, more political work Bourdieu (2003) was concerned with the politics of globalization, read mainly as the dominance of a neoliberal approach to the economy. He was interested in exploring the ways in which global neoliberal politics have dented somewhat the relative autonomy of the logics of practice of many social fields, including that of the educational policy field, which has become more heteronomous, as a subset of economic policy. Bourdieu's approach allows for an empirical investigation of the constitution of the global economic market, as well as the ways in which the media field and its logics have affected the degree of autonomy of educational policy production.

In an homologous fashion, we would argue that educational policy is a political project and yet another manifestation of the emergent politics in the age of flows and diasporas of people and ideas across the boundaries of nation-states in both embodied and cyber forms. And just as a social imaginary of neoliberal globalization has been a central component in the creation of the global market, so it has been with the global field of educational policy. A global field of education policy is now established, certainly as a global commensurate space of measurement of educational performance. Such a field does not, of course, affect all nation-states in the same way, for they are positioned differently in terms of power and the strength of national capital within the global fields of the economy and governance and have to relate to these global fields in terms of their own economic, social and political conditions. Schriewer and Martinez (2004) argue that nation-states now have significant 'reference societies' which serve as points of comparison of the performance of national education systems. While nation-states retain their significance for policy-making in education, their capacity to set their policy priorities has become relativized, as they now have to refer to the global processes in a range of different ways, including their effects in specific nations.

Drawing on Bourdieu (2003: 91), it can be argued that the amount of 'national capital' possessed by a given nation is a determining factor in the degree of autonomy for policy development within the nation. National capital in one articulation can be seen to consist of the economic, political and cultural capital (evidenced in quantity and quality of education of a country's workforce) possessed by any given nation. Here the Global South is positioned very differently from the Global North in relation to the educational policy effects of the World Bank and other international agencies. National capital can be seen to mediate the extent to which nations are able to be context-generative in respect of the global field. Under globalization and the emergence of global fields, the sovereignty of different nation-states is affected in different ways. As Jayasuriya (2001: 444) suggests, 'the focus should not be on the content or degree of sovereignty that the state possesses but the form that it assumes in a global economy'. It is possible of course to resist the global dominance of neoliberalism. The state is not powerless in the face of globalization, but different states have varying capacities to manage 'national interests'. This capacity should clearly be a focus of research on education policy. It should be noted, however, that within nation-states this capacity to resist neoliberal globalization varies. This is so because the educational policy field is multilayered, stretched from the local to the global. Mann (2000) speaks of five socio-spatial layers, namely local, national, international (relations between nations), transnational (pass through national boundaries) and global, which cover the globe as a whole. We might also add a regional layer to Mann's account. It is important to note, however, that these layers are interrelated, in ways that too are affected by the processes of globalization.

If this is so, education policy analysis demands an empirical and theoretical stretching beyond the nation, but in ways that do not overlook the importance of these layers. We have adapted Bourdieu's notion of field to examine the relations between these layers, suggesting that global, international, national and local educational policy fields represent a different way to locate the practices and products of policy. This global educational policy field encompasses the contexts of the policy cycle, offers some analytical gains in locating the effects of particular policies, and reframes the contexts, texts and consequences of policy. That is, it caters for these matters and also offers a particular way of utilizing Bourdieu's concept of field to discuss issues around the impact of different fields on one another within national fields of power, and of different scalar levels of fields also affecting one another. All three contexts of the policy cycle, the context of policy text production, the context of influence and the context of practice are affected in different ways by globalization through both its policy mediation and more direct effects. It is probably the case today that the habitus of national policymakers and of those in international organizations have a lot in common, thus facilitating flows of policy ideas and ensuring certain 'policyscapes'.

Conclusion

In this chapter we have sought to show how globalization has given rise to a number of new theoretical and methodological issues for carrying out education policy analysis. Globalization has affected theory and methodology within critical social science; these changes need to be incorporated into education policy analysis. We have argued that at the very least these changes have demanded a critical *reflexivity* and awareness of our positionality as policy analysts. This is to ensure a deparochialized approach to education policy analysis, one which recognizes the layering today of policy processes across local, national, regional and global spaces and the globalization of many policy discourses in education. The disposition for critical education policy analysis in an era of globalization requires that we recognize the *relationality and interconnectivity* of policy developments. This recognition of relationality is in response to the new spatial politics and interconnectivity within and across nations that are evident in globalization. We have also suggested the need to have a *historical orientation* to policy analysis. We have argued that while traditional rationalist perspectives took as given the policy problem as constructed by the policy, a critical approach to policy analysis needs to determine how the problem is historically constituted. We also need to deconstruct the way any given policy text in education articulates its context and history.

In stark contrast to the rationalist approach which views the 'policy problem' in its immediate context, our approach works with larger temporal and spatial frames, as does the policy ecology framework. It requires the location of any given education policy in the context of the policy ensemble of which it might be a part. It demands consideration of a temporal frame beyond incremental links to immediate policy precursors. So, for example, this temporal frame might refer to the broader discursive policy settlements, the social imaginaries, such as Keynesianism or neoliberalism, the assumptions of which underpin a policy. Further, and particularly in relation to the nations of the Global South, we would suggest that policy analysis in education needs to consider both the colonial past and the colonial present, as both are manifest in policy pressures from beyond the nation, and the contestation involved in respect of post-colonial political aspirations in relation to contemporary education policy.

Critical policy analysis demands recognition of the significance of the *positionality* of the education policy researcher, the type of policy being analysed and the location of the site of policy production. It requires an awareness of the broader historical constitution of the context or ecology in which a policy is articulated, requiring the analyst to have a critically reflexive disposition. 'Critical' here means that we deconstruct the many 'taken-for-granteds' in policy processes and policy texts. But as part of this reflexivity, we must also articulate our positionality and political stance – our value position. Our own value position is informed by a commitment to work progressively towards a more equal and democratic future that recognizes and respects differences.

This means that critical education policy analysis must offer a critique of the assumptions built, either explicitly or implicitly, into any given policy with a view to showing how they might either support or undermine the values of democracy and social justice. Beyond critique, another purpose of critical education policy analysis is to suggest how policy could be otherwise – to offer an alternative social imaginary of globalization and its implications for education. In the remainder of this book we seek to illustrate this approach to policy analysis, not as a recipe for carrying out policy research, but as a way of showing how policy analysis can open up a dialogue about globalization and its educational possibilities.

4 Education policy and the allocation of values

Introduction

Education is a deliberate, purposive activity directed at the achievement of a range of ends which could potentially include the development of knowledgeable individuals who are able to think rationally, the formation of sustainable community, and the realization of economic goals benefiting both individuals and their communities. The term 'education' has normative implications: it suggests that something worthwhile is being intentionally transmitted, and that something valuable is being attempted. Thinking about education thus necessarily involves considerations of values. But where are these values to be found? What might be their content? Whose values are to be privileged? How should they be justified? These questions have long been the subject of philosophical deliberations. Philosophers of education have long sought to elucidate how education might serve various moral, social, political and economic ends. Some have suggested that education is intrinsically worthwhile, and that it is designed to produce knowledgeable, responsible and serious-minded people, while others have articulated educational goals in more instrumental terms. Some have developed and justified educational values in terms of what they believe to be the nature of human beings, knowledge or rational thought, while others have viewed education in functional terms, as a component of social or economic systems.

In this chapter we want to argue that, useful as these philosophical discussions are, it is not possible to simply derive education policies from a particular value position. A philosophical articulation of an educational goal does not in itself suggest a particular policy prescription – what ought to be done in a given set of circumstances. So, for example, a commitment to social equality by policymakers does not in itself imply the policies that ought to be pursued. Much depends on how the idea of social equality is interpreted and how it is reconciled with a range of other values, such as efficiency and freedom. Also important are the competing political interests involved in policy development. In a democratic society these interests are clearly negotiated, resulting in policy outcomes that most stakeholders can live with. Policy involves compromises and trade-offs. Also relevant in the development of a policy are pragmatic considerations relating to what is in fact possible, for example the level of resources that are available to implement a policy. Equally, policymakers have to consider the ways in which policies are to be allocated, so that those who are subject to them can more or less adhere to the values they embody.

What this suggests is that policymaking is a fundamentally political process: it involves major trade-offs between values. Public policies in education, in particular, have to deal with a range of values, such as equality, excellence, autonomy, accountability and efficiency, simultaneously. This means policymakers have to assemble, organize and order them, configuring them in such a way as to render them more or less consistent. This requires privileging some values ahead of others, and re-articulating their meaning. So, for example, in recent years, a commitment to market values in education has not entirely involved rejecting a concern for social equality, but it has required that the meaning of equality be re-articulated. Similarly, a commitment to system accountability may sometimes conflict with the values of autonomy, requiring autonomy to be redefined so that this conceptual conflict does not result in loss of policy legitimacy.

In the development of education policies, then, values are negotiated through a range of political processes. However, in light of what we have discussed in the previous chapters, it should be clear that these negotiations no longer take place only within the national political context, but also in an emerging transnational space. National policymakers now feel obliged to recraft education policies in relation to what they interpret as the emerging imperatives of globalization, aligning them loosely to the values negotiated at the national or local levels. They take note not only of the comparative data produced by international organizations, but also of the educational values that have become globally dominant, expressed in a neoliberal social imaginary.

In this chapter we suggest that there is an unmistakable global trend towards a convergence in thinking about educational values. This results in policymakers and experts in differing social, political and economic traditions often presenting a similar diagnosis of the problems confronting educational systems and proposing similar solutions and programmes of educational reform. There is thus a global shift towards a neoliberal values orientation, manifested most clearly in privatization policies and in policies that assume the validity of market mechanisms to solve the various problems and crises facing governments. In education policy discourses, this has involved a reorientation of values from a focus on democracy and equality to the values of efficiency and accountability, with a greater emphasis on human capital formation allegedly demanded by the new knowledge industries, and required by nation-states to participate and compete successfully in the global economy. This does not mean that the social values of equality and democracy have been abandoned, but rather that they have been re-articulated, subordinated to dominant economic concerns. In this way, policies do not simply express a particular value, but bring a host of them together – they order, organize and enact them in a particular configuration.

Philosophical traditions

Issues concerning how best to think about educational values have been much debated for most of the past century. In the early part of the 20th century, Whitehead (1929) wrote a highly influential book about the aims of education, in which he insisted that educational values needed to be expressed in explicit terms derived from our theoretical assumptions about the nature of knowledge and its transmission, learning and human nature. Education, he argued, should actively 'utilize the knowledge and skills that were taught to students to a particular end', of 'producing men [*sic*] who possess both culture and expert knowledge in some special direction' (ibid.: 1); and that it should 'impart an intimate sense for the power and beauty of ideas coupled with structure for ideas together with a particular body of knowledge, which has peculiar reference to the life of the being possessing it' (ibid.: 10). Whitehead's conception of educational values was thus linked directly to the structure of knowledge that was judged to be intrinsically worthwhile, applicable equally to all those who wished to be educated, and necessarily good for all societies in the same way.

Some 40 years later, Hirst and Peters (1970) similarly argued that the aims of education should be tied to its 'knowledge condition'. Educational values, they argued, specify something general and formal, a conceptual truth about the very concept of education, as involving a 'family of processes leading up to desirable states of mind in people involving depth and breadth' (ibid.: 26). They viewed the production of these states of mind as the main aim of education. The problem with this analytical approach to thinking about educational values, however, is that it leaves a range of important questions unaddressed: for example, how might the desirable states of mind be determined?; which family of processes is appropriate?; and how might we apply this definition to a society that is dynamic, democratic and multicultural, where there exist contrasting and competing value positions about educational priorities? The approach proposed by Hirst and Peters clearly fails to link educational values to particular social and historical formations. Instead it articulates them in terms of highly formal conditions, justified through a transcendental argument that largely eschews any consideration of changing economic, political and social circumstances. Nor does it recognize that educational priorities are an outcome of political negotiations over competing interests. In short, this analytical tradition of thinking about education is both ahistorical and apolitical.

This analytical tradition stands in sharp contrast to the functionalist sociological tradition, the main focus of which is on socialization processes through which the young are inculcated into a given society. One of the founders of this tradition, Durkheim (1972), viewed educational values in this instrumental fashion. Educational processes, he suggested, reflect underlying processes in society because an educational system is a construct built by society, which 'naturally' seeks to reproduce its collectively held beliefs and norms through its institutions. Educational systems thus contain the imprint of past stages in the development of a society, even as each era seeks to develop that imprint in its own image. According to Durkheim, education reform requires us to first understand these imprints by analysing them and, only then, to consider how a society could be developed through the reconstruction of its educational system. For Durkheim, then, educational values express 'societal needs' at a given time and place. Society constructs its educational system to promote and reproduce its ideal of how human beings should live and relate to each other in meeting societal needs.

If Hirst and Peters's analytical approach to thinking about educational values is too universalistic, the functionalist sociological tradition rests on a view of society that is too specific and instrumental. The functionalist tradition leaves little room for social critique and radical transformation, but ties educational values largely to instrumental ends. Moreover, it assumes the borders of a society to be clearly definable and fixed, overlooking the importance of intersocietal relations. Moreover, issues of power and politics relating to the determination of 'societal needs' are left unaddressed, thus privileging hegemonic conceptions over values that might be oppositional, suggesting alternatives to existing social realities and imaginaries.

The pragmatic tradition of thinking about educational values, associated with the work of the American philosopher John Dewey, cuts across the binaries between the formal and material, the universal and particular, the instrumental and non-instrumental, as well as the contrast between the intrinsic and extrinsic aims of education. Dewey provided his most considered account of educational values in *Democracy and Education* (1916). Educational values, he argued, cannot be found outside the activity of education; they are located within the educational act itself. An aim of education, therefore, should be a natural outgrowth of the existing conditions, and should be formed in the process of realizing it. It should 'enable individuals to continue their education'. In this sense, 'the object and reward of learning is continued capacity for growth' (ibid.: 81). Dewey specifies three conditions that he says are found in all good educational aims. First, 'an educational aim must be founded upon the intrinsic activities and needs (including original instincts and acquired habits) of the given individual to be educated'. Secondly, 'an aim must be capable of translation into a method of cooperating with the activities of those undergoing instruction'. And finally, 'educators have to be on their guard against ends that are alleged to be general and ultimate' (ibid.: 85). Beyond these general conditions, Dewey insists that educational values should grow out of the context of the educative activity itself.

Dewey's account of education has been criticized for its lack of specificity, for example by Suppes (1995). However, Suppes acknowledges this lack might be deliberate on Dewey's part, for he was reluctant to prescribe a pre-specified ideal of the educated person, a single greatest good, a universal. Educational values, for Dewey, have to be negotiated within the process of education itself, so long as 'there is adequate provision for the reconstruction of social habits and institutions by means of wide stimulation arising from equitably distributed interests. And this means a democratic society' (Dewey 1916: 78). As Noddings (1995) suggests, Dewey might well have said that the primary educational value is to produce people who will understand, appreciate and use the 'method of intelligence'. However, even this level of specificity might have conflicted with Dewey's contention that educational values should arise out of the specific contexts in which people find themselves, for he had noted that contexts change in ways that demand different educational responses. Indeed, it is not surprising that the context in which Dewey was writing greatly affected his own analysis of the relationships between society and education. His was an era of strong nationalisms. His remarks were therefore located within a national imaginary, characterized in the United States by various sentiments about democracy and about the role of education in producing certain kinds of citizen.

For Dewey, while educational values are often articulated in formal terms, explicitly specified in legislation, statutes or policy documents, they can also be implicit in social practices representing established ways of doing things in various informal arrangements. They can also be expressed implicitly in plans of action or programme descriptions. They therefore have to be discerned and teased out in a particular context, and then made explicit for the purposes of analysis. Educational values are often embedded within a broader context of social relations and practices, or as we have noted in Chapter 2, in a 'social imaginary', a framework that is at once descriptive and prescriptive of conceptions of how educational practice is best directed towards certain outcomes and is organized around a set of values. In this sense, educational values are embedded in policies in a range of complicated ways within a social imaginary.

An analysis of education policies therefore requires not only an examination of their specific content but also an investigation of the context that provides them with meaning and legitimacy. Since education policies cannot simply be inferred from a particular value position, policy analysis requires an understanding of how multiple, sometimes competing, values are brought together, organized and configured in a policy statement and are allocated in an authoritative manner. Policy analysis needs to show how some values are glossed over while others are highlighted, re-articulated or sutured together in any given policy text.

Values and education policy

According to Deborah Stone (2001), public policies in most liberal democratic societies are structured around five key values – equity, efficiency, security, liberty and community. They are, she argues, 'often invoked as justifications for a policy, for a government action, or for the government not taking action' (ibid.: 37). They are also used as criteria for analysing policies and evaluating programmes. Yet, Stone insists, none of these values admits a simple and determinate definition; each of them is ambiguous and is subject to competing interpretations that make it the object of political struggle. She maintains that the concepts of equity, efficiency, security, liberty and community are continuously constructed and reconstructed, and in public policy deliberations the priority of one value over others in particular is constantly negotiated. Seldom are any of these values completely abandoned, but some values are foregrounded while others are masked or re-articulated, given a weaker meaning.

The idea of equity, for example, relates to issues of 'who gets what, when and how'. Issues of distribution of material and human resources often lie at the heart of public policy controversies. Anyone familiar with debates in the United States about affirmative action would vouch for the complications that arise in assessments of how the notion of equity should be interpreted. Equity can be viewed, for example, in a weak sense, as simply implying formal access to provisions without any examination of the social and economic conditions that permit such access. Stronger notions of equality, those associated with the policies of affirmative action, in contrast, emphasize the need to pay attention to the historical conditions that define people's capacity to benefit from state provisions – not simply to issues of access, but also to outcomes.

Those who reject affirmative action policies do not also by and large favour redistributive measures. Yet they do not entirely reject the importance of equality, but seek to subordinate it instead to the idea of liberty. The values of equality and liberty are not always reconcilable, for sometimes people's liberty needs to be constrained in an effort to provide greater equity of opportunity and outcomes. The debate thus revolves around the question of what kind of interference is acceptable as a price of distributive justice. In public policy deliberations, then, there is always a certain level of conflict between values. This conflict is resolved in a number of ways, for example by trade-offs between values, by sidelining a particular value, or redefining or re-articulating its meaning (Hall 1996).

Similarly the idea of efficiency is not a self-evident, morally neutral one. To show how this is so, we might ask a more basic question: 'Efficiency in terms of what?' As the philosopher Alasdair MacIntyre (1981) points out, there are strong grounds for rejecting the claim that efficiency is a morally neutral concept. Rather, it is 'inseparable from a mode of existence in which the contrivance of means is in central part the manipulation of human beings into compliant patterns of behavior' (ibid.: 71). Efficient organizations are those that get things done with a minimum of waste, duplication and expenditure of resources. But organizations can tolerate some measure of efficiency if other more worthy values are at stake. Within the logic of input and output measures of efficiency, who determines what is the correct output goal, how multiple goals should be compared and evaluated, and how input costs and factors are counted are more than merely technical questions; they also involve specific political judgements. In public policy processes, then, the value of efficiency has to be assessed in relation to the other equally important values of equity, liberty, community and security.

Much has been said since September 11, 2001 about the notion of security as an important public policy objective (Klein 2007). Security is considered to be one of the key governmental responsibilities. But security is a complicated idea, which refers not only to physical security of people, but also to their economic, social and psychological well-being. The idea of security can never be reduced to a set of objective conditions. And if this is so, it often conflicts not only with the idea of liberty, but also with the idea of community. In assessing security we need to count not only material resources, but also symbolic meanings provided by resources. Should a government secure not only the needs of individuals but also their relational needs, such as a sense of community? The Bush administration in the United States used a very narrow definition of security, but this clearly had implications for public policies, as the values of liberty and community in particular were both sidelined and subordinated (Saltman 2007).

What this discussion demonstrates is that public policies are always about trade-offs, compromises and of course politics, sometimes informed by narrow personal or sectional interests but more often by ideological differences. The political Left has generally been thought to work with notions of equity and community, while the Right has emphasized the values of liberty and security, as well as efficiency. This contrast, however, is somewhat misleading, since no public policy in liberal democratic countries can entirely ignore any of these values. The debates between the Left and the Right are more accurately characterized as being located within a discursive struggle over meaning, as each side seeks to re-articulate and realign differently the meaning and significance of key values associated with public policies. In policymaking there are compromises, not only in policy content but also in the ways in which policies are allocated, characterized, represented and promoted.

In education policy, David Labaree (2003) has observed that education has traditionally involved struggle over three distinct but often competing values: democratic equality, social mobility and social efficiency. He argues that while these values are not mutually exclusive, historically one has been given precedence over the others. So, for example, in post-World War II social democracies the idea of democratic equality became dominant in many parts of the world, interpreted in Scandinavian countries from a social democratic perspective but in countries like the United States from a more liberal perspective. In socialist countries a very different definition of equality was promoted. In many post-colonial countries equality became something of an ideological mantra in educational thinking, even if it was seldom realized. In other countries social mobility and meritocracy were placed ahead of social equality.

For Labaree the concept of democratic equality has long suggested the need for education to facilitate the development of democratic citizens who can participate in democratic communities in a critically informed manner. Its focus is on equal access and equal treatment of all citizens, and on regarding education as a public good. This implies that maximum benefit to society can only be realized if every member of a community is educated to realize their full potential. The primary purpose of education is, then, the creation of productive citizens able to maximize personal fulfilment, not simply efficient workers. This view, however, does not imply a denial of the importance of vocational training, but stresses that such training must be located within the broader role that education must play in the development of a socially cohesive democratic community. The purposes of education, from this perspective, are thus more social and cultural than economic, focused more on the community than on the individual.

If the democratic equity view of education focuses on its role in promoting the public good, the idea of social mobility gives precedence to education's role in providing individuals with a range of private goods that they can exchange within the labour market for money, power and prestige. The social mobility view thus regards education as both inherently rivalrous and desirably competitive, serving the function of allocating economic benefits and social status to individuals. It suggests that social rewards should be based on both effort and intelligence. It maintains that the market rewards those who work harder and have inherently superior skills and talent. Yet the social mobility view does not deny a role for education in promoting social equality, but insists on leaving the processes of social formation to the market. It suggests that the only role public policy must play is to strengthen structures that enable each individual to have formal access to educational institutions within the market. It thus emphasizes individual choice, freedom for students to gain in their own way the knowledge and skills they will require for finding a place within the labour market and thus achieving social mobility. The focus here is on competition and the ability of the market to reconcile the values of not only equality and liberty but also efficiency.

A third view of education values highlights its role in achieving social efficiency. While the social mobility view focuses exclusively on individuals, the social efficiency view requires education to play a more important instrumental role in developing workers able to contribute to the economic productivity of nations and corporations alike. Its focus is not as much on the needs and development of individuals as on the efficiency with which educational systems operate. The emphasis is on the system's capacity to make an adequate return on investment, assessed in terms of its contribution to producing workers with knowledge, skills and attitudes relevant to increasing productivity within the knowledge economy. In this way, education is viewed as both a public and a private good: public because it contributes to the economic well-being and social development of a community; and private because it serves individual interests within a competitive market. However, it is important to stress that the notion of the public good that the social efficiency view promotes is markedly different from social democratic conceptions, which regard education as intrinsically good, and not linked instrumentally to organizational efficiency, economic outcomes and productivity.

Knowledge economy and policy constructions

In recent years, however, it is the social efficiency view of education that appears to be increasingly dominant, especially among large corporations and intergovernmental organizations, as well as in many national governments. As we have noted, it assembles the traditional values associated with public policy – equity, efficiency, security, liberty and community – ordering them in a particular fashion, giving each of them a specific meaning that is located within a broader discursive structure. This structure is now constituted by a social imaginary that not only defines the ways in which values are interpreted, but also points to the manner in which policies should direct practice and enable us to conceive of possibilities and futures. It is through this neoliberal imaginary, as Appadurai (2001: 15) has pointed out, that citizens are now disciplined and controlled, by states, markets and other powerful interests, but it is also the faculty through which collective patterns of dissent and new designs for collective life are conceptualized. The hegemonic power of the neoliberal imaginary is not absolute, and is constantly resisted.

In the context of globalization there are different and competing ways of interpreting the contemporary realities of global interconnectivity and interdependence, and of deriving educational implications from them. Yet these competing imaginaries do not exist in a neutral space, but in a context in which neoliberalism has become dominant. It is in terms of this imaginary that most recent statements of educational values around the world appear to be couched. These statements are expressed in a language that is magisterial in tone and assumes the authority of its claim, a language that demands consent and legitimacy. It brings factual and normative aspects of policy together in an effort to forge a shared implicit understanding of the problems to which policies are proposed as solutions. In this way the authority structure within which policies are located demands a shared social imaginary.

In an effort to secure this authority, we have noted, intergovernmental organizations (IGOs) have played an important role in shaping particular discourses of globalization and their supposed implications for rethinking educational values. Organizations such as the OECD, the EU, APEC, UNESCO and the World Bank have become major sites for the organization of knowledge about education, and have created a cajoling discourse of 'imperatives of the global economy' for education. Recognizing that developments in communication and information technologies have enabled increased circulation of ideas, images and ideologies across national borders, they have created a space within which ideas are now explored, exchanged, promoted and steered.

Their efforts have led to policy borrowing, transfer, appropriation and copying of ideas across national boundaries as never before (Phillips and Ochs 2004). Policy debates around the world now display an almost universal deepening of a shift from social democratic to neoliberal orientations.

There is an enormous pressure on educational systems not only to increase the amount of formal education young people are now required to have, but also to align the content of this education with the alleged requirements of the global economy. As a result, new requirements of policy have emerged, resulting in the corporatization and marketization of education. This has involved greater and new demands for accountability and surveillance, creating new pressures on teachers' work. As public resources for education in most countries have declined, there has been a growing emphasis on increasing the role of the private sector and user-pays approaches. Yet amidst all this change, and despite pressure on educational systems around the world to diversify – to meet the diverse needs that systems have – educational systems have seemingly mimicked each other, pursuing a common set of solutions to their fiscal and organizational problems. Indeed they have even interpreted the requirements of reform in a broadly similar fashion.

At a very general level, a new human capital theory has informed discussions of educational values. The old human capital theory had postulated (Becker 1964) that expenditure on training and education was costly, but that it should be treated as an investment, since it is undertaken with a view to increasing personal incomes and can be used to explain occupational wage differentials. The new human capital theory extends this claim to the requirements of the global economy and to the competitive advantage of individuals, corporations and nations within the transnational context. The new theory is technically complex and has been the subject of much debate. There are a number of strands to its claims. However, in its popular form, it considers all human behaviour to be based on the economic self-interest of individuals operating within free competitive markets. It assumes that individuals are equally free to choose. It also assumes economic growth and competitive advantage to be a direct outcome of the levels of investment in developing human capital. It suggests that, in a global economy, performance is increasingly linked to people's knowledge stock, skills level, learning capabilities and cultural adaptability. It therefore demands policy frameworks that enhance labour flexibility, not only through the deregulation of the market, but also through reform to systems of education and training, designed to align them better with the changing nature of economic activity.

In its most radical form, the new human capital theory not only requires reform of systems of educational governance, it also demands a reconceptualization of the very purposes of education. The OECD (1996) has suggested, for example, that the advances in information and communication technologies have so transformed the nature of knowledge production and utilization, the organization of work and labour relations, modes of consumption and trade, and patterns of cultural exchange, that education now needs to produce different kinds of persons who are better able to work creatively with knowledge, are flexible, adaptable and mobile, are globally minded and interculturally confident and are lifelong learners. What this view implies is that learning for learning's sake is no longer sufficient, and that education does not have any intrinsic ends as such, but must always be linked to the instrumental purposes of human capital development and economic self-maximization. This should not, of course, be taken to mean that ethical and cultural issues are no longer relevant to education, but rather that they should be interpreted within the broader neoliberal social imaginary. In this way, this view rests on what George Soros (1998) has called 'market fundamentalism', a kind of conceptual schema within the framework of which values associated with public policies must now be interpreted and, if necessary, re-articulated.

In this framework, the idea of a knowledge economy features prominently (Kenway *et al.* 2006). It suggests that globalization has fundamentally altered the relationship between the production of knowledge and its economic application; and that the emergence of knowledge-intensive activities and the production and diffusion of information technologies have led to the development of new models of work organization (Paul 2002). One of the countries to embrace and use the notion of knowledge economy early was New Zealand. The so-called 'New Zealand experiment' (Peters 2001) assumed that a knowledge-driven economy is one in which the generation and exploitation of knowledge play the predominant part in the creation of wealth. It maintained that in the industrial era, wealth was created by using machines to replace human labour, but the new jobs in the knowledge economy are to be found increasingly in high-technology industries such as telecommunications and financial services.

Knowledge, of course, has always been central to discussion of education and the economy. But the new discourse of the knowledge economy marks a number of major shifts about the changed significance of knowledge. According to Drucker (1999), knowledge as an input is now quantitatively and qualitatively more important than capital, especially given the rise of new forms of trading of knowledge products, including of course education itself. In its landmark report, the OECD (1996) has presented perhaps the most magisterial account of the knowledge economy. Basing its views on the 'new growth theory', it argues that the growing codification of knowledge and its transmission through communications and computer networks has led to the emerging 'information society', creating new economic opportunities based on an economics not of scarcity but of abundance. Unlike most resources that deplete when used, knowledge can be used and may actually grow through application.

This discourse of knowledge has now become commonplace around the world, from the OECD countries to the newly industrializing countries of Asia such as Singapore and India, to countries such as China and Vietnam where Communist Parties remain in political control but which now speak of 'market socialism'. Every national system, so it seems, is now developing its education policies to take advantage of the knowledge economy. Everywhere it is assumed that the knowledge economy will require a larger proportion of workers to be prepared for highly skilled jobs, workers who have competencies linked to their ability to use new technologies and their cultural attitudes towards change, even if most of the new jobs are in low paid and highly casualized service industries jobs. In a rapidly changing world, it is believed, these competencies must involve certain behavioural features such as adaptability, organizational loyalty and the ability to work in culturally diverse contexts and to provide leadership.

This conception of education involves a new approach to human capital development, grounded not so much in the amount of schooling individuals have, but in the learning attributes they are able to develop, with which to deal effectively and creatively with unfamiliar and constantly changing conditions of work. It emphasizes the development of broad generic skills such as communication skills, problem-solving, the ability to work independently, often under pressure, to take responsibility for decisions and to obtain field-specific knowledge quickly and efficiently and ascertain its commercial potential.

In the knowledge economy, knowing facts and theories is thus less important than an understanding of the world of social relations and the networks through which knowledge is converted into innovation and commercially viable products. The principles of flexibility and dynamism demand skills of finding out the relevant information and using it commercially. These skills are considered more important than formal, codified, structured and explicit knowledge. Against these assumptions, the new growth theorists such as Foray and Lundvall (1996) suggest that a nation's capacity to take advantage of the knowledge economy depends on how quickly it can become a 'learning economy'. Learning, Foray and Lundvall argue, should not only involve the ability to use new technologies in accessing knowledge, but should also mean using technology to better communicate with other people about ways of improving productivity. They maintain that in the knowledge economy, individuals, corporations and nations will create wealth in proportion to their capacity to learn and share innovation. If this is so, learning must be continuous and not restricted to formal schooling.

Lifelong learning

The contemporary notion of lifelong learning is thus linked to various claims about the knowledge economy, located as they are within the neoliberal imaginary of globalization. Yet the idea of lifelong learning is not new. It first emerged during the 18th century, and was associated with a range of concepts such as individualism, social equality and social progress, as well as social processes such as industrialization, secularization, urbanization and rationalization. It expressed a particular image of the social world and a way of thinking about it. The idea of developing reason featured prominently in this image. It was believed that human progress was only possible through the application of reason and science, and that this required not only formal schooling, but also education that was ongoing, shaping the ways in which people thought about and lived their daily lives. Knowledge was thus considered crucial for both individual advancement and social progress. In the 19th century, industrialization required workers to be trained in the new technologies of work, with the expectation that further changes would require a disposition for lifelong education. To meet this demand, Mechanics' Institutes were set up by various industrialists, first in Scotland and then throughout the world, to provide adult education, particularly in technical subjects. The industrialists ultimately benefited from having more knowledgeable and skilled employees (Candy and Laurent 1994).

Inspired by the ideas of the French Enlightenment in particular, the notion of 'lifelong self-education' was central to Thomas Jefferson's political theory. As early as 1776, Jefferson proposed a *Bill for the More General Diffusion of Knowledge*, which sought to establish public libraries throughout America so that the general population could develop knowledge and skills he considered necessary, not only for a republican society but also for the general pursuit of happiness (Boyd 1950). According to Tozer and his colleagues (2002), most American educational theorists since Jefferson have agreed that a fundamental purpose of education is to prepare the student for lifelong learning. John Dewey (1916), for example, viewed lifelong education as a key component in his instrumentalist theory of democracy. One of Dewey's British contemporaries, Yeaxlee (1929: 28) saw education as inseparable from life itself, and argued that for life to be vivid, strong and creative, it demanded 'constant reflection upon experience, so that action may be guided by wisdom, and service be the other aspect of self-expression, while work and leisure are blended in perfect exercise of body, mind and spirit, personality attaining completion in society'.

In the 1960s the notion of lifelong education proliferated as educators sought a new vision for a more democratic and socially just society. Initiatives in workers' education, informal education, radical education, adult education, community education and the like involved attempts to transform education away from formal rigid and authoritarian traditions to more informal approaches that highlighted the importance of experiential and informal learning. According to Raymond Williams (1989), adult education was crucial for an 'organically grounded struggle' towards a genuine democracy and a socialist vision of society. Without lifelong education, he argued, resources of hope and struggle could not be sustained. In the United States, a similar progressive tradition in community education developed around a distinctive set of educational values and historical social purpose. In South America, a parallel tradition inspired by Paulo Freire (1972) viewed lifelong learning as a way of mounting a popular struggle against exploitative capitalism. Freire believed that education should not involve one person acting on another. The idea of lifelong learning also found favour among feminist, civil rights and other social movements. In the 1970s, education policy experts even at organizations such as the OECD saw lifelong education, viewed as recurrent education, as a way of keeping educational expenditure down and yet still expanding educational access to meet the increasing and changing human resource needs of an economy hit by inflationary pressures and decline in productivity.

As diverse as these approaches to lifelong learning were, each was based on the assumption that if education were to serve broader social purposes, it needed to be continuing. The current policy notion of lifelong learning continues this tradition, but is evidently located within the neoliberal imaginary of globalization. It celebrates the values of social efficiency and the ability of individuals and countries to compete in the global knowledge economy. Effectively it re-articulates older, more liberal humanist constructions of lifelong learning. Promoted vigorously by international organizations, it does not simply imply the importance of learning new knowledge and gaining new skills on an ongoing basis. Rather, it is located within a broader discourse of economic competitiveness. As Field and Leicester (2000: xvii) point out, this discourse has arisen primarily from changes in the economy, including such developments as 'the rapid diffusion of information and communication technologies, the constant application of science and technology, and the globalization in trade of goods and services'. This observation mirrors the OECD's contention (1996) that the 'increased pace of globalization and technological change, the changing nature of work and the labour market, and the ageing of populations are among the forces emphasizing the need for continuing upgrading of work and life skills throughout life'. These developments, the OECD suggests, have made constant investment in education necessary for individuals and nations alike.

While the current policy notion of lifelong learning is highly varied and diffuse, some of its key features nonetheless stand out (Evans 2003). First, the idea of lifelong learning stresses the need to acquire and update all kinds of abilities, interests, knowledge and qualifications from the preschool years to post-retirement. Second, it places emphasis on all forms of learning, including formal learning such as a degree course followed at university, and non-formal learning such as vocational skills acquired at the workplace. Third, it shifts the focus of learning from 'knowing that' to 'knowing how', giving rise to new conceptions of the ways in which learning is defined, arranged, valued, utilized and promoted. Fourth, it stresses the benefits of informal learning such as intergenerational learning, for example where parents learn to use the new information and technologies through their children, or where learning takes place in informal settings such as work or leisure. Fifth, it holds individuals responsible for their own education, viewing it as an economic investment. Sixth, it prescribes a system-wide network of 'learning pathways' extending from early childhood through to all stages of adulthood in both formal and informal educational settings, fulfilling social and economic objectives simultaneously by providing long-term benefits for the individual, the enterprise, the economy and society more generally. And finally, it promotes the development of knowledge and competencies that enable each citizen to adapt to the knowledge-based society and actively participate in all spheres of social and economic life, increasingly shaped by globalization.

Each of these shifts is arguably informed by an underlying focus on social efficiency, within the broader discourse of which even the values of democratic equity and social mobility are now incorporated. For example, it has been argued by the OECD that a focus on efficiency can in fact lead to greater equality and opportunities for social mobility. Without the ability to perform effectively in the global labour market, the OECD suggests, the potential of workers for social mobility is severely reduced. Nor is the concern for equity overlooked by the advocates of lifelong learning. As the OECD (1996) suggests:

> A new focus for education and training policies is needed now, to develop capacities to realize the potential of the 'global information economy' and to contribute to employment, culture, democracy and, above all, social cohesion. Such policies will need to support the transition to 'learning societies' in which equal opportunities are available to all, access is open, and all individuals are encouraged and motivated to learn, in formal education as well as throughout life.

Ultimately, the dominant ideas of both knowledge economy and lifelong learning are predicated on the assumptions of social efficiency, viewed largely in terms of economic efficiency. Indeed, economic efficiency now appears to be regarded almost as a 'metavalue', subsuming within its scope aspirations such as social equality, mobility and even social cohesion.

The idea of lifelong learning has thus been rethought, broadened and linked to the production of 'self-responsibilizing' individuals (Rose 1999). According to UNESCO (2006: 13), not only must learning 'adapt to changes in the nature of work, but it must also constitute a continuous process of forming whole human beings – their knowledge and aptitudes, as well as the critical faculty and the ability to act'. Lifelong learning should thus be promoted through a system-wide network of 'learning pathways', extending from early childhood through to all stages of adulthood in both formal and informal educational settings, fulfilling 'social and economic objectives simultaneously by providing long-term benefits for the individual, the enterprise, the economy and the society more generally' (OECD 1996). In both of these accounts, social mobility becomes a functional outcome of economic efficiency, and the egalitarian impulse is largely collapsed, becoming subordinate to the overriding goal of developing human resources needed for the changing global economy.

This neoliberal notion of lifelong learning assumes education to be a private good, providing benefits to the individual consumer. As a private good, education is viewed as a commodity that can provide an individual advantage over others. At the same time, however, education becomes something that can be used to differentiate people in terms of their economic value. In this way, education is more geared towards fulfilling the needs of the market than those of communities. Educational systems that do not meet explicit functional economic goals are dismissed as inefficient and ineffective. Indeed, popular media and corporations propagate this largely ideological assumption, calling for reforms designed not only to produce workers who are self-directed, self-capitalizing and self-sufficient learners, but also to hold teachers and educational bureaucracies more accountable (Edwards 1997).

What this discussion suggests is that the current discourse of lifelong learning is motivated more by a political agenda of social control (see Coffield 1999) than with social transformation through education. It is based on an assumption that human societies are necessarily competitive, and that social efficiency can only be achieved through a reliance on market principles. However, such a view intensifies the divide between valuable and non-valuable people and places. It assumes a moral economy in which people are believed to be motivated largely by self-interest, with little capacity for forms of altruism and cooperation other than those linked to self-capitalization, as a way of maximizing return on capital. Education itself is assumed to be a form of capital, exchanged in the marketplace largely for personal benefit. Lifelong learning is thus considered necessary not as a way of creating an informed and self-reflexive community, but as an investment with which individuals, corporations and nations can maximize their economic advantage.

Privatization and the politics of choice

Linked to this emphasis on the market are the ideas of privatization and choice in education. In recent years, both have been promoted as major panaceas for the challenges facing education in the era of globalization. Proposals for reform by governments and corporations alike have emphasized the efficiencies that can be obtained from the transfer of services provided by the public sector to a range of private-sector interests, and by giving greater choice to the educational consumer. Yet these notions are highly ideological, located within the neoliberal imaginary of globalization.

As a construct, the idea of privatization emerged in the 1970s as an attempt by a number of western countries such as the United States to separate decision-making in the areas of public policy from the execution of service provision. Three decades later it has become globally pervasive, increasingly assumed to be the only way to ensure that public services, including education, are delivered efficiently and effectively (Ball and Youdell 2008). It has come to symbolize a new way of looking at public institutions and the role of the state in managing the affairs of its citizens. Under this broad philosophical orientation, many possible activities are construed as privatization, ranging from selling state-owned enterprises to contracting out public services to private contractors, be they individuals or corporations. According to Bray (1996), privatization of education takes at least three forms: transferring ownership of public institutions, shifting sectoral balance without redesignating existing institutions, and increasing government funding and support for private institutions. Bray might have added to this list, contracting out functions and services. Indeed, contracting out and enterprise sales may perhaps be the most influential modalities of privatization in the contemporary public sector. We can thus see why Ball (2007) speaks of 'privatizations' to capture these various meanings and practices.

Just as privatization appears in several forms, so do the reasons governments give in favour of privatization. Most of the reasons are couched in economic terms. It is argued that privatization leads to cost-effective delivery of public services, and that it enhances the productivity of government agencies. Governments also suggest that the power of private property rights, market forces and competition brings out the best in public-sector employees. Thus, when the public sector is forced to compete against private contractors, service delivery is necessarily more efficient; when public institutions are thrust into market environments, they become much more organizationally agile and innovative, with greater commitment to reform. Economic arguments in favour of privatization also view it as necessary for growth, for meeting increasing levels of demand for particular services, including higher education. Such arguments necessarily assume the welfare state to be a thing of the past, withering away, no longer capable of meeting the requirements of both society and individuals, who are increasingly interested in managing their own affairs and do not trust the state to look after them.

Many of these arguments have become commonplace, even if most cannot be substantiated with any hard data. So, for example, that private contractors are more efficient and cost-effective in delivering services without compromising on quality is a contention that has repeatedly been shown to be both groundless and perhaps even unverifiable (Boyer and Drache 1996); yet this does not seem to stop advocates of privatization from asserting it in a mantra-like manner. The fact is that economic arguments on their own cannot justify privatization. To try to do so is to grossly underestimate the political nature of the privatization agenda, and also to misunderstand the role of ideology in promoting it. In the end, the political context in which privatization is promoted is inherently ideological. It is based on an almost ontological assumption that the private sector is intrinsically more productive and efficient than the public sector.

Such an assumption is based on a philosophical conception of society as constituted by self-maximizing individuals with the free capacity to choose, as well as a conception of government as necessarily inimical to individual interests. Accordingly, public institutions are regarded as distant and unresponsive organs of government which pose serious threats to individual property rights, initiatives and freedom. According to this neoliberal view, individual freedom is not the only value that is endangered by government institutions; justice is as well. Justice, it is assumed, is compromised because of the perennial desire of governments to redistribute wealth that is never theirs and to seek to control human affairs that are best left to individual discretion. While neoliberalism accepts that some redistribution and control may be necessary, it suggests that the Keynesian welfare state exceeded its democratic authority and is no longer relevant to contemporary economic and social life, especially under the cultural conditions of globalization. Of course, the global financial crisis of 2008 has once again opened public and political discussions about these claims.

Freedom, justice and efficiency are thus key ingredients underpinning neoliberal ideology, which have increasingly been redefined in the self-image of that perspective. These social concepts, developed with particular meanings and significance within social democratic traditions, have been systematically re-articulated. Within the neoliberal discourse, the idea of freedom, for example, has become tied to a negative view of freedom as 'freedom from', rather than a positive view of freedom as 'freedom to' in terms, for example, articulated by Amartya Sen (1999), who has defined freedom in terms of the capabilities that people have to exercise choices and live decent lives, free from poverty and exploitation.

Similarly, the idea of justice has been reduced to property rights, rather than being inclusive of personal rights (Bowles and Gintis 1985). A property right vests in individuals the power to enter into social relationships on the basis and extent of their property, while personal rights are based on simple membership in their social collectivity. Personal rights involve equal treatment of citizens, the capacity to enjoy autonomy, equal access to participation in decision-making in social institutions, and reciprocity in relations of power and authority. The neoliberal view of justice, on the other hand, is located in the processes of acquisition and production rather than in the need to build community and social lives that are characterized by human dignity for all. Such a conception of freedom necessarily privileges the ruling capitalist class, which is able to access property rights within a system of asymmetrical power relations and labour exploitation (Apple 2001).

The neoliberal construction of efficiency, as we have already noted, is equally problematic because it cannot be interpreted neutrally, as neoliberal theorists often do, without reference to the more fundamental moral and political criteria against which it might be measured. Nothing is efficient in its own right. In an organizational setting, efficiency drives always involve control over people, achieved through either sanctions or hegemonic compliance. What this brief discussion shows, then, is that to embrace the interpretation of the concepts of freedom, justice and efficiency in neoliberal terms is to accept a certain preferred mode of existence, to become drawn into processes of governmentality described by Foucault (1991).

Philosophical assumptions relating to this preferred mode of existence underpin most theories of privatization. Chief among these are public choice theory, agency theory, the theory of transaction cost analysis, the new public management theory, and property rights theory. Each of these theories assumes the key rationale for privatization to be the need to increase economic efficiency through better organizational performance and control, as a means of increasing the well-being of citizens. Public choice theory is based on the fundamental notion that self-interest dominates human behaviour and that human beings are essentially 'rational utility maximizers'; that individuals can express their personal preferences much more effectively through market exchanges than, say, through political participation; and that the role of government should therefore be restricted to establishing high-level policy objectives rather than delivering the services per se. Agency theory views the delivery of services through an organization as a series of contracts which, if optimally established and operated, can generate significant levels of efficiency. The theory of transaction cost analysis suggests that organizational costs of transacting business can be minimized and made more efficient through vertical integration, best achieved through the privatization of all functions of an organization, except those that are regarded as absolutely central to organizational mission.

The idea of new public management (Lane 2000) shares its assumptions with theories of agency and transactional cost analysis, and applies them to the public sector. It emphasizes a range of concepts that have become commonplace in higher education around the world. Collectively these concepts amount to what Waters (1995) refers to as 'organizational ecumenism', a single idealization of appropriate organizational behaviour. These concepts include generic management skills; quantified performance targets; devolution; the separation of policy, commercial and non-commercial functions; the use of private-sector practices such as corporate plans and flexible labour practices; 'just-in-time' inventory; monetary incentives; cost-cutting; and above all the privatization of the so-called non-core functions and services. It thus emphasizes a preference for private ownership and prescribes, wherever possible, the use of contracting out and competition/contestability in the provision of public services.

Aligned to these concepts is the theory of property rights, which argues that private ownership of the assets of an organization results in superior profitability and effectiveness. In each of these theories, the emphasis on the principles of efficiency, effectiveness, productivity and profitability is paramount. These theories moreover assume that these principles are generic and apply equally to all kinds of organization, be they commercial or service-oriented, private or public. As organizations increasingly work in the international sphere, these theories seek to universalize these principles, eschewing those organizational practices that are situated within local and national cultural traditions.

However, what these theories mask is a range of philosophical assumptions about how society and its institutions are best organized. Insofar as these theories provide empirical justification for their various claims about efficiency and productivity, they do so within a self-referential framework in which its principles are assumed to be self-evidently good, even when they might conflict with other equally important goals. Public agencies like schools and universities have multiple and complex goals; yet these theories focus only on a narrow range of goals, making it difficult if not impossible to measure the justificatory claims that are made by their proponents. For unlike commercial businesses, performance in the public sector cannot be aggregated up to a single valid measurement of an agency's effectiveness. Yet most advocates of privatization try to do precisely this, often treating efficiency as a foundational principle, an end in its own right. In so doing, they clearly show how ideologically driven arguments in favour of privatization really are. Since no one can really object to efficiency and profitability, the neoliberal emphasis on these principles appears self-evident, and hence highly persuasive. Yet it is only when they are juxtaposed with other equally worthy service-related goals that they become contestable. And insofar as these contests are obscured by a narrowly defined language of freedom and justice, as we have already noted, the emphasis on efficiency and effectiveness obscures the powerful elite capitalist interests that privatization serves. The idea of privatization thus functions as an ideology.

The idea of choice may be viewed as a form of privatization and is similarly beset with a range of contradictions. As a policy construct, it emerged in the 1970s and quickly became a central policy prescription of the New Right and libertarian alike. The idea that parents should be able to choose which school their children attend appealed not only to the libertarians, with their ideological commitment to the market, but also to those social conservatives who promoted the family values agenda. In the UK, the Education Reform Act of 1988 embodied a highly regulated version of the school choice (Whitty *et al.* 1998), allowing parents to choose among government-run schools. In the USA, the ideology of choice has given rise to a range of policy initiatives including vouchers, charter schools, magnet schools and even home schooling. Other countries too have followed the lead from the United States and the United Kingdom, albeit in a highly regulated fashion (Forsey *et al.* 2008; Chakrabarti and Peterson 2009).

According to Brighouse (2003), the generic case for school choice is made on a number of grounds, many of which are derived from the highly controversial economic theories of Milton and Rose Friedman (1990). First, choice is a fundamental right that parents have over their children, and therefore any interference by the state in its exercise is illegitimate. Second, it is argued that the standard bureaucratic model of education alienates parents from their school, potentially creating a disjuncture between their values and those of state-mandated school practices. Third, it is suggested the costs of schooling can be driven down by choice, and that private schools can provide education at a much lower per-pupil cost than public schools. This is a variant on the efficiency argument that is central to the neoliberal belief that the state provisions are necessarily inefficient and perhaps even ineffective. Fourth, it is argued that choice is more likely to produce greater diversity of schools, and educational entrepreneurs experiment and innovate in an effort to meet the diversity of educational needs within the market. Finally, it is believed that there is something fundamentally inequitable about a system that effectively gives parental choice to the wealthy, thus depriving the poor from being able to enjoy diversity of provisions.

What must be clear from this account of the diverse reasons for school choice is that these arguments address each of the five values that Stone (2001) identifies as basic to all public policies, namely equity, efficiency, security, liberty and community. Whatever the merits of these arguments, however, it is also clear that values of efficiency and liberty are dominant, while issues relating to the role of education in building and sustaining community are sidelined. Equity considerations are also expressed in a way that appears disingenuous, since equity is already framed in market terms. The poor do not have the capacity to pay for private education. The idea that inequity can be eliminated without extending choice to all, by depriving the wealthy of choice, is not even entertained by these arguments, which are based on liberalism that assumes that 'individual persons are the sole intrinsic objects of moral concern' (Brighouse 2003: 5). But these arguments for school choice are neoliberal in the sense that they are opposed to state intervention in people's lives in favour of market principles with which to organize social life. They are thus located within a neoliberal social imaginary that drives policy-makers into assuming the limits of community formations.

Conclusion

In this chapter we have discussed some of the ways in which, under the conditions of globalization, educational values have been interpreted through a neoliberal imaginary and how this, in recent years, has reconfigured the discursive terrain within which educational policy is developed, articulated and enacted in countries around the world. We have argued that this imaginary has redefined educational values in largely economic terms, linked to the concerns of social efficiency. It has emphasized the importance of market dynamics in the organization of education around a view of education as a private good. It has linked the purposes of education to the requirements of the global economy. However, there is nothing inevitable or necessary about locating globalization within this imaginary. It is indeed possible to understand the facts of global interconnectivity and interdependence in radically different ways, with implications for rethinking educational values that do not simply call for a return to some romanticized past, but require us to engage with transformations brought about by recent developments in information and communications technology in ways that do not prioritize the economic over all other human concerns.

While there is no sign that the neoliberal imaginary of globalization is in decline, it is becoming abundantly clear that it has given rise to a range of contradictions that can no longer be ignored. For example, the promotion of the value of efficiency over other values has left many educators, schools and educational systems feeling disenfranchised, especially when they are expected to conform to unrealistic accountability regimes and deliver outcomes for which they have not been adequately funded or resourced. Their professionalism has been sapped of any real meaning, as they are required to become efficient and effective in contexts that are much more culturally, economically and politically complex than many governments and IGOs often assume. At the same time, the policy shift towards privatization has compromised the goals of access and equality and has widened inequalities not only across nations, but also within the same communities. It has made the goals of gender and racial equity more difficult to realize. Indeed, while hegemonic neoliberal globalization has greatly benefited some countries and groups of people, it has had disastrous consequences for others, whose economic prospects have declined and whose cultural traditions have become eroded.

5 Curriculum, pedagogy and evaluation

Introduction

In his highly influential paper 'On the classification and framing of educational knowledge', Basil Bernstein (1971) referred to curriculum, pedagogy and evaluation as the three message systems of schooling. He used the notion of 'message system' to name those aspects of schooling which have the greatest socialization impact and which link schools and their message systems to the broader culture and the reproduction of that culture and associated social system. He observed that 'How a society selects, classifies, distributes, transmits and evaluates the educational knowledge it considers to be public, reflects both the distribution of power and principles of social control' (ibid.: 47). The selective tradition of the curriculum, then, is linked to broader issues of social power. Relatedly, Bernstein (2004: 196) viewed pedagogy as a 'cultural relay', suggesting it is a 'uniquely human device for both the production and reproduction of culture'. For Bernstein, the idea of evaluation included strategies of monitoring and assessing performance. He regarded these three message systems as inextricably linked, with changes in one affecting shifts in the other two.

Traditionally, issues relating to curriculum, pedagogy and evaluation have not been a major focus in education policy studies. Education policy studies and curriculum studies have usually been considered as separate arenas of theory and practice. Education policy studies have tended to focus on almost all aspects of educational processes except those relating to curriculum, pedagogy and evaluation. Policy studies have thus, for example, addressed issues of funding and equity, but have not usually linked them to their effects on practices of curriculum, pedagogy and evaluation. The fields of curriculum and education policy have thus been considered as separate, located in different academic and organizational spaces. Indeed, at times in the realpolitik of education policy there have been real tensions between the statutory authorities that oversee curriculum and examinations and departments of education that focus more on policy and staffing matters. This separation has served to sideline issues of curriculum, pedagogy and evaluation in policy discussions and in the development of education policy studies. Yet it is these three message systems which frame the core of teachers' work, which inform their logics of practice. Perhaps it is for this reason that teachers are often unaware of policies that have implications for their work. Further, we would suggest that the achievement of some policy goals in education requires that the policy has some impact within the message systems.

In this chapter we want to explore the politics of the three message systems within the broader framework of education policies, showing how they are inextricably linked, and how for policies to be effective they must engage more directly with issues of practice. We want to suggest that in the context of globalization, education policy reform is now intimately linked to the ways in which curriculum, pedagogy and evaluation are being reframed. But as we have already noted, globalization is a contested notion, and it is in the framing of these message systems that competing interpretations of globalization become evident. Indeed, as we have already noted, reforms with respect to curriculum, pedagogy and evaluation are now increasingly presented in terms of a discourse of the challenges and opportunities precipitated by globalization. A key challenge is couched in terms of the role of the message systems for preparing students for participation in a global economy, thus enhancing national competitiveness. This has implications for reimagining the nation, and the role of the message systems in transforming identity and citizenship and promoting social cohesion.

This focus on global competitiveness of nations has extended the scope of Bernstein's message systems, which now include a major concern for testing and accountability. Increasingly, systems of education around the world have begun to steer their systems using standardized testing regimes, both national and international. Indeed, it could be argued that testing now constitutes a fourth message system, through which central policymakers seek to steer local practice through various demands and structures of accountability. Indeed, testing has become a central element in policy regimes. Such testing could be seen as a reductive version of the potentially broader evaluation message system.

In what follows, we discuss a range of examples of how both within nation-states and across them, there have been intense policy debates about how best to reframe curriculum, pedagogy and evaluation around the requirements of testing. Testing itself is centred on an assumption that globalization demands new forms of skill, knowledge and dispositions, as well as better, more efficient and effective systems to be achieved through more robust and coordinated regimes of accountability. In line with the overarching argument of this book, these systems of accountability can also now be seen to have a global element to them.

Interpreting global imperatives

To demonstrate the policy significance of curriculum it might be useful to consider moves towards national curriculum in England and Australia. The

Education Reform Act (1988) of the Thatcher government in the UK saw the creation of national curriculum in schooling in England for the first time. Until that point much more authority and power had been situated at the local authority level (and with various examination boards), the site also of most progressive anti-racist and equal employment opportunity legislation. Thatcher and subsequent UK governments have continued to strengthen the hand of the national government in education policy in England vis-à-vis local authorities. The Thatcherite move for a national curriculum was ideologically driven; at one level it was about what her New Right ideology saw as defeating the 'producer' or 'provider capture' of teachers of the institution of schooling, their perceived political stance and similarly in respect of the local authorities; at another level this was about the production of national citizens of particular kinds, ones looking more to the glories of the past than the future perhaps – what has been referred to as a 'curriculum of the dead' and linked to the New Right political project of cultural restoration and new individualism (Ball 1994). These rationales and policy intentions can be contrasted with those of the subsequent New Labour government, who see national curricula as ensuring the types of skill and human capital necessary to the post-industrial economy and the competitiveness within the global economy of the national one.

The situation in Australia has been that schooling, according to the Constitution, has been the responsibility of the states rather than the national government in the complex federalism of Australian education policy (Lingard 2000). Curriculum and assessment policies and practices have thus been determined within state jurisdictions. However, the Hawke and Keating federal Labor governments (1983–1996) sought to create a national curriculum justified on a number of grounds, including the need for a national focus on schooling to produce the requisite human capital thought necessary for national economic competitiveness, as well as efficiency arguments and a (spurious?) argument about the interests of students who were mobile across state borders. The result, though, of this version of federalism in schooling was the creation of National Curriculum Statements and Profiles. This was almost a lowest common denominator agreement or perhaps an agreement at a broad level of abstraction. Schooling and curricula were still, by and large, controlled at the state level.

Across the early stages of the conservative Howard government elected in late 1996, which was at least in its early period more federalist in orientation than the preceding Labor governments, the commitment to a national curriculum weakened somewhat. In its latter stages, however, the Howard government (1996–2007) once again raised the question of the need for a national curriculum, for a uniform national system of assessment or examination and for national standardized testing. This move had economic and more overtly ideological motivations to do with the select tradition of school curricula, particularly in history, linked to the broader culture wars, and the teaching of literacy (Snyder 2008). This received, by and large, bipartisan support from the then Labor opposition, or at least the call for a national curriculum did, if not so much the ideological drive. Central to Labor's electoral platform in the late 2007 federal election was a so-called 'education revolution', which can be compared with Tony Blair's 1997 election policy mantra of 'Education, Education, Education', and a key component part of this was a Labor commitment to a national curriculum for schools, at least in English, Maths, Science and History in the first instance. We would make the point, though, that the federal/state political structure in Australia will mean that a national curriculum will always be mediated to some extent by federal structures and state interests. This mediation can be contrasted with the possibilities for national developments in respect of the message systems in a unitary form of government, such as in New Zealand.

We mention these two national curriculum examples to make the point, which is the rationale for this book-length study of contemporary education policy, that globalization has affected education policies of all types. Curricula are no exception. Indeed, curriculum reform has been linked to the reconstitution of education as a central arm of national economic policy, as well as being central to the imagined community the nation wishes to construct through schooling. Both are responses in their own ways to the perceived pressures of globalization. The former is concerned with the development of what are perceived to be the skills and dispositions thought necessary to the so-called knowledge economy and globalization; the latter is concerned with constructing the imagined community which is the nation in the context of the heightened flows of migrants and resulting multi-ethnic nature of national community. This has dented the (always erroneous) assumption of the homology between nation and ethnicity. Further, all nations on the globe are attempting to improve both the quantity and quality of their human capital. This of necessity involves a focus on curricula and, as we will discuss later, a focus on assessment and testing and new accountabilities as part of the emergent 'audit culture' (Power 1997). In particular, the focus on curricula is often about how to cater for a broader senior schooling cohort than has historically been the case and how to balance academic curricula and more vocationally oriented education. In some nations there has also been a focus on early childhood education in an attempt to challenge the social class/educational success nexus. This is also linked to the project of enhancing the totality of the nation's human capital and ensuring greater retention in the long term to the end of secondary schooling and higher participation rates in university education.

The Scottish curriculum reform *A Curriculum for Excellence*, published in November 2004, is exactly about that policy pressure, on what has been the academic focus of curricula in Scotland, delivered in comprehensive secondary schools. The desired outcomes from schooling according to *A Curriculum for Excellence* are the production of 'successful learners', 'confident individuals', 'responsible citizens' and 'effective contributors', which frame the design of the curriculum for ages 3–18 years (Scottish Executive Education Department 2007).

In Queensland, Australia, the creation of the Queensland Studies Authority, which deals with curricula, assessment and testing across the school career from preschool to the end of secondary schooling and tertiary entrance, had as one rationale the need for a so-called 'seamless curriculum' across the compulsory years of schooling and the related need for complementarities with post-compulsory curricula. The policy desire was to see all students complete 12 years of schooling or its equivalent. This Authority replaced two other statutory authorities that had dealt with P–10 curricula and upper secondary curricula respectively.

The Brown Labour government in the UK is committed to increasing the school leaving age to 18 years by 2015 and seeing 50 per cent of the relevant age cohort attending university. This policy commitment has pushed matters of upper secondary curricula, examinations and qualifications to the forefront of policy concerns. These considerations have precipitated some defence of the more traditional A-level academic curricula, as well as a range of challenges to it. Further, apparently improved student performance over time on this and the GCSE examinations has seen some calls to make the exams more difficult, a clear articulation of the sorting and selection functions of schooling and a concern for 'standards'.

The final point to be made at this stage about globalization and curricula is that while the pressures on curriculum reform might be similar throughout the globe, the reforms which result always have a vernacular character as they build incrementally on what has gone before within specific educational systems. As Taylor *et al.* (1997: 16) have argued in respect of incremental relations in policy development, we can argue similarly about curriculum change: 'There is always a prior history of significant events, a particular ideological climate, a social and economic context.'

This vernacular reform of curricula set against globalized policy discourses is very evident when one considers moves in the ASEAN countries collectively to develop a post-national approach to curricula and pedagogies aimed at enhancing regional economic activity and creating a postnational or regional identity (Koh 2007, 2008). Political structures also mediate curriculum reform possibilities, with the various moves to a national curriculum in Australia and the mediation by federalism and state interests being a good case in point. The same is the case in the federal political structure of the USA, but Bush's *No Child Left Behind* reforms have also affected curricula and pedagogies in US schools (Hursh 2008), which are, as in Australia, under the jurisdiction of the states. Hursh (ibid.) argues that in those states without mandated curricula, the testing necessitated by the federal *No Child Left Behind* legislation has constructed a de facto curriculum. One could go further back in US education policy history and trace the effects of the federal report *A Nation at Risk* (National Commission on Excellence in Education 1983) to see the ways this report as a de facto policy affected education policy production in the states and the resultant all-consuming focus on standards and accountability (Weaver-Hightower 2008: 157).

The fallout in Germany following the poor German performance on the first PISA in 2000 (Grek 2009) also saw national attempts at school reform which were mediated by the German federal political structure, where the states or *Länder* control schools, and where the *Länder* had been strengthened vis-à-vis the national government following the fascism of the Third Reich. Further, we would note that any proposed changes to high-status curriculum fields always come up against vested interests of various kinds and always provoke resistance to change. Bernstein (2001a: 368) also suggests that alternative knowledges and pedagogical practices are more likely to be taken up in low-status institutions than in high-status ones.

As education has been reconstituted as central to the economic competitiveness of nations in the context of a global economy, many educational systems have instituted high-stakes, standardized testing to try to drive up educational standards. This has been the case in England, particularly as developed by New Labour governments after 1997, which utilized league tables of performance and other data sets for school improvement agendas more than for parental choice reasons as part of a quasi-market in schooling. A commitment to markets and parental choice was the rationale for the introduction of league tables of performance for earlier Conservative governments of Thatcher and Major from 1979 until 1997. The use of performance data for enhancing the educational outcomes of all students has been taken a step further by the trial in England of *Making Good Progress* (Department for Education and Skills 2006), which attempts to utilize data on the individual performance of students to reframe classroom practices geared to improvement.

The instigation of such testing regimes has usually been resisted by teachers and their representative bodies, such as teacher unions and professional associations, because of the perceived negative (that is, narrowing and reductive) effects of such testing on both curriculum and pedagogy, as well as on teacher professionalism, which is reconstituted by these reforms. In the strongest policy mechanisms of this kind, such as in England with Standardised Attainment Tests (SATs) at Key Stages 1, 2 and 3 (primary schooling) and in the standardized testing which dominates schooling in most states of the USA, and strengthened by the demands of the federal Act *No Child Left Behind* (Hursh 2008), we see almost a transfer of educational authority from the professional teacher to the standardized tests and those who construct them. Apple (2001) actually sees this new class of technicians involved in such test construction as beneficiaries of such policy regimes. The point we would make is about the contrasting dispositions and logics of practice of test creators and classroom teachers.

At another level, such testing can be seen to be central to the new accountabilities which are part of what Power (1997) called the 'audit society', which in turn is part of new public management which now sees central policy steer at a distance. This new public management approach sees overarching goals set at the centre, with the site of practice being accountable for the achievement of these goals measured against performance indicators, standardized test results and the like. The audit culture has manifested in particular ways in education systems, linked to accountabilities and summative assessment. Teachers appear to be more comfortable with formative assessment, which they see as potentially enhancing student learning – what has been called assessment *for* learning.

It is this set of developments which can be encapsulated in the idea of 'policy as numbers' (Rose 1999), which sees outcome data of various kinds becoming central to policy developments within education systems. A good case in point is Queensland, where school students have performed badly on the National Assessment Program – Literacy and Numeracy (NAPLAN) and where consequently the government instigated a policy review seeking recommendations to overcome this situation. One recommendation of the Interim Report of that review was that Queensland students be made more test-literate.

Given our concern with globalization and education in this book, we would also note here that this policy as numbers approach has a global manifestation in, for example, the OECD's Programme for International Student Assessment (PISA), which seeks to constitute the globe as a commensurate space of measurement of performance of students at the end of compulsory schooling on literacy, science and maths. PISA's international comparative measures of 'quality' and 'equity' in the national performance of students have taken on strong policy salience within national systems and are on the radar of education ministers in participating countries. Fifty-seven countries participated in PISA in 2006; that is, almost as many non-OECD member countries (27) participated as member countries (30), with a real expansion of participating countries projected for the next round of PISA in 2009.

When Bernstein spoke of the three message systems of schooling, he made the additional point about the symbiotic relationships between the three systems. We have added testing to these message systems, and would make the same point about testing: that is, that it also sits in a symbiotic relationship to the other three message systems. What this means in effect is that changes in one message system, often assessment and testing, or curricula, have effects on the others. This is well exemplified by the case of high-stakes standardized testing at state level in the USA, which has been shown to lead to 'defensive pedagogies' (McNeil 2000). Delpit (2006: xiii), writing in the new edition of her influential study of educational disadvantage in the USA, *Other People's Children*, comments in the following way on changes in US schooling brought on by President Bush's *No Child Left Behind Act*:

> Since the publication of *Other People's Children*, the country's educational system has become caught in the vice of the *No Child Left Behind Act*, which mandates more standardized testing of children than the country has ever seen, with more

> and more urban school districts adopting 'teacher proof' curricula to address low test scores. Along with school consultants whose sole purpose is to police teachers' adherence to scripted lessons, mandated classroom management strategies, and strict instructional timelines that ignore the natural rhythms of teaching and learning.

On this very same point David Hursh (2008) has written a book-length study of the symbiotic relationship in the USA between this reality of high-stakes testing and what he calls 'the decline of teaching and learning'.

In England (and in respect of schooling we need to disaggregate the UK into its constituent parts – Scotland, Wales, Northern Ireland and England), as already noted, the New Labour government has attempted to drive up school quality and achieve school improvement through a very strong emphasis on Standardised Attainment Tests (SATs) and student performance on GSCE and A-level public examinations and the publication of related league tables of performance and target-setting for schools. The Improving Schools Programme (ISP) is one such national strategy in England that seeks to use data for whole-school improvement. *Making Good Progress* is yet another of these developments with an individual student performance focus. These 'policy as numbers' moves have affected pedagogies, thinning them out and reducing curriculum content to that which is valorized in tests and examinations – a manifestation of the symbiotic relationship between the message systems.

Hartley (2003) and Ranson (2003) have clearly demonstrated how in England the 'secret garden' of the curriculum is secret no more, and how the reductive effects of testing and the related policy regime, including accountability measures, ensure that schools cannot achieve the policy goals of producing creative thinkers and entrepreneurial dispositions linked to the perceived human capital demands of a globalized knowledge economy. Educational policymakers in Singapore have likewise become aware of the reductive effects of a testing and performance-driven schooling system on the production of independent, creative thinkers (Koh 2004).

In research one of us conducted in Queensland, Australia on teacher classroom pedagogies (Lingard *et al.* 2001; Lingard, Hayes, Mills and Christie 2003; Hayes *et al.* 2006; Lingard 2007), we found that there was not enough intellectual demand in the pedagogies we observed in about 1000 classroom lessons to have the desired learning effects for all students, and especially for students from disadvantaged backgrounds lacking the requisite cultural capital. We hypothesized a number of reasons for this, including the amount of curriculum content coverage demanded by syllabus documents, a crowded curriculum, class sizes, and the emphasis on support and care in early policy documents rather than on intellectual demand. Allan Luke, a co-researcher on that project, has commented regarding this lack of intellectual demand in the pedagogies observed: 'the testing, basic skills, and accountability push had encouraged narrowing of the curriculum' and was also affiliated with the finding of a 'shaving off of higher order and critical thinking and a lowering of cognitive demand and intellectual depth' (Luke 2006: 123). This is a very good exemplification of the symbiotic relationship between the message systems.

Another example relates to the differential implementation of the 'Assessment is for Learning' (AiFL) policy in contemporary Scottish education policy. This is a policy about formative assessment as central to good pedagogy and good student learning, which conceives of the multiple purposes of assessment (both formative and summative) as including assessment *as*, *of* and *for* learning. This policy, based on the academic research and theorizing of Black and colleagues (2003) about formative assessment, has been taken up enthusiastically in many Scottish primary schools, but not so profoundly in junior and senior secondary schooling, where public exams focused on summative assessment still hold much stronger sway. Indeed, AiFL is constructed as a policy for the 5–14 age group, but ought to have relevance for all of schooling.

Further evidence of the symbiotic relationships between assessment policy and curricula and pedagogical effects can be found in the situation in England with GCSEs, where the government has constituted the percentage (more than one-third) of students achieving five A–C grades on this examination as the Gold Standard for measuring school quality. Schools have been set targets for getting more than a third of their students to achieve this Gold Standard. Gillborn and Youdell (2000) have shown how this policy frame has had triage effects, with schools and teachers focusing their concerns on those students just below this threshold with the potential to achieve it, and neglecting others without this potential. Lipman (2004) in her study of educational 'reform' in Chicago, demonstrated similar triage effects in respect of standardized testing and the focus on 'bubble kids', those close to achieving standards and required proficiency levels.

Since the early 1970s the Queensland school system has had no public examinations. Rather, at the senior levels at the end of secondary schooling, students participate in school-based, teacher-moderated assessment during the last two years of schooling, which includes all schools, both government and non-government, and which further moderates teacher assessment via a standardized Core Skills Test based on common curriculum elements across all senior curricula. These moderated and aggregated student results are used to determine tertiary entrance scores. When the Howard government made moves towards a national curriculum, one of their targets was this Queensland approach to assessment. This Queensland approach has produced very assessment-literate senior teachers in Queensland (Lingard *et al.* 2006), with the nature of the Core Skills Test also having a positive impact upon pedagogies through its emphasis on higher-order outcomes. Often, in contrast, standardized tests are used to measure minimum standards, with resultant negative impact upon pedagogies and the breadth of the curriculum.

Up to this point we have talked mainly about curriculum, assessment and testing, rather than directly about pedagogy. This is because educational systems have tended not to have policies about pedagogies. For example, in Scotland there is a statutory authority responsible for examinations and qualifications, the Scottish Qualifications Authority, and another responsible for curricula, called Teaching and Learning Scotland. However, there are no explicit policy discourses about pedagogy. This is the norm across educational systems, rather than the exception. Pedagogy has thus been the domain of teacher professional autonomy, while teacher identities have been constructed largely around teaching children for primary teachers and teaching subjects for secondary teachers. Pedagogies are central to teacher professional practices and yet have not been a central aspect of their identities (Lingard 2009). How one imparts knowledge framed by a mandated curriculum and testing and assessment regimes was the space of teacher professional autonomy. Policy about pedagogies was usually not explicit, but rather implicit in curricula and assessment and testing. A very good example here is the Literacy Hour in England introduced by the Blair government in an attempt to improve literacy standards through the imposition of allotted time and a particular approach to literacy teaching. This policy enumerated what teachers had to do in the space of the literacy hour each day. As such, there was an at least implied pedagogy in the literacy hour policy, but one always subject to some pedagogical recontextualizing by classroom teachers (see Marsh 2007).

In New South Wales, Australia, the state department has a recommended policy for schools on quality pedagogy, a model developed out of the Queensland productive pedagogies research referred to earlier (Lingard *et al.* 2001; Lingard, Hayes, Mills and Christie 2003; Lingard 2008). In our view there are some potential dangers in mandating policy about pedagogies. Such mandating tends to dissociate pedagogies from epistemological and knowledge concerns and deny teacher professional mediation of policy (Lingard and Mills 2007: 236). We need to recognize the significance of pedagogies (and assessment practices) to what teachers can achieve with students, but any research-based or policy models of pedagogy attempt to universalize a model. There are competing logics between policy production and the characteristics of pedagogical practices. As Coburn and Stein (2006: 42) note, teacher practice is 'always local, situated, emergent, and linked with prior practice'. In contrast, and as Bourdieu (1998b: 59) has argued, central to the capitals possessed by the state and the broader field of power is the 'monopoly of the universal', that is, policy assumes and demands universal applicability. In Bourdieu's terms there is a clash between competing and different logics of practice of the policy-producing state and teacher pedagogical practice (see also Hardy and Lingard 2008 and Rawolle and Lingard 2008). It is thus our view that because of these different logics of practice, eventually some technization of practice will probably result from pedagogies being a policy focus (Alexander 2004). This technization is often read by teachers as potential deprofessionalization.

It seems to us that in respect of improving pedagogical practices, some level of trust of teachers and their professionalism is needed within a supportive professional development framework and the creation of teacher professional learning communities within schools. This demands investment in teacher professional development. However, a lack of trust has been central to relationships with professional practices in health and education policy, for example, in England. It might also be important for the 'pedagogizing' of teacher identities, so that teachers begin to articulate their specific professional expertise as pedagogical (Lingard 2009).

Throughout this book we have emphasized the point that education policy in the context of globalization has become a focus of economic policy. We might call this the economization of education policy. While we are dealing largely with school curricula and the other message systems of schooling in this chapter, education policy and these matters are significant in all sectors of education, including higher education. We would make a related point that many policies in specific public policy domains other than education, for example health, social welfare and the law, have become quite educational in orientation as well. Bernstein (2001a, 2001b) wrote of the 'totally pedagogised society' to refer to the ways in which pedagogy has salience across a range of public policies, across the society and across professional and policy practices. Indeed, Bernstein (2001b: 377) claimed that 'the State is moving to ensure that there's no space or time which is not pedagogised'. In a sense this is linked to talk of the knowledge economy and also linked to the neoliberal subject as responsible for his/her continuing education, conceived as an investment in the self, across the life-cycle. This is lifelong learning in its neoliberal guise, rather than a more humanist or social democratic one. There are openings here for education policy studies, as well as for curriculum studies. There is also an important opening for pedagogical considerations in contemporary social theory (Lingard *et al.* 2008a).

In Chapter 3 on analysing education policy we argued that globalization demanded that education policy analysis be deparochialized (Appadurai 2001). The totally pedagogized society means that education policy studies need to be deparochialized in another way – beyond the 'traditional' institutions of education. This picks up on what Young (1996) called the de-differentiation of educational institutions. Education policy studies might be concerned, for example, with pedagogies associated with the 'health promoting school' being produced by health departments or with one's consumer rights as part of economic policy and so on.

In the remainder of this chapter we consider specific examples of the ways in which globalization has affected curricula, assessment and testing policies. The first case study is of a curriculum reform which was trialled in a number of Queensland schools across Years 1–9, which had a research base and which was an attempt to reconceptualize curriculum and align it with assessment and pedagogies in the context of globalization. The subsequent section deals with two curriculum examples from the Global South and demonstrates how the positioning of these two Global South nations, Pakistan and St Lucia, frame policy development and possibilities for curriculum, at least discursively, with implications for the character of curriculum and the implementation of curriculum policy. In the conclusion to the chapter we will return briefly to a consideration of the distinctions between the fields of education policy studies and curriculum studies and what this means for considering the message systems as policies.

The *New Basics* and productive pedagogies

We have already mentioned the productive pedagogies research in Queensland, Australia (Lingard *et al.* 2001; Lingard, Hayes, Mills and Christie 2003; Hayes *et al.* 2006) which created a model of effective pedagogies and documented the actual pedagogies utilized in about 250 classrooms and in about 1000 lessons across the state in both government primary and secondary schools. The model of pedagogies developed, derived from the US work by Newmann and his colleagues (1996) on 'authentic pedagogy', a wide range of critical pedagogy literature from the sociology of education, and from statistical analysis of maps of actual classroom pedagogies. The statistical analysis revealed a multidimensional model of 'productive pedagogies' consisting of four dimensions, namely intellectual demand, connectedness, supportiveness, and working with and valuing difference. The research found very supportive and caring classrooms with not enough intellectual demand and connectedness in the pedagogies and with very little working with and valuing difference. On the latter, we need to recognize that the bureaucratic structures of schooling have tended to encourage a pedagogy of sameness, rather than pedagogies of difference (Trifonas 2003; Lingard 2007). Writing about the USA, Dimitriadis and McCarthy (2001) have suggested that even in the present time of multiplicity of identities, pedagogies have tended to tame and regulate as a response.

Earlier in this chapter we also suggested a number of hypotheses regarding why this lack of intellectual demand exists. We will return to these in considering the New Basics reform in Queensland. We would note, though, that the caring character of pedagogies documented in the study was very important and perhaps indicative of the social worker role that many teachers must adopt today in their professional practices. In some schools, particularly those located in very disadvantaged communities, often those adversely affected by the fallout from neoliberal globalization, such a teacher role is central to supporting young people and in some cases is responsible for holding school and broader communities together.

The Queensland School Reform Longitudinal Study (QSRLS; Lingard *et al.* 2001), which developed the concept of productive pedagogies, has been influential in a number of educational systems and research communities, including New South Wales, Australia, where it forms the basis of that system's quality pedagogy model; and in Singapore, where a large research project is being conducted to further develop models of pedagogies which make a difference (Luke and Hogan 2006).

We would also make the point that the QSRLS argued on the basis of its evidence that of all the school-based factors, it was teacher pedagogies and assessment practices which made the greatest difference to student learning outcomes, while at the same time recognizing the significance of student socio-economic background to successful school learning. There are some significant policy insights to be drawn here.

Governments would prefer to see teachers and schools and their practices as being the sole solution to a whole range of social problems, including improving the quality of outcomes and the issue of equality of educational opportunity. However, as Bernstein observed a long time ago, education cannot compensate for society. In a somewhat similar vein, Ladson-Billings (2006), writing about the so-called 'achievement gap' between white and black students in the USA, has rejected that concept and spoken instead of an 'educational debt', consisting of an historical debt, an economic debt, a socio-political debt and a moral debt. This means that schooling alone, including pedagogies and curriculum reform, cannot address the 'educational debt'. In effect, what both Bernstein and Ladson-Billings are saying is that an unequal society will usually have unequal provision of schooling and thus not be able to offer equality of educational opportunity for all.

The PISA results have confirmed that it is those societies that are more equal in income, wealth and other economic ways – that is, that have small Gini coefficients of inequality – that provide real equality of educational opportunity and where the social class/school success nexus is weak (Green *et al.* 2006). In Australia, the Rudd Labor government has recognized that more educational equality is dependent upon quality teacher practices and less societal inequality, and demands positively-discriminating funding for 'disadvantaged schools'. The broad political and policy question is how to convert that research recognition into education policies which have the desired effects. The matter of policy learning is an interesting one in this respect. In respect of education it is clear that redistributive policies are required in the broadest public policy sense and also specifically within education.

The QSRLS also had influence in Queensland. The state department of education, now called Education Queensland, took up the model of pedagogies and committed to its implementation across the systems through professional development work and the like. It has currently commissioned subsequent research to ascertain the outcomes of that commitment to productive pedagogies on classroom practices and, by implication, on student learning outcomes. We would make the point, though, that such 'implementation' needs to work with teachers through professional development and the creation of teacher professional learning communities in schools. Further, the utilization of a research-based model of pedagogies in classrooms still requires professional mediation and the adaptation of the model to the specificities of the classroom. This is yet another manifestation of the competing logics between systemic policy and research on the one hand, and professional practices on the other – a clash between the claim to the universal and the specificities of practice.

The QSRLS had another significant policy effect in Queensland. Professor Allan Luke, a member of the QSRLS research team, was seconded to Education Queensland for the period 1999–2000 as Deputy Director-General with responsibility for strategic thinking about the future of schooling in the context of globalization and the findings of the QSRLS. The outcome of Luke's time as Deputy Director-General was the creation of a New Basics curriculum trial (2000–2004) in more than 50 Queensland government schools across Years 1–9. This project argued the need for alignment between curricula, pedagogies and assessment practices – the QSRLS had starkly demonstrated the lack of alignment between the three and the need to reconceptualize curricula in relation to the pressures of globalization, while rejecting a high-stakes testing and accountability regime as the way to achieve better quality and more equitable outcomes. An early Education Queensland booklet on the New Basics stated on this point (Education Queensland 2000: 3):

> At its heart, then, the New Basics Project is about renewing our work as educators, getting back to the basics of curriculum, pedagogy and assessment, with a clear focus on improving student outcomes through increasing the intellectual rigour of their work. It isn't a simplistic paint-by-numbers system, and it doesn't buy into the argument that lots of tests or lots of outcomes will solve the complex problems we face. Instead it is based on a commitment to teachers' professionalism. It recognizes their capacity for intellectual decision-making and their commitment to their students.

This is an important statement, representing the reconceptualist character of the New Basics. In the introduction to this chapter we noted how standardized testing relocates professional authority away from teachers to the creators of standardized tests. In the Queensland system with the New Basics trial there was, in contrast, the important recognition that teacher professionalism and professional skills were central to strengthening the intellectual rigour of classroom practices, which the QSRLS had shown was necessary for achieving high-quality student outcomes for all.

The New Basics worked on the assumption that the crowded curriculum was an important factor in the lack of intellectual demand in pedagogies and that more assessment-literate teachers were necessary to achieving better outcomes for all students. As such, the New Basics curriculum frame sought to reduce the remit of the curriculum, to 'unclutter' the curriculum as it were, and worked with the productive pedagogies and with what was termed a Rich Tasks approach to assessment practices. The New Basics also required the incorporation of new technologies into students' collaborative work across the New Basics and Rich Tasks.

Earlier in this book, mention was made of the mediatization of education policy. It is interesting to note here that the title of this curriculum reform trial, the 'New Basics', was derived from market research which demonstrated that the title New Basics appealed to a broad cross-section of the community – from progressives, who liked the notion of 'new', to conservatives, who liked the concept of 'basics'. This offers some important insights into educational change processes today and the significance of the semiotics of policy statements and naming. We would also note how the context of the New Basics reform, constructed in its own documentation, was replete with the descriptor 'new'. Indeed, this documentation spoke of 'new student identities', 'new workplaces', 'new technologies', 'new times', 'new citizenship', 'new knowledges' and 'new epistemologies' as part of the globalized context of the reform and the need for it. This proliferation of 'new' is an example of what Fairclough (1992) has referred to as 'overwording'.

A booklet for teachers in those schools participating in the trial described the New Basics in the following way:

> The New Basics are futures-oriented categories for organizing curriculum. Essentially they are a way of managing the enormous increase in information that is now available as a result of globalization and the rapid change in the economic, social and cultural dimensions of our existence.

The New Basics are clusters of essential practices that students need if they are to flourish in 'new times'. Apart from globalization, contributors to these new times include a shift towards local service-based economies, new and constantly changing technologies, complex transformations in cultural and social relationships, fluid demographics and a sense of uncertainty about the future (Education Queensland 2000: 1).

The clusters of essential practices were represented by the following curriculum organizers: life pathways and social futures; multiliteracies and communications media; active citizenship; and environment and technologies. Each of these transdisciplinary categories was framed by a question: respectively these were: 'Who am I and where am I going?'; 'How do I make sense of and communicate with the world?'; 'What are my rights and responsibilities in communities, cultures, and economies?'; and 'How do I describe, analyse and shape the world around me?'.

We can see in this descriptor of New Basics and the essential practices, globalization as the constructed context of the reform. Globalization is constructed as both context and rationale for the reform. We also get the sense of the uncertainty of the present and the future, and implicitly some notion of the dispositions needed to be acquired through schooling to cope with this insecurity (and risk) – dispositions geared to change, to working with differences of multiple kinds (including forms of literacy), and working with and across the local and the global. We can also see that considering curricula, as with policy, as the authoritative allocation of values, is a useful thing to do, while recognizing that globalization has challenged the meaning of this conceptualization.

The QSRLS had demonstrated the need for more assessment-literate teachers, and that teachers of the senior years in the secondary school, because of more than 30 years of teacher ownership of school-based, teacher-moderated assessment, as opposed to a system of external examinations, were more assessment-literate than other junior secondary and primary teachers. The New Basics trial recognized this and developed a suite of transdisciplinary tasks in three-year spans across Years 1–9. There were a small number of Rich Tasks for each cycle (Years 1–3, 4–7, 8–9), which were developed by assessment experts, and each of which required knowledge and skills from at least two clusters of the curriculum organizers. Research about the implementation and achievements of the New Basics reform, including the Rich Tasks, showed how important shared teacher moderation in a learning community was to the enhancement of teacher assessment skills.

The New Basics trial has been completed and evaluated. The points to note here, perhaps, are that it linked to a government-funded research project; involved close relationships between education researchers and policymaking; and was a reform based clearly in respect for teacher professionalism and recognition of the changes in school curricula, pedagogies and assessment practices thought necessary to achieving the quality outcomes now demanded of schooling systems, given the competitive pressures of globalization. The New Basics schools were supported throughout the reform by quarantined funding support and critical friends. It is interesting as well to recognize that the New Basics left untouched the senior years, where curricula remained based around subject disciplines and where the sorting and selection processes of schooling continued to affect the provision of schooling. In that respect it is interesting that the QSRLS showed some primary schools which seemed to break the social class/quality of pedagogies/achievement nexus, whereas this was not the case in respect of secondary schooling.

Some important lessons from the New Basics trial include the significance of attempting to align the three message systems of curriculum, pedagogy and assessment through building teacher capacities and through recognizing that such change requires the development of teacher professional learning communities of various kinds and that this capacity building takes time. There is very often a mismatch between political time frames for policy trials and the time required to institutionalize effective change. Politics and effective educational change are situated within different temporalities, a reality often ignored by political expectations about education policy and reform. Targeted funding support is necessary to achieve change of the kind envisioned by the New Basics, as is continuing political commitment at both the political and bureaucratic levels. It is interesting to note that while curriculum in the Queensland education system is under the jurisdiction of the Queensland Studies Authority, a statutory authority with some independence from government, the New Basics reform was under the jurisdiction of Education Queensland, and trialled at the same time as the Authority was implementing a new P–10 curriculum constructed around Key Learning Areas (KLAs). It is also worth noting that some schools which were not formally part of the New Basics actually utilized the New Basics approach to curriculum organization.

In relation to the argument of this book, though, the interesting thing about the New Basics reform was that its rationale was linked to the perceived changes wrought by globalization, socially, politically, culturally and economically, and its attempt to reconceptualize curriculum and assessment practices that would produce workers/citizens for this changed world. While the New Basics reform continues to have effects in schools, this policy reform moment seems to have passed, with the government unable to commit to the funding levels necessary to roll out the reform across the entire system.This situation is likely to be exacerbated by recent policy development in Australia at the national level, promoting a national curriculum and new forms of national testing, including NAPLAN. The global financial crisis also makes it less likely that in the foreseeable future governments will commit to the funding necessary to productive implementation of a reform of the message systems such as the New Basics in Queensland. Furthermore, and in line with the argument of this chapter that testing has become a central policy steering mechanism in education systems, the Queensland government's policy attempt to enhance student performance on NAPLAN, the national literacy and numeracy tests, and other global test measures such as PISA, probably means the approach to reforms such as the Rich Tasks through the enhancement of teacher knowledge and professionalism is a thing of the past or at least not core to contemporary education reform.

Two cases from the Global South

The previous case study and other examples of curriculum policy used to this point have been from nations of the Global North. In this section we consider in contrast some aspects of curriculum policy in two nations of the Global South, namely Pakistan and St Lucia, a tiny Caribbean island nation. Our concern is with globalization as the context of these policies. Here we acknowledge Tikly's (2001) point that we need to consider the specificities of the ways particular nations are located in relation to global pressures and policy framings. In this respect, nations of the Global North are positioned very differently from those of the Global South. As Tikly states (ibid.: 152):

> It has been a shortcoming of much of the existing literature on globalization and education that the specific contexts to which the theory is assumed to be applicable have not been specified. It is problematic to assume that there is one superior vantage point from which global forces can best be understood.

First we will consider the curriculum aspects of *Education in Pakistan – A White Paper*, which was initially released under the then Musharraf government in December 2006 and subsequently fine-tuned and redistributed in February 2007 (Aly 2007b). (See Lingard and Ali (2009) for a fuller analysis of the *White Paper*.) Despite the change of government following the February 2008 election, it seems that the *White Paper* still has considerable policy salience, as it is the basis of the Draft Education Policy posted on the new government's website in May 2008 (ibid.).

The first thing we ought to say about the *White Paper* is that it is written in English, a signifier of the colonial past and perhaps of the global present of Pakistan, despite Urdu being the lingua franca and national language. This means that the *White Paper* was probably not accessible by many teachers who would ultimately be responsible for implementation of the policy. Since the creation of the nation in 1947 on partition from India, policy implementation has been an ongoing issue in Pakistani education – a common problem in nations of the Global South whose broad policy frames are often set by donor agencies such as the World Bank, with implications for implementation. Indeed, it has been observed that given the massive task of providing primary education for all, including girls, and staffing schools with qualified and committed teachers, education policy in Pakistan has been a continuous exercise of target revision (Ali 2006). The current political turmoil in Pakistan, under the Presidency of Zardari, has made concerns with educational provision and quality even more problematic and has probably widened the quality gap between public and private provision.

Since the creation of Pakistan in 1947, Islam has been an important tool for unifying the nation across ethnic and language groups. Pakistan's first Constitution, created in 1956, declared Pakistan an Islamic Republic. Schooling and specifically curricula have been important in relation to Islam and constituting national citizens. The *White Paper* is significant in relation to these matters, as it creates the context of the reforms envisaged and also creates a history of education, as well as an imagined and desired future (Lingard and Ali 2009). In Chapter 1 we mentioned how policies often construct the problems to which they are putative solutions; the same is the case with context. As Seddon (1994: 6) notes, context can 'be worked up as a slogan or more concrete narrative which is used to construct a story of the past, present and future'. This is the case with the *White Paper*, as will be demonstrated, with implications for broad policy framings of curriculum in respect of a secular/Islamic binary. It is also significant in respect of these matters that the Musharraf military coup of 1999 resulted in the ending of international aid assistance to Pakistan, with real implications for governmental spending on social policy, including education. However, after September 11 and the wars in Afghanistan and Iraq, the Musharraf government aligned with the USA and Bush's so-called 'war on terror'. This resulted in the recommencement of western aid to the country. For example, the US aid agency USAID committed $100 million for education development in Pakistan between 2002 and 2007 (Kronstadt 2004).

In terms of Islam, President Musharraf articulated an 'enlightened moderation' to depict Pakistan as a moderate, tolerant and modern nation and Islam as fully compatible with modernity, science and economic development. Musharraf's enlightened moderation actually worked with a fundamentalist/moderate binary in relation to Islam, speaking back to the west an Orientalist construction of Islam and rearticulating a construction dominant in the west following September 11 (Appadurai 2006). This enlightened moderation appealed to moderates inside Pakistan and also to western nations, especially the USA and the UK, and to international donor agencies. The initial pages of the *White Paper* distance the Pakistani government from dogmatic and fundamentalist ideologies, which it is suggested have been the cause of a lack of research and questioning minds in Pakistan. Previous education policy is seen to be implicated in this situation. Indeed, an argument can be sustained that the *White Paper*, whose first pages clearly articulated an enlightened moderation, had as its prime implied readership the west and donor agencies. This is an example of Tikly's point about the significance of specific location of any given nation in relation to the various aspects of globalization; here, the strategic significance of Pakistan to US interests and US aid to Pakistani interests.

The issue of Islam is dealt with in the *White Paper* specifically in relation to the framing of school curricula. Indeed, because of the centrality of Islam to identity in Pakistan, each education policy has had to address this matter, either explicitly or at least implicitly. As background, the *White Paper* constructs an historical analysis of education policies since 1947 in relation to Islam. This is an example of the policy constructing its own context, its own historical provenance. The basic conclusion that can be drawn from a reading of the historical matrix in the *White Paper* is that the overarching objective of education policy in Pakistan relates to 'Islamic-ness'. The matrix 'demonstrates' that after 1979 the process of Islamization of schooling became a strong goal of education policy, and also explicitly framed curricula and teacher training. Against this backdrop, the *White Paper* argues the pressing need to 'free ourselves of dogmas and to chart a path where the entire citizenry of Pakistan will be prompted, through a sensible education system, to realize personal and collective goals of individual and social empowerment' (Aly 2007b: 3).

The ideological context constructed by the *White Paper* then suggests that hitherto Islamic ideology has been central to education policy in Pakistan and that Islamization of schooling has restricted development. This Islamic ideology has been treated as dogma, which has constructed a negative external image of Pakistan and limited modernization because of the apparent incompatibility between fundamentalist Islam and science and modernity. In contrast, the *White Paper* conceives of (moderate) Islam as compatible with modernity. Enlightened moderation is to frame school policies and curriculum 'through a sensible education system', with more secular schooling and religious education being regarded more as the responsibility of the family.

Other manifestations of the specific global positioning of Pakistan as a nation of the Global South are also evident in the *White Paper*. For example, globalized education policy discourses frame its structure and headings, such as 'Governance and Management', 'Quality', 'Equity' and 'Access to Education'. Chapter 11 is entitled 'Linkages with Principal Social Issues' and links education and schooling to matters of population growth, health, democracy and the environment, all of which are closely linked to the UN *Millennium Development Goals*. Further, the broader Washington and post-Washington 'global' consensus of markets, devolution, privatization and good governance, which has driven aid policies, can be found throughout the *White Paper* and can be seen as the global policy context constructed by it (see Robertson *et al.* 2007 for discussion of the Washington and post-Washington consensus).

Next we will consider briefly the *Education Sector Development Plan: 2000–2005 and Beyond* in the small Caribbean island nation of St Lucia (Lingard and Jn Pierre 2006), again to demonstrate Tikly's point about the significance of global positioning, and we would add history, to global policy effects and resistances at specific national locations. This Plan is framed by the globalized policy discourse of lifelong learning rearticulated as individual responsibility for self-development across the life-cycle and framed by a human capital rationale. Central to education policy development in a small nation such as St Lucia, one with strong post-colonial aspirations, has been a reliance in both funding and policy terms on donor agencies. As future Prime Minister Kenny Anthony (1990: 13) commented in 1990, 'education in St Lucia has always suffered from undercapitalization. Reliance is usually placed on foreign aid to provide capital expenditure to satisfy the needs for infrastructure.' This has placed the nation in a mendicant position in relation to such agencies, which has limited the capacity for autonomous policy development at the national level which would take account of the specific educational and curriculum needs of St Lucia and its cultural history and current post-colonial aspirations.

'Conditionalities' associated with aid have real policy effects, including in the curriculum. On this very point Jules, Permanent Secretary of Education involved in the development of the Plan, noted: 'The differential of power within the international arena gives to the multilaterals that power of definition and selection to determine whose knowledge is worth incorporation into best practice and the new common sense' (Jules 2006: 16). Donor agencies and the global positioning of nations such as St Lucia have had real policy effects. We would also note the significance of St Lucia's membership of regional coalitions, CARICOM (Caribbean Common Market) and OECS (Organization of Eastern Caribbean States), both of which seek to establish a regional identity and a larger market and economic entity amongst small

Caribbean nations and both of which are responses to and manifestations of globalization.

Policymakers and educators in the Caribbean, then, have been concerned that education policy development has largely been a series of responses to international demands, with little consideration given to implementation and local conditions and post-colonial aspirations. Indeed, each new policy framed by donor agencies appears to arrive before the previous one has been implemented. The Plan tried to work against this situation by involving very broad consultation in its development, quite easy to do in a very small nation of approximately 160,000 people. The World Bank in fact praised St Lucia for this process of policy development, which also ensured better understanding of the policy in terms of subsequent implementation. Further, with the policy covering all education sectors and being in place for ten years, the Ministry was seeking to mediate future donor agency policy effects. The hope was that new donor policy requirements would be incorporated into the overarching policy framework articulated in the Plan and thus the St Lucian Ministry would retain some autonomy in policy development and not simply be continually responding to policies and policy ideas which had their gestation elsewhere. Thus, despite the mendicant position of St Lucia vis-à-vis donor agencies, there was still some sophisticated resistance evident in the framing of the *Education Sector Development Plan*, which sought to mediate the effects of donor agencies and globalized policy discourses. This resulted in what we can see as the vernacular globalization of the Plan and translation as a two-way process central to the post-colonial situation (Young 2003: 142). This political and policy mediation can also be seen as an attempt at strengthening 'national capital' in Bourdieu's (2003) terms, thus enhancing the policy capacity of the nation vis-à-vis that of donor agencies. The consultation process, the cross-sector coverage and the ten-year time frame of the Plan were central elements of this strategy to enhance the mediating capacity of educational policymakers in St Lucia through the strengthening of national capital (Lingard and Jn Pierre 2006).

However, colonial residues are still evident in St Lucia schooling and education policy in the hegemony of English as the language of instruction in the schools and the neglect, indeed denial of *kweyol*, the national language in schooling. Such residues are also evident in the neglect of indigenous knowledges in the school curriculum which, particularly at the secondary level, remains very academic in orientation and dominated by public examinations, manifesting the continuing effects of colonialism. This is evidence of what Gregory (2004: 9) has called 'the colonial present' set against post-colonial aspirations. Further, as a rearticulation of globalized policy discourses, the Plan emphasized human capital development and global economic competitiveness to the neglect of other forms of capital, such as social and cultural capitals, at a time in St Lucia of increasing influence of US popular culture and culture industries and a policy desire to build national and regional identities through schooling.

Tikly's observation, noted earlier, that the positioning of a nation in geopolitical terms in relation to globalization is central to understanding the effects of globalization, is confirmed by the considerations of education and curriculum policy in Pakistan and St Lucia. So too is the broader policy point that history, including colonial history, is central to understanding contemporary policies, as well as understanding contemporary globalization and its effects in education and curriculum policy within specific nations. However, global pressures of various sorts are resisted and mediated in varying ways, resulting in vernacular globalization.

Conclusion

In this chapter we have argued that globalization has given rise to a new discourse of education policy, with serious implications for rethinking the three message systems described by Bernstein. However, we have noted that this discourse has been enacted differently around the world, resulting in a wide variety of policy prescriptions. Indeed, these prescriptions have been vigorously debated along different political axes within the nation-state. Yet the pressures for change have emerged not only from within national systems, but also from international sources, most notably IGOs. This has particularly been the case in respect of nations of the Global South. There is clearly now a globally converging discourse about how education policies should reshape curriculum, pedagogy and evaluation. So, for example, in England and Australia the political authority to determine and manage the curriculum has steadily moved from local/state to the national level. Such a transfer of political authority has been justified in terms of efforts to ensure better articulation between education and economic policies in order to achieve national competitiveness within the global economy. This emphasis is located within a neoliberal imaginary based more on the values of the market and system efficiency than on goals of democratic equality and community.

The focus on human capital formation for greater competitiveness has created a demand for more robust regimes of testing. Within nation-states, testing has increasingly reshaped notions of worthwhile knowledge as well as pedagogical practices and has affected teacher professionalism. But beyond testing at the national level, international comparisons have also become important. In policy terms, comparative performance on testing regimes such as PISA has even become a surrogate measure for determining the quality and effectiveness of national educational systems. Indeed, it is no longer possible to understand education policy without an appreciation of the central role that testing and accountability regimes now play in policy development and evaluation. Testing has also become the key instrument with which policy-makers steer practices at the school level. We have also shown how the other message systems of curriculum and pedagogy have been affected not only by what are seen to be global imperatives, but also by history. On the latter, the history of colonialism continues to affect these message systems in the nations of the Global South, as illustrated in our examples drawn from Pakistan and St Lucia. Policy as numbers in the nations of the Global South has been manifest as indicators of achievement of the UN's Millenium Development Goals, which we deal with in more detail in Chapter 7.

In the nations of the Global North the emphasis on testing has become central to the development of new regimes of accountability, giving rise to new forms of educational governance that no longer assume traditional rule-bound bureaucratic processes, but direct individuals towards particular policy priorities and practices. If policy is the 'authoritative allocation of values', testing plays a major role in reallocating particular values. Given the centrality of the message systems to systemic governance, particularly new forms of testing, we have argued that education policy studies needs to think about these message systems as policies. We think this chapter has demonstrated the veracity of that claim. In the next chapter we discuss these issues in relation to new ways of thinking about educational governance.

6 From government to governance

Introduction

In the previous two chapters we explored some of the ways in which globalization is transforming the conceptualization of educational values, and the manner in which the three message systems of education – curriculum, pedagogy and evaluation – are now reconfigured in line with the changing conceptions of those values. Around the world, education is increasingly seen in terms of human capital formation, implying the development of educational policies that seek to prepare students for new kinds of work and labour relations. In this way, educational policies are driven more by the values of the market and system efficiency than by cultural and community values such as justice and democracy. In order to make educational systems more efficient and effective, policymakers have become more concerned with testing than ever before. Through various regimes of testing, both national and international, they have sought to steer educational practices relating to curriculum, pedagogy and evaluation towards the values of the market.

Increasingly, efficiency has become a kind of metavalue within the framework of which other more ethical and cultural purposes of education are now interpreted. Efficiency is usually taken to mean achieving the best possible outcomes with a given level of funding. Often this is reframed as 'doing more with less', with policies often seeking so-called 'efficiency dividends'. The related notion of effectiveness is usually conceived as achieving the allocated set of objectives within given time frames. In this chapter we will argue that this emphasis on efficiency and effectiveness has given rise to a particular conception of accountability, as well as a new way of thinking about educational governance.

There is now much rhetorical talk, especially in the developing countries and within international development agencies, about 'good governance'. This talk is often concerned with such issues as transparency of decision-making processes, forms of devolution, technologies of measuring educational performance, the development of appropriate performance indicators, international benchmarking, new standardized testing regimes, mechanisms of quality assurance, rigorous accountability systems, multiple sources of educational funding, effective uses of public resources, public/private partnerships and so on. Even this short list shows how each of these concerns is couched in terms of a focus on efficiency, defined mostly in terms of the extent to which educational systems are responsive to the perceived labour market needs of the global economy. Such a policy discourse highlights technical concerns – issues of means – that often mask real political debates about educational ends. But beyond this preoccupation with the technical, this discourse also points to a new way of thinking about educational governance.

What is clear is that, just as globalization has transformed the discursive terms in which issues of educational policies linked to curriculum, pedagogy and evaluation are now considered, so too has it shifted the ways in which issues of educational governance are addressed. The neoliberal imaginary of globalization has led to a new way of thinking about how schools, technical colleges, universities and educational systems should be governed. This view of educational governance shows remarkable signs of convergence around an education policy discourse proselytized by a range of international organizations including the OECD, the World Bank and UNESCO, and embraced readily by national systems in the Global North and the Global South alike.

In this chapter we will argue that under the conditions of globalization there has been a notable shift in the ways in which education is now governed. This shift involves a move from government to governance. This suggests that national governments are no longer the only source of policy authority, but that the interests of a whole range of policy actors, both national and international, have now become enmeshed in policy processes. This is the overlay of Westphalian and post-Westphalian realities which we have written about throughout this book. The bureaucratic administrative state also has been replaced by polycentric arrangements involving both public and private interests. In managing social relations, the state no longer simply relies on rules and their hierarchical impositions, but seeks also the production of self-regulating individuals. Ideologies now play a greater role, for example, in relation to the ideas of individual choice and markets. In this way, the processes of the allocation of values and the structure of state authority are transformed. However, this shift to governance is not uniform around the world but is negotiated locally, as these processes are mediated by local histories, cultures and politics.

From government to governance

The concept of governance is derived from the recent literature in political science, where it is now usually taken to indicate a change in the structures and modus operandi of government (Roseneau 1997). This change occurred around the time of the end of the Cold War and the emergence of the hegemony of neoliberal capitalism on a global scale, a shift sponsored in the first instance politically by Thatcher in the UK and Reagan in the USA and later supported by governments around the world, including Deng Xiaoping in China. Government is usually taken to refer to the political party, parties or political coalitions that control state structures (the public service) and state practices (e.g. introducing legislation, law making, policymaking, creating regulations and appointments to the judiciary) within any given nation at any given time. Government in this sense could be seen to function within a nation-state and within the bureaucratic structures of the public sector.

Governance signifies changes in this form of government linked to the effects of globalization. These changes are related to the application of new public management across the public sector, including across the state's administrative structures and practices, resulting in what is often referred to as 'the new managerial state' (Clarke and Newman 1997). Here we see the ecumenical move of private-sector structures and practices inside state structures (Waters 1995), all facilitated by the flows associated with what Thrift (2005: 6) calls the 'cultural circuit' of capitalism, where business schools, management consultants and management gurus, along with international organizations, proselytize management and leadership practices of a particular kind across both private and public sectors which have become more alike and more intertwined. These changes are also linked to the 'freeing up' to some extent of the market vis-à-vis the state and the incorporation of market and private-sector relations inside state structures. The latter has seen the emergence of, for example, a global higher education market (Marginson 2007), and the creation of quasi-markets in schooling systems across the globe (Apple 2001; Ball 2008).

There is a global element to the move from government to governance as well, intimately related to the new scalar politics of globalization (Brenner 2004; Robertson *et al.* 2006a, 2006b; Dale 2006). The new scalar politics, what Brenner (2004) calls the 'rescaling of statehood', has not seen the decline of the nation-state as predicted by some post-national theorists such as Strange (1996), but now works differently in the context of neoliberal globalization. As Roger Dale (2006: 27) has put it, 'It seems to be widely accepted that states have at the very least ceded some of their discretion or even sovereignty to supranational organizations, albeit the better to pursue their national interests'. To supranational institutions such as the EU, which Dale is talking about, we would add the plethora of other governmental and non-governmental organizations which now exist beyond nations, but which have real effects within nations. It is this new post-Westphalian politics which has been the backdrop to the move from government, thought of as functioning within national borders, to governance, acknowledging effects from beyond national borders and the involvement of agencies other than public ones.

Education policy and the education state have not remained unaffected by these changes in state structures and practices and the new scalar politics. It is those changes which have been 'most economically rendered in the conception of a shift from "government" to "governance"' (Dale 2006: 27). It is these matters of educational governance as a subset of the move from government to governance which are the focus of this chapter.

One aspect of the new managerial state associated with the transition from government to governance is the new public management. This has been layered into the structures and practices of the older bureaucratic state structures. This new public management (NPM) sometimes also called 'corporate managerialism', has been a structural and practice response to the new flows of globalization and the related speeding up of policy change and indeed the centrality of a discourse of change in contemporary policy regimes (Clarke and Newman 1997). The older bureaucratic structures and practices were deemed to be too slow, indeed sclerotic, in the face of the 'needs', 'requirements' and 'demands' of what could now be seen as transnational (rather than multinational) corporations and global capitalism (Yeatman 1998). The OECD has been one international organization that has been central to sponsoring this view of the older state structures and practices. It has argued (OECD 1995: 7) that bureaucratic state structures were 'highly centralized, rule-bound and inflexible' and stressed 'process rather than results'.

This critique implicitly suggests some of the positives seen to be associated with the new public management (Lynn 2006). NPM's focus is on results or, in 'management speak', its focus is on outputs and performance, rather than inputs and processes. Further, these were to be achieved efficiently: that is, at the lowest possible cost. Efficiency has also been accompanied by the discourse of effectiveness, which is here taken to mean achievement of goals and objectives. This has witnessed a new way of steering policy implementation and outcomes through the establishment of objectives and creation of indicators of performance in relation to objectives. This has seen a flattening of state structures and new relationships between the 'centre' and the 'periphery' within state structures.

Such restructuring or 'cultural re-engineering' (Ball 2008: 47) has reconstituted the character of the relationship between education departments, which establish policy goals and create related accountability regimes, and schools, which now have to focus on achieving these policy goals and meeting the required accountability demands. In policy cycle terms, this is a new type of relationship between the context of policy text production and the context of policy practice or implementation. This involves steering at a distance via performance measures (including testing) as a new form of outcomes accountability, as part of the stress on outcomes rather than processes or inputs of the new public management. With this change, more tasks are devolved to the practice site, but we should not see this as deregulation, but rather as a form of 'reregulation' (Ball 2008: 43) or what du Gay (1996) has called 'controlled decontrol', constituted through the performative culture of testing, league tables, benchmarking, performance indicators and the like. This structure and modus operandi are based in many ways on a low-trust culture and, implicitly, surveillance. As Clarke *et al.* (2000: 6) note, state structures are now 'viewed as chains of low-trust relationships, linked by contracts or contractual type processes'.

The idea of new public management shares its assumptions with theories of agency and transactional cost analysis, and applies them to the public sector. It emphasizes a range of concepts that have become commonplace in educational governance around the world. Collectively these concepts amount to what Waters (1995) refers to as 'organizational ecumenism', that is, a single idealization of appropriate organizational behaviour. These concepts include generic management skills; quantified performance targets; devolution; the separation of policy, commercial and non-commercial functions; the use of private-sector practices such as corporate plans and flexible labour practices; just-in-time inventory; monetary incentives; cost-cutting; and above all the privatization of the so-called non-core functions and services. New public management thus emphasizes a preference for private ownership and prescribes, wherever possible, the use of contracting out and competition or contestability in the provision of public services.

Central to the new form of governance and the new public management are attempts to decentralize educational management systems, even if there is considerable variance in the ways in which the notion of decentralization is conceptualized. The term 'decentralization' is used differently in different nations, revealing their distinctive organizational histories. It is often used interchangeably with the idea of devolution. The OECD, in its 1995 report, *Governance in Transition: Public Management Reforms in OECD Countries*, uses the term devolution as 'a catch-all term for the granting of greater decision-making authority and autonomy' under specific conditions (OECD 1995: 157). It used 'devolution' as a single term to avoid confusion over its meanings.

However, it is possible to define three different modes of decentralization: democratic devolution, functional decentralization and fiscal decentralization. These variations are useful because they suggest that ideas about governance cannot be divorced from assumptions about the educational purposes they often embody. They also clearly demonstrate the contested terrain of all the concepts that underpin the new form of governance. The idea of democratic devolution, for example, is more in line with democratic equality than are notions of functional and fiscal decentralization, which are institutionalized to achieve greater social efficiency.

The enhancement of democratic participation, local control and community decision-making are major characteristics of devolution. This form of governance typically involves major power shifts in control from the central ministerial level down to local community levels, promoting the aims of democracy, equality and the public good. When decentralization of governance is viewed in functional terms, local institutions are not given the autonomy to govern, seeking to realize their own priorities, independent of the dictates of the central government. Rather, functional decentralization involves the transfer of specific functions of the central government to the local or regional level, framed today by objectives and indicators of success established by the policy centre.

Advocated in the name of social efficiency, functional decentralization is often linked to technologies of accountability and transparency as a part of the larger notion of public management or good governance. Local agencies are theoretically given increased flexibility to manage their affairs, but these nonetheless have to conform to the performance goals and targets set by the central government. Sometimes these goals and targets are linked to fiscal shifts within patterns of governance changes. Fiscal decentralization typifies the transfer of monies and control over funding sources to local institutions. To achieve greater social efficiency, the central government no longer collects and distributes funding, but allows local institutions to generate their financial resources, though not relinquishing control over how these funds are spent. The use of locally generated funds is nonetheless audited, not only to ensure transparency but also to ensure that funds are used for purposes specified by central authorities, and utilized to realize performance targets.

This pressure to decentralize has come from a wide variety of sources, but is legitimated most profoundly by international policy organizations such as the OECD, UNESCO, and APEC as part of a broader agenda of multilateralism in education and the Washington consensus. Nations are increasingly seeking to cooperate with organizations such as the OECD, APEC, APEID (Asia Pacific Program of Educational Innovation for Development) and APPEAL (Asia Pacific Program of Education for All) to align educational policies with each other. But the agendas of these organizations are increasingly converging around similar understanding of the forms of educational governance required for a globalizing world. As an example, from 2000 the attention of APEC's Educational Ministries was placed on quality assurance and accountability as a means of monitoring education. The EU has a similar focus (Grek *et al.* 2009). In APEC's Joint Statement from the third APEC Education Ministerial Meeting in 2004, the top priorities included balancing local-site autonomy with national goals. The focus is placed on greater school-based management and autonomy, while also emphasizing increased standards of accountability to meet national goals and enhance international cooperation, international benchmarking and quality assurance systems.

The politics of performance

The performance targets associated with the new public management have effects on professionalism, reframing professional practices and in some ways distorting them. Thus professionalism has been reconstituted by these changes, which have been manifest in specific ways in educational systems and in schools around the world (Gewirtz *et al.* 2009). The moves in education are part of the displacement of older-style bureau professionalism by the new forms of governance and new policy technologies (Gewirtz 2002: 2–3). These changes have in turn reconstituted the roles of school principals and teachers. School heads have become new managers, and are expected to implement policies set elsewhere and have their schools achieve according to various league tables of performance and sets of performance indicators. In outlining the effects of the new public management in education, Gewirtz (ibid.: 32) says:

> The new management discourse in education emphasizes the instrumental purposes of schooling – raising standards and performance as measured by examination results, levels of attendance and school leaver destinations – and frequently articulated within a lexicon of enterprise, excellence, quality and effectiveness.

It should be noted here that Gewirtz is talking about the English schooling system. However, such pressures are playing out in educational systems across the globe, but always in ways that are mediated by local politics. In considering the specificities of any national educational system we must therefore always also recognize the effects of globalization from below.

We can name the new state structures associated with the move to governance as 'post-bureaucratic'. However, here 'post' does not simply mean 'after'; rather, we would see it more as building upon, developing out of, in tension with, the bureaucratic structures and practices that preceded it. Thus, the state remains bureaucratic, with many of the features of classical bureaucracy foreshadowed some time ago now by Max Weber; what we have are new hybrid mixes of bureaucratic and NPM structures and relationships.

The emphasis on outcomes and performance within the new public management has seen the proliferation of performance indicators and various league tables of performance measures across the last two decades or so in all public-sector departments. This phenomenon has been called 'policy as numbers' (Rose 1999; Ozga and Lingard 2007) and is also linked to a culture of performativity (Lyotard 1984; Ball 2008). The OECD (1995: 8) sees the NPM as being central to 'developing a performance-oriented culture'. One important element, then, of the new form of governance is the construction and use of comparative performance and outcome measures. As Ball (2006: 144) points out, who controls these fields of judgement becomes crucial, and such fields become sites of contestation.

This governance through comparison has occurred within systems and within nations, but also internationally, indeed almost globally. The concept of governance was actually used in political science in the early 1990s in relation to 'global governance' to depict the significance of a wide range of intergovernmental and non-governmental international organizations in the governance of nations in the post-Cold War period (Roseneau 2005). Additionally, part of the steering at a distance of new state structures is achieved through constraints related to the emphases on performance and performance measures. These constraints now work at a number of multilayered levels from the global through the international to the regional, national and subnational.

Regionally we can think about the educational indicators which have been central to the construction of a new supranational European education space (Dale 2006; Lawn 2006). Indeed, even the creation of statistical categories and agreement upon them, as has occurred with the alignment of educational statistics of the OECD, Eurostat (the statistical arm of the EU) and UNESCO, have policy effects in nations. It has been demonstrated how this action had policy effects in the net-benefactor nations of the EU as part of a broader policy convergence in education driven by a policy as numbers approach by supranational (EU) and international (OECD) agencies and by reports from both types of agency (Lawn and Lingard 2002). These effects worked through what has been called a 'magistrature of influence' operating above these nations, and have ensured some policy convergence as a result of this form of global governance, which was also part of the move from government to governance within these particular nations.

With the globalization of the economy and the apparent reduction of the economic sovereignty of nations, particularly in policy terms with the hegemony of neoliberalism, international comparative measures of performance have become a global aspect of the new governance. Mundy (2007: 348) calls this 'standard-setting multilateralism'. This mode of governance reconceptualizes education policy in economic terms, as involving the production of the human capital, in quantity and quality terms, thought necessary to ensure the global competitiveness of the putative national economy. As Brown *et al.* (1997: 7–8) state: 'Indeed the competitive advantage of nations is frequently redefined in terms of the quality of national education and training systems judged according to international standards.'

Such education quality measures have become surrogates for the strength of the national economy. Nations still control their education and training systems, even though they are now framed very often by globalized educational policy discourses; there is a global dimension to the move to governance. The nation-building and citizenship formation functions of national education systems are very much linked to 'the structuration of the Westphalian world order – that is, world order as a society of states' (Mundy 2007: 346). Because of this level of national mediation, education policymaking, unlike economic policymaking where free-trade ideology has made national economies more porous, is still seen as largely a national task, yet standard-setting multilateralism has helped reorder national policies in education.

Nóvoa and Yariv-Mashal (2003) have written very insightfully about the global character of this new form of governance through comparison. They talk about how the 'national eye' today governs in conjunction with the 'global eye', noting that 'the attention to *global* benchmarks and indicators serves to promote *national* policies in a field (education), that is imagined as a place where national sovereignty can still be exercised' (ibid.: 426). The metaphor of the eye here is significant, as Barthes (1979: 9) has noted, 'The eye is reason, evidence, empiricism, verisimilitude –

everything which serves to control, coordinate, to imitate.' Benchmarks, indicators and the like make the nation, and indeed the globe, legible for governing (Scott 1998).

This interplay of the global and the national is most evident in the observation of Rodney Paige (2003), George W. Bush's first federal secretary of education, in his response to an OECD report on educational performance:

> The report documents how little we receive in return for our national investment. This report also reminds us that we are battling two achievement gaps. One is between those being served well by our system and those being left behind. The other is between the US and many of our higher achieving friends around the world. By closing the first gap, we will close the second.
>
> (Paige, quoted in Hursh 2008: 84)

It is this emphasis on global comparison that explains the growing importance that national systems attach to international student assessment programmes such as the OECD's Programme for International Student Assessment (PISA), established in the late 1990s, to measure the literacy, numeracy, science literacy and sometimes problem-solving capacities of students at the end of compulsory schooling (aged about 15 years) and the Trends in International Maths and Science Study (TIMSS) of the International Association for the Evaluation of Educational Achievement (IEA).

The OECD's educational indicators, published annually now as *Education at a Glance*, measuring and describing relationships between system inputs and system achievements or outcomes (Henry *et al.* 2001), have also become part of what we might see as an emergent global education policy field. With UNESCO and the World Bank, the OECD is developing global educational indicators which apply to the developing nations of the Global South. This is yet another example of global governance through comparison and of the globalization of the policy as numbers approach linked to new forms of accountability, what Nóvoa and Yariv-Mashal (2003: 427) call 'the politics of mutual accountability'. This politics of mutual accountability is a central element of the transition from government to governance and an important component of global governance in education.

Such mutual accountability on a global scale, along with the performative policy as numbers form of accountability at national level, are part of what Power (1997) has called the 'audit culture'. This audit culture is closely aligned with the new public management, its emphases on efficiency and effectiveness ('value for money') and the associated shifts in regulatory styles in the work of the state (ibid.: 42). The rise of quality assurance and a quality assurance industry and market has also catalysed the audit culture. The audit culture is central to the new form of governance. There is also a connection with the rise of managers and the discourse of managers and management in the public sector. In that, as Power (ibid.: 67) demonstrates, 'the audit explosion represents a decision to shift evaluative cultures away from social scientific towards managerial knowledge bases'.

This cultural shift has also been accompanied by a 'rebalancing' of the relationships between the state and the market. The older Keynesian settlement of states intervening in and against the fallout of the market to protect the 'national economy' and 'national citizens' was replaced by a post-Keynesian settlement which gave priority to the market and individual choices over the state and collective concerns to do with the common good, which had been the focus of state structures and policies in western nations in various forms from the end of the Second World War through until the end of the Cold War and the politics pursued by Thatcher and Reagan. In giving priority to the market and its freeing up, privatization has become a key policy element of governance.

As we have already noted, the idea of privatization refers to the transfer of services provided by the public sector to a range of private-sector interests. As a political construct it represents an attempt to separate decision-making in the areas of public policy from the execution of service provision. And it has come to symbolize a new way of looking at public institutions and the role of the state in managing the affairs of its citizens.

Contracting out and enterprise sales may perhaps be the most influential modalities of privatization in the contemporary public sector. Stephen Ball's (2007) exhaustive mapping of private-sector participation in public-sector education in the UK demonstrates the multiple meanings of privatization in education, as well as the huge changes which have occurred in the move away from the earlier Keynesian settlement. He talks of first-order privatizations to refer to the enhanced private presence in relation to 'ownership, organization forms, financial relations, etc' and their second-order effects in terms of citizenship, democracy and governance. Additionally he speaks of 'commercialization' in education where schools are involved in commercial advertising and consumerism.

Drawing on Hatcher (2000), Ball makes a distinction between exogenous and endogenous privatization. He states:

> 'Where the former involves private companies entering education to take over directly responsibilities, services or programmes, the latter refers to changes in the behavior of public sector organizations themselves, where they act as though they were businesses, both in relation to clients and workers, and in dealings with other public sector organizations' (Ball 2007: 14).

Endogenous privatization involves the construction of quasi-markets in education and students and parents as consumers rather than as citizens with democratic rights and freedom. Here, freedom becomes reconstituted as consumer choice in education (Apple 2001). Underpinning such marketization and privatization is the neoliberal, possessive, self-interested individual, a central element of the neoliberal social imaginary, which we have written about in Chapter 4.

From hierarchies to networks

The move from government to governance is also accompanied by a move from hierarchy to network, from classical hierarchical vertical bureaucratic relationships to more horizontal networked relationships. Castells (2000: 458) argues that there is some decentralizing of power associated with the networked society, nationally and globally, and that today 'function and power' are 'organized in the space of flows'. Appadurai (2006) has similarly spoken of the emergence globally of cellular politics as distinct from older-style vertebrate politics, which operated at the national level. This is a distinction somewhat akin to that described in the move from hierarchy to network, from government to governance. Appadurai (ibid.: 25) argues in respect of vertebrate politics:

> The modern system of nation-states is the most marked case of *vertebrate* structure, for though nations thrive on their stories of difference and singularity, the system of nation-states works only because of its underlying assumption of an international order, guaranteed by a variety of norms.

In the context of globalization, Appadurai sees the new cellular politics emerging alongside these vertebrate structures in what we would see as a hybrid interplay of Westphalian and post-Westphalian structures and practices. These new networked or cellular relationships in the context of neoliberalism and privatizations in the public sector, including education, involve both public- and private-sector players and those located both within nations and globally.

Rhodes (1997) draws a distinction between policy communities and policy networks. Policy communities, he argues, are more coherent and structured than policy networks, and surround any given policy field and usually consist of policymakers, professionals, interest groups and so on. Networks are more loosely coupled arrangements. (See Hudson and Lowe (2004 Ch. 8) for a useful, brief coverage of the policy network literature.) We would make the point here, though, that today in the context of globalization, both policy communities and policy networks have been stretched out globally and now also include private-sector participants. These extended communities and networks are part of the new governance. Rhodes (1997: 15), one of the earliest writers about governance in political science, says that it refers to 'a *new* process of governing'. While also acknowledging that governance refers, *inter alia*, to 'the minimal state; corporate governance; and the new public management', Rhodes actually defines governance in terms of networked relationships. He notes, '*governance refers to self-organizing, interorganizational networks* characterized by interdependence, resource exchange, rules of the game and significant autonomy from the state' (ibid.).

The global context of the move to governance is also related to the move from a Westphalian to a post-Westphalian mode of international relations, which we outlined in Chapter 2, with the latter referring to new post-national global spaces and relations. It is the emergence of the post-Westphalian reality, which initially provoked talk of 'governance without government' on a global scale (Roseneau and Czempiel 1992). The Commission on Global Governance (1995: 2) of the UN defined this global take on governance in the following manner: 'primarily as intergovernmental relationships, but it must now be understood as also involving nongovernmental organizations, citizens' movements, multinational corporations, and the global capital market. Interacting with these are the global mass media.' Again, though, we see the contemporary world as manifesting a complex hybrid mixture of both Westphalian and post-Westphalian politics.

This move from government to governance has been manifested in the emergence of a globalized post-Keynesian policy consensus. Related has been the emergence of a more polycentric state (Ball 2007) and new education policy production rules, along with what Ball (2008: 41–54) calls new policy technologies. Policy technologies, he suggests, 'involve the calculated deployment of forms of organization and procedures, and disciplines or bodies of knowledge, to organize human forces and capabilities into functioning systems' (ibid.: 41). He sees the market and privatizations, new public-sector management, and the plethora of outcomes and performance measures associated with performativity, as these new technologies of governance.

In considering the emergence of a European education policy space, Dale (2006: 33) argues that new governance activities might include funding, ownership, provision and regulation, and that there are now a number of institutions of coordination within educational governance, including the state, the market, the community and households. In considering the 'pluriscalar governance of education', Dale layers in three scales of governance in education, namely the subnational, the national and the supranational. We would suggest there is also, potentially at least, a regional layer. It is these matters that force us to talk of new forms of educational governance. We would make the strong point, however, that all of these matters require empirical verification in considering how they are played out in any given educational system at any time.

In this section we have documented various features that constitute the new form of educational governance. These features include the new public management, privatizations, marketization, and networked and cellular politics, all linked to the new scalar and post-Westphalian politics associated with globalization. This new form of governance does not simply negate what has gone before, but rather builds on what has gone before in specific and hybrid ways. A range of international organizations have played important roles as 'institutionalizing mechanisms' (McNeeley and Cha 1994) of this new form of governance, including the OECD in relation to the nations of the Global North and the World Bank, and IMF and UNESCO in relation to the nations of the Global South. In what follows we consider some aspects of the new form of educational governance in a little more detail. We look at the changing role of international organizations and the emergence of a global commensurate space of measurement linked to 'multilateral standard setting' and processes of 'mutual accountability'. We conclude by considering how this new form of governance helps to constitute new educational subjects and new consumer citizens through the processes of what Foucault would call 'governmentality'. For Foucault, governmentality as a concept deals with the 'conduct of conduct' and emphasizes the ways in which the new neoliberal subjects become self-governing. As such, it is an effect of governance.

New forms of governance: the role of the OECD

We have argued up to this point that a range of international organizations have been important in the new forms of governance in education. For the rich countries of the world, the Organization for Economic Cooperation and Development (OECD) has been an important component of this global level of governance. Other agencies such as the World Bank and UNESCO and the aid programmes of developed nations have played a central role in the new form of educational governance in the nations of the Global South (Mundy 2007; Jones 2007; Jones and Coleman 2005). Globalization, as we will argue, has also changed the role of the OECD.

Established in 1961 out of the Organization for European Economic Cooperation (OEEC) and funded under the Marshall Plan by the USA for the economic reconstruction of post-war Europe, the OECD has variously and simultaneously been described as a think tank, a geographic entity, an organizational structure, a policymaking forum, a network of policymakers, researchers and consultants, and a sphere of influence (Henry *et al.* 2001: 1). In formal terms, the OECD views itself as an intergovernmental organization of 30 of the world's most developed countries, which produce two-thirds of the world's goods and services, and which are committed to the principles of a market economy and a pluralistic democracy (OECD 1997), with a commitment to human rights being a new, more recent requirement for membership.

Although primarily an economic organization, since its inception the OECD has emphasized the role education must play in both economic and social development. Within the organization, however, there has been much debate about the ways in which economic and educational policies might be related. In the 1970s and 1980s in particular, the European countries sought to 'tone down' the dominant US versions of market liberalism within the OECD, with their own distinctive social democratic agendas, refusing to view education and social policies as secondary to, or instruments of, economic policies. Haas (1990: 159) has suggested that the OECD could best be viewed as 'a rather incoherent compromise between the United States and the European members', especially with respect to the role education plays in the total polity.

Indeed, as Papadopoulos (1994: 11) points out, in the OECD's original charter there was no independent structural location for education, though there was always an 'inferred role', derived from early human capital formulations of links between economic productivity and educational investment. In the early days those links were conceived somewhat narrowly in terms of boosting scientific and technological personnel capacity and, by extension, of improved and expanded science and mathematics education in schools.

It was not until 1968 that the Centre for Research and Innovation (CERI) was established within the OECD, partly as a result of a growing recognition within the organization of the 'qualitative' aspects of economic growth – 'as an instrument for creating better conditions of life' – and, along with that, a more comprehensive view of education's multiple purposes. By 1970, the organization recognized a fuller range of objectives of education – a less 'economistic' view of education policy, as Papadopoulos (1994: 122) puts it, enabling it to attach equal importance to education's social and cultural purposes. For most of the 1970s and 1980s, then, the dominance of economic concerns within the OECD was tempered by the recognition of the social dimensions and purposes of economic growth and development.

This is not to deny the existence of ideological tensions within the OECD. Any analysis of the debates until the mid-1990s, both within the organization's committees and its secretariat, reveals an ideological cleavage between social-democratic and neoliberal policy stances. These tensions, however, were resolved in the way the OECD worked: without any prescriptive mandate, it operated through processes that involved its 'traditions of transparency: of providing explanations and justifications for policy, and of engaging in critical self-appraisal' (OECD 1998: 102). As Martens *et al.* (2004: 15) point out, the OECD does not have any legally binding mandate over its members, nor does it have the financial resources at its disposal to encourage policy adoption. It thus seeks to exert influence through the processes of 'mutual examination by governments, multilateral surveillance and peer pressure to conform or reform'.

Papadopoulos (1994) provides a convincing historical account of how, until the early 1990s, the OECD's educational work could be characterized as involving a struggle between its concerns for promoting economic efficiency and growth, on the one hand, and education's broader social purposes on the other. However, since the mid-1990s this tension is no longer so evident, we argue, as education is once again increasingly viewed in instrumental terms, as a handmaiden to the organization's primary interest in economic matters. With a greater focus on the changed context in which education now works, and armed with new discourses of globalization and the knowledge economy, the economic efficiency perspective now dominates the OECD's educational work – which is now increasingly more technical and data-driven – and has replaced the earlier normative debates about the multiple purposes of education.

The OECD acknowledges as well that the way it works and the manner in which it relates to its members have changed (OECD 1996a: 15):

> OECD has evolved greatly in the globalizing world economy. It has been 'globalizing' itself, notably through new Members and dialogue activities ... Further, analysing the many facets of the process of globalization, and their policy implications, has become the central theme in OECD's work, as the challenges and opportunities of globalization have become a high priority of policy-makers in OECD countries.

The OECD now asserts – perhaps accurately – that 'a broad consensus exists on many aspects of the policy requirement for a globalizing world economy'. In this way, the OECD has made considerable use of the idea of globalization in both redefining its policy programme and in reconceptualizing its relationship to member countries, often prescribing the manner in which they should interpret and respond to the pressures of globalization and take the opportunities offered by the global economy. We would also argue that the OECD itself has been a central agency in establishing this consensus of which it speaks.

However, in articulating the logic of globalization in this manner, the OECD appears to 'reify' the economic relations it regards as 'globalizing', treating them as if they were self-evident and inevitable. This has the effect of masking some of the normative assumptions underlying its conception of globalization, treating them as if they were beyond political debate. It associates globalization with technological revolutions in transport, communications and data processing, but only explores their economic implications, and not the cultural transformations to which they have also given rise.

Insofar as the OECD (1995) considers the political aspects of the global economy, characterized as informational, networked, knowledge-based, post-industrial and service-oriented, it suggests a radically revised view of the roles and responsibilities of the state. It assumes that the old centralized bureaucratic state structures were too slow and sclerotic and 'out of sync' with the emergent needs of transnational as opposed to national capital and corporations (Yeatman 1998b). It therefore calls for a minimalist state, with a greater reliance on the market. It argues for new devolved forms of governance that are more compatible with the so-called 'demands of the global economy'.

A problem with this account is that it views globalization in terms of an objective, inexorable set of social processes. This focus on description, however, overlooks the fact that globalization is also a subjective phenomenon which involves actual human agents interpreting the conditions of interconnectivity. Nor does it permit the possibility that it may be a deliberate, ideological project of economic liberalization that directs people towards more intense market forces (see Bourdieu 2003), and that it is based on a politics of meaning that seeks to steer them towards a certain taken-for-grantedness about the ways in which the global economy operates and the manner in which culture, crises, resources and power formations are filtered through its universal logic. It thus 'ontologizes' the processes it describes, seeking to create subjects who view policy options through the conceptual prism of an assumed logic.

Given this representation, the OECD no longer seems to entertain the broader philosophical debates about the purposes of education, but locates them instead within its presumed normative commitment to globalization's ideological forms, articulated in terms of a neoliberal logic of markets (Rizvi 2007). This depoliticization of educational issues leads the organization to reconceptualize its policy work in mostly technical terms, concerned with questions of how best to understand the so-called imperatives of globalization; how education can be a more efficient instrument of economic development; how greater accountability of educational systems can be ensured; and how education should develop social subjects who view the world as an interconnected space in which informational networks play a crucial role in sustaining market activity.

Indeed, within this neoliberal economic logic the OECD now accords greater importance to education than ever before. So much so that in 2002 it established a separate Directorate for Education, something it had resisted for most of its history. In establishing the Directorate, the secretary-general of the OECD (2002) stressed that 'education is a priority for OECD Member countries, and the OECD is playing an increasingly important role in this field. Society's most important investment is in the education of its people.' This observation is clearly based on the OECD's interpretation of the requirements of the global economy, in which knowledge is assumed to be a key ingredient and in which innovation and commercialization of knowledge are considered major drivers of economic development.

Given these normative convictions it is not surprising, then, that much of the educational policy deliberations at the OECD are concerned with technical issues, as is evident in its work programme for 2005–2006, which suggests that internationally comparable statistics and indicators must underpin the educational work of the OECD, and that the ultimate outputs of its policy recommendations must be designed to increase both the quality and the equity of education systems. Listed as major concerns are issues of equity in access and outcomes, quality, choice, public and private financing, and individual and social returns to investment in learning. Underpinning this list is the conviction that education is a major factor in contributing to human capital formation and economic growth, and that policy research in education should therefore be directed to this end.

With this conviction firmly in place and in the context of globalization, the OECD's mode of working has undergone substantial shifts. According to Papodopoulos (1994: 14), the OECD's general approach to education between 1960 and 1990 was based on international cooperation, which involved its education committee identifying problems around which such cooperation was felt to be useful. Country educational policy reviews were conducted on a voluntary basis, and followed 'a *sui generis* pattern in terms of their methods of investigation, coverage and periodicity'. The secretariat in turn brought to the education committee newly emerging policy concerns around which it was authorized to conduct thematic reviews. And although these reviews made recommendations, there was no mechanism for ensuring that they were implemented, beyond encouragement and advice.

In more recent years, however, while the OECD has retained this general rhetoric of international cooperation, the balance between the political work of the education committee and the technical tasks performed by the secretariat has shifted. With a greater agreement over the organization's ideological position, the debates within the committee are no longer as intense, and are replaced by the setting of work priorities and a consideration of the administrative issues of coordination and monitoring. The OECD now devotes more resources to the collection of comparative performance data in education than it has ever done before.

More recently, the OECD's outreach and impact have been greatly extended through its work with 'non-member economies' and through the global recognition of the technical expertise it has acquired in comparative performance assessment. Its Directorate for Education, for example, has developed a Unit for Co-operation with Non-member Economies (NME), the terminology used by the OECD to refer to non-member countries. The Directorate's interest in NMEs is based on the view that in the context of a global integration of economic activity it is no longer possible to understand the economic competitiveness of its own members without focusing also on comparative issues and monitoring the challenges posed to them by transitional economies, especially those that are now achieving higher levels of economic growth.

The OECD's perspective on globalization has also led it to develop formal links with a number of other international organizations, with the expressed purpose of helping to bring the OECD's institutional and policy expertise and technical know-how to NMEs. It has worked, for example, with the World Bank and UNESCO on the development of a World Education Indicators (WEI) project. WEI is a joint initiative of these organizations designed to provide a set of comparative educational data about transitional and developing economies. The OECD's role in the project has been to provide technical advice based on its long history of work with performance indicators. But as Rutkowski (2007) points out, this role is grounded in the OECD's neoliberal precepts, and it is difficult to separate the OECD's technical expertise from its normative assumptions about the role education must play in the development of the global economy.

These normative assumptions now constitute a global ideology that both informs the OECD's policy work in education and has become central to its multilateral relations with NMEs and international organizations alike. This has occurred within the broader context of the changes in the ways in which nation-states now relate to and work with each other. As we have noted throughout this chapter and indeed throughout this book, the traditional concept of the nation-state as a fundamental unit of world order, a unitary phenomenon characterized by its relative homogeneity with a set of singular purposes, has been replaced by a fragmented policy arena permeated by transnational networks as well as by domestic agencies and forces. This is the new governance and post-Westphalian reality.

This multilateral cooperation does not occur in a politically neutral space, but in a space that is characterized by asymmetrical relations of power. The flows of information and policy ideas are skewed towards the most powerful countries and their political interests. However, as facilitators of information flows and policy dialogue, international organizations have acquired greater power and influence than ever before. In the past, the OECD viewed itself as a forum for open dialogue with its members, but it is now clear that it has increasingly become a policy actor in its own right (Rizvi and Lingard 2006, 2009). The OECD has become a policy actor in its own right in the context of globalization, as both a response to and articulation of neoliberal globalization. Through both the construction of its agenda for policy dialogue and its technical statistical work, it displays a marked preference for certain policy priorities. Through all of its work the OECD is part of and helped constitute the new form of global governance in education, as well as within nations. Additionally, it has contributed to the construction of a global commensurate space of educational measurement, particularly through PISA and its indicators, which we consider in the next section.

Pressures towards commensurability

An important component part of the new educational governance on a global scale has been the construction of a commensurate space of educational measurement globally. The OECD has been very important in the construction of this space, through its indicators work and through its Programme for International Student Assessment (PISA). Indeed, in the context of globalization, the OECD has established a niche for itself amongst international organizations as a repository of international expertise in respect of comparative measures of the quality of educational systems. As noted already, the OECD's indicators and PISA are founded on a fundamental assumption that the international competitiveness of national economies is based on 'the quality of national education and training systems judged according to international standards' (Brown *et al.* 1997: 7–8). The OECD has been very successful in representing PISA as the most accurate and legitimate measure of comparative international educational performance. PISA demonstrates the important role that OECD now plays as a policy actor and mediator of knowledge, with an increasing capacity to shape policy priorities in education, not only among its member nations but among other non-member nations as well.

UNESCO and the World Bank have drawn heavily on the OECD's expertise in developing the World Education Indicators for the education systems of the transitional and developing economies. The OECD has also worked closely with the European Commission in developing technical infrastructure for the collection and analysis of data of various kinds, including indicators, and has provided technical advice to numerous national systems. This expertise privileges what might be referred to as 'a numbers approach' to policy work, which sidelines the broader philosophical discussions of educational purposes, focusing instead on an input/output approach, attempting to offer policy insights about the efficiency and effectiveness and equity and quality of national educational systems.

The effectiveness of national education systems is now increasingly measured against the performance data provided by PISA. Its results are taken very seriously by participating nations as a measure of the effectiveness of their education systems and the quality of their current and potential human capital (Simola 2005; Grek 2009). An example of this is the apparent education policy panic in Germany following their poor results in the first PISA of 2000. The outstanding performance of Finnish students on all PISA measures to date, on the other hand, has made Finland something of a laboratory for educators looking to improve their systems. In 2006, 27 non-member nations also participated in PISA, with more nations being pulled into this global field of comparison or global education policy field. The categories around which PISA is constructed have seldom been the subject of political debate, as comparative performance and relative rankings have assumed centre stage.

PISA was developed in the 1990s and was based on the 1999 OECD report, *Measuring Student Knowledge and Skills – A New Framework for Assessment*. It is conducted every three years to examine the applied knowledge and skills of students at the end of compulsory schooling at age 15. Thus its tests are not based on national curricula; rather, they are constructed in a purpose-built way by a contracted consortium of expert agencies with the support of technical advisory committees. A lot of sophisticated test development is done to ensure as far as possible culture-fair testing and accurate translation. In this way, PISA creates its own data, rather than drawing national data into a space of international comparison. PISA regards as crucially important its claim to comparability and a commensurate space of international comparison – a space of uniform measurement, or what Desrosieres (1998) refers to as a 'space of equivalence'. Our argument here is that PISA contributes to the constitution of a global space of equivalence as a part of the new form of educational governance.

As the histories of national statistical systems have shown (Desrosieres 1998; Porter 1995), within the national framework there was always greater concern about the creation of a national commensurable space of measurement than about validity, more about issues of reliability and comparison than about ontology. The same is the case with PISA. It too claims to have created a global commensurable space of measurement of the effectiveness of schooling systems in terms of the capacities of students at the end of compulsory schooling in the 'application of knowledge to real-life challenges'. Its architects suggests that PISA is constructed in a policy-relevant way and is concerned to ascertain the dispositions of students at the end of compulsory schooling for lifelong learning. As a consequence, while there might still be some technical debates about the nature of the tests, most of the national and international media and political responses to PISA results are about the league tables of performance and comparative national positioning. In this way, the technical is favoured over the political, and the popular social imaginary of the knowledge economy is sustained. As Rose (1999) has argued, policy as numbers tends to do this – the power of numbers is such that they 'render invisible and hence incontestable – the complex array of judgments and decisions that go into a measurement, a scale, a number' (ibid.: 208).

While PISA deals with literacy, mathematics, science and sometimes problem solving, it also requires students to complete a questionnaire about themselves, their backgrounds and study habits, while background data on the school in terms of resources, size and the organization of the curriculum are also collected. This allows for the generation of some very useful correlational policy data between variables such as socio-economic background and performance, which has helped reignite equity debates both within the OECD members and elsewhere. However, as Berliner (2007) points out, PISA's technical focus means that its own analysis of equity matters is located within a very narrow definition of equity in education, as formal access to educational institutions. It eschews the broader political issues about educational justice, both within and across nations.

As noted, we suggest that PISA has contributed to the constituting of a global commensurate space of measurement of educational performance, which is an important element of the new form of educational governance. Here we will draw upon histories of statistics which demonstrate the political, technical and cognitive work necessary to the emergence of both the nation and national statistics and their overlap with each other (Porter 1995; Desrosieres 1998). To use Scott's (1998) analysis of a state optic for governing – national statistics made the nation legible. We make the analogy with the significance of indicators and data to the construction of the globe as a legible, governable policy space.

A number of histories of statistics demonstrate the intimate and interwoven relationships between the development of state administrative structures, what Bruno Latour (1987) calls a 'centre of calculation' – and the development of standardization, methodologies, technologies and related cognitive schemes of statistics and scientific thinking (Hacking 1975, 1990; Porter 1995; Desrosieres 1998). Concerning statistics, Desrosieres (ibid.: 8) notes, 'As the etymology of the word shows, statistics is connected with the construction of the state, with its unification and administration.' He goes on to show how statistics combine the authority of the state with the authority of the scientific world. Indeed, he and Porter (1995) both demonstrate the necessity of the modern state and statistics to each other. The nation constituted as a 'space of equivalence' is necessary to the construction of statistics (Desrosieres 1998), but also statistics and numbers which elide the local are equally important to the construction of the nation. This constitution of a single space of equivalence is an affirmation of Porter's (1995: ix) observation that 'quantification is a technology of distance'. Porter (ibid.: 37) observes that 'the concept of society was itself in part a statistical construct'. While this involved technical advances, it also reflected political and administrative work as well. As Desrosieres (1998: 9) argues, 'Creating a political space involves and makes possible the creation of a space of common measurement, within which things may be compared, because the categories and encoding procedures are identical.'

While the focus up to this point has been on the historical constitution of national statistical systems and their relationships to the nation conceived as a space of equivalence, an analogy can be made with the collection of data, statistical information, and in education, performance data and educational indicators, to the construction or fabrication of a global space of measurement as a space of equivalence, a commensurate space of comparative performance. Such data, while not all of a piece, is central to the project of making the globe legible, central to the global aspect of educational governance. While the creation of national systems of statistical collection eradicated localized systems of measurement, the emergence of the globe as a commensurable space of measurement has *not* obliterated national data collection systems, but is now an aspect of the governance of education, globally and within nations.

OECD statistical work, including indicators and PISA, can be seen to be contributing to the constitution of an emergent global education policy field. We might also have considered the indicators work of the EU and the constitution of the EU as a commensurate space of equivalence (Grek *et al.* 2009). We can see at play here social-spatial networks of the national, international (between nations), transnational (passing through nations) and global (Mann 2000). There is as well a complex interplay between these layers of the new scalar politics with brokering occurring at the national level (Grek *et al.* 2009).

Conclusion

We have outlined those changes in the structures and practices, policy orientations and policy production rules associated with the move from government to governance. This transition is taken to pick up on the now more polycentric state with private-sector involvements and principles, for example markets, operating inside the state structures and framing its policies and policy practices. There is also a global layer to this transition. A large number of intergovernmental and non-governmental organizations existing above the nation now have policy effects inside nations and national education systems. This is the new scalar politics, which is central to the new forms of educational governance. As Held and McGrew (2005: 11) argue, 'the contemporary era has witnessed layers of governance spreading within and across political boundaries', transforming state sovereignty into a shared exercise of power. Furthermore, with the emergence of new patterns of political interconnectedness, 'the scope of policy choices available to individual governments and the effectiveness of many traditional policy instruments tends to decline' (ibid.: 13).

We dealt with the OECD as a case study and demonstrated how the OECD itself has been affected by globalization, taking on more of a policy actor role, while also articulating a particular neoliberal version of globalization and the need for reculturing and re-engineering the state through new public management and market orientations. We also demonstrated how the OECD has been a central agency in the development of multilateral standard setting in education through our discussion of PISA and educational indicators. We could have spent time looking in some detail at the effects of other such international organizations, and we would stress that they are not all of a piece, for example the World Bank. This would have demonstrated the emergence of the Washington and post-Washington consensus which neatly dovetails with the agendas we have outlined in our discussion of the move from government to governance. The World Bank and a range of other intergovernmental organizations have their effects in the nations of the Global South and of course there are asymmetrical power relations between such agencies and these nations. Our point here, however, is that this is all part of the new scalar politics, central to the move from government to governance and the emergent new forms of educational governance across the globe. With our discussion of multilateral standard setting in the indicators work and PISA of the OECD, we also showed the emergence of a global education policy field which is now a part of educational governance.

Of course there are still governments within nations, which putatively control policy agendas. The extent of this autonomy or sovereignty is affected by the amount of national capital possessed by a given nation. However, what we have also demonstrated in this chapter is how there are now effects coming from the new scalar politics and effects derived from the involvement of new private-sector policy players, resulting in the more polycentric or hollowed-out state at national levels.

We want in this conclusion to briefly touch on another concept related to the move from government to governance, namely 'governmentality'. Foucault (1991) used this concept to refer to the production of self-governing individuals, that is, individuals who act in particular ways as they are positioned by dominant political and policy discourses. Governmentality today is an effect of the form of governance we have been describing and analysing. Underpinning the new forms of governance in the context of neoliberal globalization is a possessive, self-interested individual. The discourses and policies which constitute and emanate from the new form of educational governance seek to create this new individual. Rose (1999) has argued that this is the new 'self-capitalizing' individual, one who has to continually invest in his or her own education, professional development and lifelong learning so as to actively and productively participate in the globalized economy and labour market. In some education systems there have actually been attempts to constitute individuals with more entrepreneurial dispositions, so as to better meet the perceived demands of fast globalized capitalism and this more individualistic and competitive world. The cultural circuits of globalized capitalism also produce concepts such as the 'knowledge economy', proselytized by international agencies such as the OECD, which also help to discursively create that of which they speak. The new governance and its effects through governmentality are based on a philosophical conception of society as constituted by self-maximizing individuals, as well as a conception of government as necessarily inimical to individual interests and a vibrant economy and society.

The new form of educational governance, through the policy technologies we have written about in this chapter, also seeks to produce new players within education. Here we can see the new educational manager as an effect of the new forms of governance. Further, and as we have noted, we can see the reconstitution of the role of the school principal or head as one who seeks to maximize the educational performance of students in the school set against performance targets, thus eliding and weakening other educational purposes, as we demonstrated in chapter 4. This also has effects on teachers in the move away from bureau professionalism. In respect of the production of new teacher subjects, Stephen Ball (2006: 145) has observed, 'the policy technologies of education reform are not simply vehicles for the technical and structural change of organizations but also mechanisms for reforming teachers (scholars and researchers) and for changing what it means to be a teacher, the technologies of reform produce new kinds of teacher subjects'. It is this self-governing that results, which is captured by the Foucauldian concept of governmentality, and which in turn can be seen to be an effect of the new forms of educational governance.

Ball (2006) actually talks about the debilitating impact of the new forms of governance and governmentality effects when he suggests that the performative, performance-oriented culture in English school reform actually frays the very soul of the teacher, who feels that the situation inhibits the achievement of authentic practice. In some manifestations, the culture of performativity provokes individual and organizational fabrications (ibid.), as both need to be seen to perform within the new audit culture. Here, fabrication is used in its dual meaning of creating and falsifying; the latter aspect can result in goal displacement, with individuals and organizational units spending more time on self-representation than actually working at achieving their 'real' goals. Such fabrications, as Ball (ibid.: 153) notes, are 'both resistance *and* capitulation'. There is, of course, resistance of various kinds and at various levels to the new forms of governance we have outlined in this chapter. These are matters we will discuss further in the concluding chapter of this book, when we look at globalization from below and a range of anti-globalization movements which seek to imagine other globalizations.

7 Equity policies in education

Introduction

At least since the 1950s, most educational systems around the world have been concerned with issues of equality. They have used public policy as an instrument to ensure greater participation in education in an attempt to reduce levels of social stratification. Their commitment to equality in education has been based on the principles of both economic efficiency and social justice. They have regarded a better-educated population as necessarily good for the economic development of a nation while, on social justice grounds, they have viewed education as a basic human right, and essential for social cohesion. A commitment to these principles has led governments, often with the assistance of international development agencies, to invest heavily in education and develop programmes to enhance educational participation. And indeed they can claim major success in reducing levels of illiteracy, increasing access to educational institutions and, to some extent, achieving greater equality of social outcomes. Such progress, however, has been uneven both within and across nations and across social groups, particularly in relation to indigenous populations and low socio-economic groups.

The extent to which the contemporary processes of globalization have institutionalized, or perhaps even extended, this unevenness is a subject of heated debate among economists and sociologists alike. The principal division is between those who argue that neoliberal policies associated with globalization have created a more unequal and impoverished world and those who suggest that they have created unprecedented levels of economic growth that has enabled wealth to be spread and poverty reduced. In this chapter we will review this debate. We will argue that while globalization has in fact reduced some aspects of structurally imposed impediments to social equality, it has also reinforced and even extended social hierarchies. We will consider three major policy initiatives – the *Millennium Development Goals* (MDGs), gender equity policies in education and programmes designed to address the 'digital divide' – and argue that each of these is based on a narrow conception of educational justice, conceptualized largely as access to institutions, sidelining broader issues of treatment and outcomes.

Such an approach is necessarily narrow because it does not consider the dynamics of educational experiences and their social and economic outcomes, as well as the historical conditions that produce inequalities. While a commitment to formal access to educational institutions is clearly necessary, it is not enough to achieve educational justice. Since comparative international data shows a weaker correlation between socio-economic disadvantage on educational outcomes in those societies with low Gini Coefficients of inequality (Green *et al.* 2006), a different conception of educational justice is clearly warranted, one that places greater emphasis on the social and economic conditions under which learning takes place, on pedagogical quality, and on the redistribution of resources. This means that a commitment to social justice in education requires both broader reforms in social and economic policy, and reforms in education policy and professional practice. Formal access to schooling does not always translate into effective equity outcomes. Indeed, simple access can be counterproductive, setting up expectations which, if not realized, have the potential to create considerable social alienation among those who have invested time and effort in education without the promised rewards.

The era of globalization has underlined the fact that equality is a relational matter. Global economic integration means that international trade, for example, benefits some countries at the expense of others (Buckman 2004). It also has differential effects on income, culture, society and the environment. According to Scholte (2000: 260), globalization involves 'stratified access to global space'. He shows how global communication is concentrated amongst professional and propertied classes of the North; how, while there are increased opportunities for women, these are often on lower terms and conditions than men; and how global money and credit are disproportionately available to the already privileged. Nation-states have traditionally been called upon to redress these inequalities but, as we have already noted, in the context of globalization their power has declined significantly. What this means is that claims for justice now need to be couched in global terms, directed at the transnational networks and institutions where much of the power now resides. If this is so, we suggest that the very concept of justice now needs to be globalized, articulated in terms that do not assume that the responsibilities for justice lie exclusively within the nation-state.

Globalization and inequalities

There is nothing new about social inequality. Stratification by class, gender, country, race and the like pre-dates the contemporary period of globalization. The question then is, 'How has globalization altered forms of social differentiation in the contemporary era?' In what ways and in what respect have the spread of transnational links, a global informational economy, globalization of cultures and the ideology of neoliberalism in respect of markets and the economy created new and distinctive patterns of exclusion? To what extent has globalization created new threats to human security? And in relation to education in particular, in what respects has neoliberal globalization created new patterns of unequal social outcomes, both within and across national spaces?

As noted earlier in this book, international organizations such as the World Bank and the OECD, and to a lesser extent UNESCO, have been vocal and vigorous proponents of neoliberal globalization. They argue that globalization of trade, for example, is not only good for international business, it is also a good way to empower the poor. On the other hand, the critics of globalization maintain that neoliberalism only enriches the global elite at the expense of ordinary workers and poorer countries and that it also eliminates the capacity of national governments to respond effectively to social inequalities. To a large extent this debate is driven by 'the old partisanship of the push and pull distributing versus market advocating politics' (Ray 2007: 141). Central to this debate are issues of measurement of globalization's effects. Depending on which measures of globalization as well as of inequality within and between nations are used, one gets the results one wants regarding the extent and effects of globalization. In this debate, even the interpretation of the available empirical evidence on inequalities and their underlying causal relations is filtered through ideological prisms.

So, for example, the advocates of neoliberal globalization argue that integration into the global economy increases economic activity and raises living standards, enhancing the capacity of national governments to invest more in education and other areas of social policy. Martin Wolfe (2005), for example, argues that over the past few decades standards of living across the globe have been increasing, and that while there are disparities in national economic performance within the Global South, these have been declining, and are due not to globalization but to national policies and domestic factors. Similarly, Dollar and Kraay (2005) contend that globalization has narrowed the gap between the rich and the poor and has contributed to the erosion of absolute poverty. Legrain (2002) claims that in 2000 global per capita income was four times greater than in 1950. Wei and Wu (2002) point to a decline in inequality in Chinese cities that are more open to globalization. The World Bank claims that the percentage of people living below $1 per day halved between 1980 and 2000, with extreme poverty falling from 28 to 21 per cent, despite population growth during this period.

The critics of neoliberal globalization (for example Pieterse 2004), on the other hand, contest these figures, and argue that poverty calculations by the World Bank involve both misleading definitions and misguided interpretations of evidence. The Bank's $1 per day calculation, for example, does not factor in inflation in the United States, and when this is allowed, the international poverty line in fact increases by 19.6 per cent. Pieterse (ibid.) objects moreover to this technical focus on poverty, which he argues depoliticizes the debate, shifting it away from more serious issues of inequality which call into question the more fundamental relations of power and class. A decrease in absolute poverty, he maintains, is perfectly possible alongside an increase in relative inequalities. A focus on inequalities rather than absolute poverty also underlines a widening gap in wealth in almost all countries in recent decades. What this suggests is the importance of examining relativities rather than absolute measures.

And this is precisely what the United Nations Development Program (UNDP) did in its report on the patterns of global inequalities, produced in 1999. The UNDP report was totally unequivocal in its conclusion that inequalities within and between countries through the 1980s and 1990s had increased. More than 80 countries, it reported, had per capita income in 1999 that was lower than it was in 1980. Even in countries that had reported spectacular rates of growth, it maintained, inequality had been rising. In China, for example, disparities were widening between the export-orientated regions of the coast and the interior. In India, wage and labour inequalities across the urban and rural divide had become even more extensive, and there was a substantial movement of farmers and rural workers from rural to urban areas in search of work. Similarly, the rich OECD countries such as Sweden, the United States and the United Kingdom had also experienced big increases in inequality.

The UNDP Report also pointed out that the income gap between the fifth of the people living in the richest countries and the fifth in the poorest countries was 74 to 1 in 1997, up from 60 to 1 in 1990 and 30 to 1 in 1960. In 1999, while the bottom fifth of the world's people living in the poorest income countries had just 1 to 2 per cent of the world's GDP, world export markets, foreign direct investment and telephone lines, the top fifth had 86, 82, 68 and 74 per cent respectively. In 1999, the OECD countries with just 19 per cent of the world's population had 71 per cent of the global trade in goods and services and 85 per cent of the world's research and development expenditures. In the decade since the UNDP Report was published, while some countries in Asia such as China and India and the so-called Asian 'tiger' economies have witnessed significant improvement on these indicators, for the bottom 100 countries things have got markedly worse, with a clear trend towards concentration of income, resources and wealth among people, corporations and countries. It is highly likely that in the current global economic crisis, inequalities both within and across nations and groups have become much worse.

Of course, it should be noted that while these trends are not the inevitable consequences of global economic integration, the ideology of neoliberal globalization has clearly served to legitimize them. Global inequalities, of course, pre-date globalization, but contemporary global processes have arguably acted to maintain and perhaps even institutionalize social stratification at both national and global levels. As Stiglitz (2002: 214) argues, globalization itself cannot be held responsible for inequalities, but its current form, and the ideologies and institutions to which it has given rise, certainly can. Stiglitz has shown how the structural adjustment schemes under the International Monetary Fund (IMF), for example, have generated falling incomes and growing poverty in many areas of the world. The serious imbalances in global trading regimes, including those negotiated at the World Trade Organization (WTO), have seriously disadvantaged countries of the Global South, as they have permitted richer countries and regional blocks such as the European Union (EU) to maintain subsidies, while exploiting the cheap labour found in poorer countries. Liberalization has driven costs down, while the rhetoric of flexibility has produced outcomes that mostly benefit the large transnational corporations at the expense of working people in developed and developing countries alike. As a result, the poor in both rich and poor countries have experienced a real reduction in living standards (Perron 2004).

The 1999 UNDP Report also suggests that, at an experiential level, globalization is creating new threats to human security. As a result of shrinking time and space, porous borders and integration of economic activities, the patterns of daily life and economic exchange and cultural traditions are disrupted. We have witnessed, for example, disruptions caused to local communities around the world by crises in the global financial system, such as the one experienced in Asia in 1997 and the one that in 2008 and 2009 has been driven by the collapse of the American housing market and major investment banks in the United States. Globalization has created conditions of economic volatility and financial insecurity, in threatening the pension plans of almost everyone. It has also led to job and income insecurity, as it has become possible for transnational corporations to relocate sites of production and move jobs to places where they can find cheaper labour.

While the increased mobility of people and cultural exchange have opened people's lives to a greater diversity of lifestyles and traditions, the opportunities of such mobility and exchange are not equally distributed. As Bauman (1998) has noted, mobility/immobility has become another dimension of inequality, with the most disadvantaged groups either becoming immobile or forced to move (e.g. political refugees). Nor are the cultural traditions of communities equally respected within the global space, which has enabled a range of exploitative practices to flourish. Under contemporary capitalism, 'organic class formation is no longer tied to territory and the political jurisdiction of the nation-states' (Robinson and Harris 2000: 12). It is linked instead to the work of TNCs committed to 'growth at any cost' and to the increasing mobility of financial capital, the global marketing of key brands and the globalization of product development. Those who work in key positions within transnational corporations have become just as mobile as the flows of capital and cultural products, resulting in the emergence of a global class. Global elites have of course always existed, but in recent decades their numbers have grown significantly and they have acquired a distinctive 'cosmopolitan consciousness' (Calhoun 2001) – hybridized cultural tastes that have often set them apart from those who remain tied to particular localities and are unable to travel.

Linked to this pattern of inequality are considerations of the informational economy. Manual Castells (2000) has written extensively on the relationship between globalization of communication and the new patterns of social inequality to which it has given rise. He examines the links between what he calls the new 'informational capitalism' and growing inequality, poverty, social exclusion and 'immiseration' on a world scale. He insists that the global division of labour has created distinctive patterns of exclusion and marginalization that cut across national boundaries. This division transcends the old core–periphery division (Wallerstein 1978); all nations are now being divided by the forces of globalization into communities of winners and losers. Castells uses the term 'Fourth World' to refer to those communities whose labour has been individualized, who are over-exploited, who are excluded from the benefits of global processes and who, as a result, are socially excluded. Social exclusion, he argues, is a process, not a condition. Who is included or excluded, he suggests, varies over time, depending on education, demographic characteristics, social prejudices and public policies. He notes moreover that

> '... the process of social exclusion in a network society concerns both people and territories. So that, under certain conditions, entire countries, regions, cities and neighborhoods become excluded, embracing in this exclusion, most, or all, of their populations' (Castells 2000).

This process induces an extremely uneven social geography which depends to a large extent on the value that particular individuals or communities are able to offer in the global networks of wealth accumulation, information and power. In this way, globalization has created new patterns of social inequality around an emerging logic of social exclusion.

Millennium Development Goals (MDGs)

In the past two decades the concept of 'social exclusion' has become central in policy discussions about the ways in which it might be possible to tackle the problems of educational inequality. It is believed that education is essential for achieving social inclusion. The European Commission (2008), for example, views social inclusion as a 'social right' to a certain basic standard of living and to participation in the major institutions of the society, which enables social and occupational opportunities to be realized. The policy idea of 'social inclusion', as used widely in Europe and now increasingly in other parts of the world, represents a form of affirmative action designed to change the conditions that might lead to the alienation or disenfranchisement of certain people within a society. It is thus linked to the considerations of social class and living standards and how these might affect access to various educational opportunities. In a more programmatic manner, social inclusion is a strategy to combat social exclusion, but in ways that are not redistributive and thus do not seek to make reparations or amends for past wrongs, as is the case with Affirmative Action policies developed in the 1970s. Rather it is a coordinated response to the very complex set of factors that produce institutional and individual marginalization.

Levitas (1998) has argued that social inclusion originated in French social policy, but that both in continental Europe and in the UK it has been a highly contested concept, with three competing meanings operating in social policy. She distinguishes between a critical social policy and redistributionist approach with a focus on eradicating poverty; a moral underclass discourse which focuses on 'criminally-inclined, unemployable young men' and 'sexually and socially irresponsible single mothers' (ibid.: 7–8); and a social integrationist discourse which emphasizes inclusion as simply inclusion in paid work. As Levitas (ibid.: 8) argues, these three competing discourses of social inclusion differ in how they represent the relationship between inclusion/exclusion and inequality more generally and have manifested in varying ways in social policy in the UK, sometimes as the dominant approach and sometimes as a pastiche of the competing constructions.

In the context of education, the term 'social inclusion' first appeared in the mid-1980s in relation to policies concerning the education of students with special needs. Advocates of inclusion policies believed that students with special needs should be educated in regular classrooms, alongside all other students. Sometimes this policy was known as 'mainstreaming'. In the 1990s, however, this concept was extended and now means something like equality of access to education generally. It forms the basis of the World Declaration on *Education For All* (EFA), proposed by the United Nations Development Program (UNDP) together with a number of other international organizations. The Declaration represents an internationally agreed set of education goals for realizing the aim of meeting the learning needs of all students by 2015. First forged in 1990 in Jomtien, Thailand, and then reiterated in 2000 in Dakar in Senegal, EFA is based on the Universal Declaration of Human Rights, which states that 'everyone has the right to education' (Article 26).

EFA has now been reformulated in a language of inclusion, which suggests that everyone should be given a chance to learn and benefit from basic education – not as an accident of circumstance, nor as a privilege, but as a right. EFA maintains that an education must lead to wider options for individuals and communities. In the words of the European Union's Delors Report (1996), education enables us *to know*, *to do*, *to live together*, and *to be*. This includes learning to live in a society and work together towards sustainable human development, respecting the diversity of human experience and circumstance and recognizing the stake that future generations have in our planet. The Declaration is accompanied by a set of targets – performance indicators used to measure the extent to which national systems of education are realizing EFA goals with the help of aid agencies, civil society and non-governmental organizations, and communities, as well as teachers and parents.

In 2000, EFA goals were given a boost with the release of another global statement, the UN's Millennium Development Goals (MDGs). MDGs are broader than EFA goals, recognizing the close links between issues of educational opportunities and social and economic conditions under which education takes place. The architects of MDGs note, for example, that universal primary education is not possible without measures to tackle extreme poverty and the spread of HIV/AIDS, and without efforts to promote gender equality. In this way, MDGs represent not only a set of eight development goals, together with 21 quantifiable targets adopted by 189 nations and signed by 147 heads of state and governments during the UN Millennium Summit in September 2000, but also a comprehensive statement relating to the ways in which issues of social inequality might be tackled in an era of globalization. The eight MDGs require all countries, by 2015, to:

Goal 1: Eradicate extreme poverty and hunger
Goal 2: Achieve universal primary education
Goal 3: Promote gender equality and empower women
Goal 4: Reduce child mortality
Goal 5: Improve maternal health
Goal 6: Combat HIV/AIDS, malaria and other diseases
Goal 7: Ensure environmental sustainability
Goal 8: Develop a global partnership for development

UNDP argues that these goals 'recognize explicitly the interdependence between growth, poverty reduction and sustainable development' and the role that basic primary education must play in realizing all other development objectives.

In a more explicit manner even than EFA, MDGs are based on time-bound and measurable targets accompanied by indicators for monitoring progress. While they recognize the importance of global partnerships, the ultimate responsibility for the implementation of these goals lies with national governments, even as the world's leading development institutions such as the World Bank are asked to play a major role. The aid programmes of many nations of the Global North are now also focused on the MDGs. To achieve these goals, international organizations are accordingly helping countries to improve their national capacity in both policy development and evaluation. A Millennium Project has been set up, for example, to provide a comprehensive set of services to support national development strategies such as the technical and financial assistance required in diagnostics and investment planning, and in strengthening national capacity for the effective development and evaluation of programmes. In the area of education, the UNESCO headquarters in Paris collects data from each country to monitor its progress towards each of the goals, producing annual reports that are widely used to consider ways of moving forward. The MDGs have thus had profound effects in the development of education policies in the nations of the Global South, which have often been expressed in terms of the extent to which the MDGs are met. Policy is couched in terms of responses to MDG indicators – another example of the contemporary focus on policy outcomes as opposed to inputs.

With only a few years to go before 2015, the progress towards meeting the MDGs has been mixed, with some significant advances together with important setbacks. The goal of cutting in half the proportion of people in the developing world living on less than $1 a day by 2015 is unlikely to be reached, with the severe economic downturn in 2008–2009 likely to further retard any progress, especially in sub-Saharan Africa. The UNDP reports that many countries were close to achieving universal primary enrolment, with the number of children of primary school age who were out of school falling from 103 million in 1999 to 73 million in 2006, despite an overall increase in the number of children in this age group. In sub-Saharan Africa, however, the net enrolment ratio has only recently reached 71 per cent. Around 38 million children of primary school age in this region are still out of school. In Southern Asia the enrolment ratio has climbed to 90 per cent, yet more than 18 million children of primary school age are not enrolled. In Western and Central Africa, girls in particular fail to enrol and stay in school. The same is the case, for example, in Pakistan. Drought, food shortages, armed conflict, poverty, lack of birth registration, child labour, and HIV and AIDS additionally contribute to low school enrolment and high dropout rates for both boys and girls in many parts of the world.

Now EFA and MDGs are certainly important initiatives in working towards social and educational equality, which while they are constructed globally are nonetheless expected to be realized within national frameworks. Their architects thus continue to view equality not in terms of global relations but in terms that focus exclusively within the nation-state. In this way they are unable to address issues of global inequalities across national boundaries. We do not know, therefore, the extent to which they might contribute to reducing the relativities across nation-states, or whether indeed any progress is being made towards closing the gap between rich and poor countries. This suggests that the notion of justice underlying EFA and MDGs is largely framed within Westphalian assumptions. The comparative figures produced by international organizations are based mostly on the numerical data supplied to them by national governments. But these figures fail to address issues of authenticity and comparability. Further, in some ways policy for these nations becomes continual adjustment of targets with a focus on quantity rather than quality (Ali 2006).

Beyond their nation-centric approach, the emphasis EFA and MDGs place on access to primary education is based both on an ethical commitment to human rights and on certain economic calculations, which suggests that one of the main reasons for supporting the goal of equality in education is the production of human capital needed for national development. There is certainly a great deal of creditable evidence to suggest that an investment in primary education provides enormous positive public as well as private benefits. Primary education is assumed to have the power to benefit communities in both economic and social realms. This has led most developing countries from Pakistan to Peru to focus most of their educational resources on primary education, neglecting to a large extent post-primary education. Yet countries must not only concentrate on primary education, but must also allocate extra resources in secondary and tertiary education if they want to maximize the possibilities of development, especially in economies that are increasingly becoming knowledge-intensive.

Both the OECD and UNESCO have argued that, to compete successfully in the new global economy, investment in all levels of education (human capital) is necessary for developing countries. Yet the policy emphasis by EFA and MDGs on universal access to primary education may be counterproductive; for in the context of limited resources and the neoliberal ideological push towards privatization, it may have led many developing countries to simply abandon support for post-primary education, leaving it to individual students and their families to foot the bill for higher education. However, since effective participation in the global economy requires a higher level of education, the policy emphasis on primary education may serve only to reproduce existing patterns of global inequalities. A multifaceted policy approach to education policy is clearly required to address social and economic inequalities.

Without good teachers who have adequate training and professional attitudes, access can never be a complete measure of equality. An externally determined and imposed curriculum, detached from local traditions and political conditions, can also endanger local cultures, as we have shown in chapter 5 in relation to Pakistan and St Lucia in the Caribbean. As discussed above, global pressures have led to universal measurements, which in turn can lead to generic prescriptions of what is to be taught and how. At the level of primary education in particular, some autonomy for local communities to determine their own curriculum seems highly desirable. However, the global trend towards greater system efficiency undermines this educational objective. What is clear is that an education appropriate to the community in which it takes place requires a more complex view of equality than that which is suggested by EFA and MDGs. Education at all levels has a whole range of purposes, not simply producing efficient workers for the changing global economy. As Amartya Sen (1999) suggests, development's goals and means should be about enhancing the freedoms people enjoy. This is surely true as well, we would argue, about education for development. If this is so, education policies designed to tackle various patterns of inequality need to be reconciled with the broader cultural concerns of education in addition to addressing issues of economic stratification. They must recognize a variety of other ways in which marginalization and social exclusion are experienced, so that education for development enhances the freedoms which flow from being literate and numerate.

Gender equity in education

Gender equity in education is an important policy priority in both EFA and MDG declarations. It is now widely agreed that without gender equality no society can claim to be socially just. It should be noted, however, that no country in the world has achieved complete gender equity; and that as a concept it is interpreted differently across religious, political and cultural traditions. Not surprisingly, therefore, policy requirements and outcomes around issues of gender equity work differently across the nations of the Global North and those of the Global South (Unterhalter 2007), with boys becoming the focus of much gender policy in the former and girls' access to schooling remaining the dominant gender issue in education policy in the latter. There is therefore considerable variance in the approaches to educational policies designed to promote gender equity.

Before considering in some more detail the issue of gender and girls' access to schooling in the Global South, we will turn briefly to a discussion of the way in which gender policies in education have developed and been contested in the nations of the Global North. While we will be generalizing here, we need to recognize that such debates are played out in vernacular ways in any given national education system, given the nature of the gender order within that society, the standing of feminist politics and the extent of the backlash against gains made for women in education and career terms from the impact of the women's movement on public policy. In most developed western nations, as already suggested, the gender policy focus has turned from girls to boys, particularly from the early 1990s (Lingard *et al.* 2009). This 'what about the boys?' policy focus followed more feminist-inspired policy interventions from the 1970s, which amongst other things sought to widen girls' subject choices and improve their educational outcomes. This policy focus appeared to have had some success, particularly for middle-class girls, who now challenge boys for the top academic outcomes at the end of secondary schooling and who now attend university in greater numbers than boys, albeit still largely in gender-segmented courses (Arnott *et al.* 1999).

However, despite the focus shifting from girls to boys, girls' improved educational attainment does not convert into equal career opportunities and equal earnings with males, even when females have comparable levels of education. Child rearing still has a much greater impact on females' careers and wage-earning capacity than on males'. The academic debate about boys' education and the turn to boys in gender policy have also challenged the essentializing of the category of boys and argue instead that policy should focus on the most disadvantaged girls and most disadvantaged boys (Lingard and Douglas 1999). The most nuanced of these considerations asks, 'Which boys and which girls?' and the evidence demonstrates that middle-class boys are still doing well at school and in careers and that middle-class girls are likewise doing well. It is poor girls and poor boys who do not benefit from schooling in the same ways as their more privileged counterparts. There are also racialized aspects to this equation, so that in Australia indigenous boys (and girls) do not do very well at all, while the same is true for African-American boys in the USA and Afro-Caribbean boys in the UK.

In contrast to this changing pattern of gender policy in the nations of the Global North has been the situation within the nations of the Global South where gender policy in education still requires a focus on girls. This has been a question even of access to full primary education, a topic addressed by EFA and the MDGs. The situation is changing a little, however, with some emergent focus on boys' issues in developing nations. This is most evident in the report commissioned by the Commonwealth Institute on boys' education (Jha and Kelleher 2006), which seems to suggest that the 'What about the boys?' policy discourse in the nations of the Global North has travelled to some nations of the Global South and been taken up as a policy issue there. Globalization in its multiple forms and manifestations has also affected the gender order and gender politics within and across nations, as Faludi (2007) has observed in her account of the impact of 9/11 on masculinities, femininities and gender politics in the USA, with some regression towards John Wayne-type masculinities and nurturant femininities.

It needs to be acknowledged that within countries of the Global South, as elsewhere, huge strides have been taken in improving the gender gap since the early 1990s. For example, as illustrated by the United Nations Statistical Division (2004), in most regions of the world the ratio of girls to boys in primary education demonstrates that participation of girls is increasing, with large gains in Northern Africa and Eastern and Southern Asia. Despite popular misconceptions about Muslim societies, enrolment ratios in South and West Asian countries have also increased significantly, even though they still rank as having the lowest gender parity in the world (Aguilar 2004). While it is true that great gains have been made in gender parity in primary education, with many countries achieving a gender parity index close to 100 per cent, the participation of girls in secondary and tertiary education remains generally lower in most developing countries. In countries with very large populations such as China and India, girls have very poor participation rates in secondary education. Women's participation in tertiary education has also grown in the past two decades, in both developed and developing countries, but at a much lower rate in the countries of the South.

Indeed, as already noted, in some developed countries women's higher education participation is greater than that for men. However, if gains are to be made in genuine equality for girls in developing nations, access is not sufficient; there must also be a more equal distribution of gender among fields of study and employment. While women are well represented in the fields of education, social sciences and humanities, and even health services, their participation in the fields of the natural sciences and engineering is still far from approaching gender parity. With growing importance attached to these fields within the global economy, associated with technological innovation and technical expertise, this inequality is more significant than it might at first appear, for it suggests that the growing access of women to tertiary education is in areas that do not enjoy similar high economic rewards, social status and prestige.

In recent years, IGOs such as the OECD, the World Bank and UNESCO have repeatedly emphasized the importance of gender equity in education, at all levels of education (Unterhalter 2007). The arguments they have advanced for greater access, however, are both interesting and revealing. Though the ideological stances of these three organizations differ, they all seem to use similar arguments in support of gender equity in education, viewing its significance largely in terms of market efficiency. According to the World Bank, 'research has also shown that women and girls work harder than men, are more likely to invest their earning in their children, and are major producers as well as consumers'. UNESCO states: 'Educating girls yields the highest return in economic terms.' Finally, the OECD urges that 'Investing in women (with respect to education, health, family planning, access to land, etc.) not only directly reduces poverty, but also leads to higher productivity and a more efficient use of resources.' Of the three, the World Bank takes the strongest position in relating gender equity to economic consumerism and efficiency. The instrumentalist logic of this argument is arguably gender-biased, which views women simply as a means to certain economic ends rather than as people who participate in education for a huge variety of reasons, not only economic but also social and cultural.

What is evident is that, given the stated benefits of greater gender equity to economic expansion and capital accumulation, the global push for the education of women is not simply a product of altruism or a moral conviction. Rather, gender equity appears to be a calculated and efficient strategy to provide corporations with a cheaper source of labour for both local and transnational companies. The neoliberal imaginary presupposes greater cost efficiencies in educating women. Other benefits are also cited, but these too are embedded within the same imaginary. For example, the World Bank states that girls' education is a top-ranked social investment, in that their education reduces child mortality, raises per capita income at a greater rate than investment in men, and reduces total fertility rates. This economic efficiency is achieved, however, only because educated women continue to receive lower pay, tend to work longer hours than their male counterparts, and remain responsible for family welfare.

An analysis of gender equity in education would not be complete without reference to the significant pressures that many NGOs, the global women's movement and powerful women have placed on governments and international organizations to improve gender equity (Bulbeck 1998). The growing mobility of people and information associated with globalization have been major catalysts for mounting awareness concerning issues of gender equality in education. With very few exceptions, governments around the world have had to react to the growing demands for gender equity. This demand has been the loudest in South Asia. The World Development Report 2009 places

South Asia amongst the worst regions in the world when it comes to women's rights. Comparative indicators for literacy, health, economic activities, work burden, empowerment and political participation show South Asia to be lagging far behind the rest of the world. Oxfam (2008), a UK-based development organization, states that in South Asia, 'research shows that despite three decades of activism by women's groups all over the world, and the issue of violence against women gaining attention in global policy debates as a health and human rights issue, the social crisis is growing'.

This is so because policies relating to gender equity in education remain tied to the neoliberal imaginary that views equity largely in instrumental economic terms. What is clear, however, is that gender equity beyond access requires a more systematic focus on the social processes that perpetuate gender inequalities, as well as demanding a broader conception of the purposes of education. While a view of education based on the principles of the market and system efficiency demands better utilization of the human resources that women represent, a stronger view of equity seeks a social transformation through which gender relations are reconfigured. This latter view highlights the importance of not only access and social inclusion, but also the need to rethink the terms of that inclusion. It envisages societies that are potentially economically, politically and socially transformed in gender terms. This requires changes not only to the ways education is administered, but changes also to curriculum and pedagogy, especially in the context of the knowledge economy, with its potential to reshape patterns of both economic and social relations.

The digital divide

In a knowledge economy, educational opportunities are shaped by access to technology. The capacity to use information technology has become fundamental to equity policies, for issues related to the 'digital divide' are now inextricably linked to the global flows of information and communication. The idea of the 'digital divide' is now commonly used to characterize global inequalities. The initiatives taken for overcoming the 'digital divide' are now considered fundamental to educational reform. Although the term 'digital divide' is a little over ten years old, it has quickly become part of a new global slogan system – so much so that it now masks, more than it elucidates, the nature of the stratifications between those who are and those who are not electronically networked. However, it does point to something significant in the ways in which social and economic development have become highly dependent on a country's capacity to participate in the new informational economy.

This new economy, as Manual Castells (2000) among others has pointed out, is characterized largely by science and technology, a shift from material production to information processing, the emergence and expansion of new forms of networked industrial organizations and the rise of socio-economic globalization. Castells argues that economic productivity is now linked to the quality of information and its management in the processes of production, consumption, distribution and trade. This is so because there has been a shift from material production to information processing industries such as healthcare, banking, software, biotechnology, media and of course education, and because global trade now involves global circuits of knowledge exchange and data processing.

If participation in these information-rich industries has become fundamental to economic development, the idea of a 'digital divide' can be viewed as a major source of underdevelopment. But how? Given the complexity of 'informationalism', as Castells calls it, the digital divide cannot simply refer to the uneven distribution of technology hardware across communities. Rather, it is a much more complicated and multidimensional phenomenon that incorporates a whole range of factors, from access to computers to the manner in which knowledge is now produced and distributed. Pippa Norris (2001) has suggested, for example, that the idea of a 'digital divide' actually refers to three distinct divides. First, the global digital divide refers to the unequal Internet access between industrialized and developing societies. Secondly, Norris talks of a 'social divide', which refers to the divide between information rich and poor in each nation. And finally, and more significantly, she introduces the idea of a 'democratic divide' to signify the differences between those who do and do not use the enormous and growing resources of the Internet to engage, mobilize and participate in public life.

But even this corrective does not fully capture the complexities surrounding the idea of a 'digital divide'. With the size of the online community doubling every year (van Dijk 2005), it is now clear that the Internet is transforming the way people live, work and play. Few now doubt that digital technologies are transforming the flow of capital, goods and services within global spaces. Such technologies have become not only an important element of economic activity but also a ubiquitous source of information. The potential impact of the Internet on the developing countries is hard to assess. On the one hand, some argue that digital technologies provide countries of the South opportunities to 'leapfrog' various stages of economic and social development, while others maintain that the information economy fundamentally favours the already information-rich societies. Voices of developing countries on the Internet are almost entirely absent. As Ferguson (2006) notes, in the neoliberal world order sub-Saharan Africa, in particular, has been pushed further into what he calls the 'global shadows', inextricably linked to the global economy yet in ways that marginalize its voices.

The Internet age thus has the potential to extend the disparities between the post-industrial economies at the core of the global economic system and developing societies at the periphery. The richer economies are able to use digital technologies to boost productivity, while the poorer societies are left in a position to play 'catch-up', which they can seldom do due to the fast-changing nature of the digital technologies and costs involved. National systems of education and international organizations are fully aware that the always shifting nature of the new technologies has the potential to reinforce existing patterns of stratification in the new economy. Indeed, the network society may be creating parallel communications systems: one for those with income, education and connectivity and the other for those without connection and without the plentiful information needed to thrive in the global economy. If this is so, the problem of the digital divide is linked to the structural exclusion of poorer nations from the knowledge economy, where know-how and information replace land and capital as the basic drivers of economic growth and productivity. This suggests the need to understand the digital divide in relational terms, rather than in terms of a deficit – of either equipment or skills.

The idea of a 'digital divide' is often discussed as an issue of access to technology hardware and Internet connectivity, as well as of know-how. Many of the policy intiatives in the developing countries to overcome the digital divide have centred on the provision of computers and connectivity. But this is a problem that can easily be resolved by higher levels of investment and the availability of inexpensive computers. The MIT Media Lab's much-publicized $100 computer, now referred to as XO-1, will soon be a reality (Negroponte 1996), as might the ways to solve the problems of broadband. But this will not close the digital divide, because even if everyone throughout the developing countries were given a free computer, they might not be able to use it. There would remain the problem of literacy and technical skills required to access the information and services available on the Internet. As Warschauer (2003) argues, discussions about the digital divide must now shift from gaps to be overcome by providing equipment, to challenges facing the effective integration of technology into communities, institutions (including education) and societies. What is more important, he suggests, is not so much the physical availability of computers and the Internet, but rather people's ability to make use of those technologies to engage in meaningful social practices.

Policymakers in the developing countries have often reiterated the importance of higher education both in overcoming the digital divide and in taking advantage of the opportunities offered by the new technologies. Indeed, if the failure to access and utilize the new technology implied an even greater marginalization from the world economy, the developing nations, it is argued, have no other option than to invest in forms of higher education that are efficient and effective, and to develop competencies and skills appropriate to successful participation in the new knowledge economy. In this respect, programmes based on the new technologies are viewed favourably, as a way of meeting the fast-growing demand for higher education in the developing countries, especially in a context of the inability of governments to allocate the resources that would be required to build and develop university campuses. It is maintained that the new technologies have the potential to increase efficiency in the provision and quality of higher education through more flexible forms of delivery, and to support initiatives that use these technologies to 'scale up' the delivery of online programmes, so long as new policies were also developed to coordinate the accreditation, recognition and quality assurance of online programmes, especially when these are offered across national borders.

The main problem with these policy initiatives, however, is that they continue to view educational equity largely in terms of access, and do not attend to the fact that the current global system of knowledge is decidedly skewed towards the west. Much of the content on the Internet is produced in the developed countries, where English is the dominant language. As Castells (2000) has pointed out, the developed countries are able to leverage the opportunities offered by the information economy to further reinforce their economic power. He has argued that while the faultlines of marginality might not necessarily follow the current divide between North and South, it is difficult to see societies where education is grossly underfunded, and where there is far too much reliance on knowledge products imported from abroad, closing the gap between these societies and the richer countries already at the core of the information revolution.

What this analysis suggests is a different approach to thinking about how the new technologies might contribute to reducing levels of global inequalities, one that encourages integration of global and local knowledge traditions. If the digital divide is to be challenged in a more serious fashion, such an approach would seek to draw upon the enormous reservoir of knowledge available on the Internet, some of which is free as a result of such democratic initiatives as Open Source and Creative Commons (Peters and Britez 2008), but would seek to develop in students a capacity to critically interrogate them for their local relevance and utility. There is a huge gap at the moment in the appropriateness of online content for marginalized populations of the world, which threatens to reproduce and perhaps even greatly increase economic and social disparities. While much support and advice can clearly be provided by international organizations, the problems of the digital divide, so stated, cannot ultimately be solved by anyone but local communities themselves. Access to technologies may in fact be a necessary condition for achieving greater equity in education; it certainly is not sufficient.

Equity policies and educational justice

In the discussion above, we have shown how each of the three policy efforts by international organizations and national governments to achieve greater equality of opportunities is informed by a very narrow definition of equity. This definition focuses largely on issues of access to educational opportunities. MDGs are directly aimed at providing universal primary education, while gender equity policies in education focus on increasing levels of participation of girls in education. Policies designed to tackle the digital divide mostly involve efforts to provide technology to disadvantaged communities, so that they too can participate in the networked knowledge economy. But none of these policies addresses the broader historical and political contexts that produce disadvantage in the first place, and none looks seriously at the conditions under which access is provided and might succeed. These policies focus mostly on quantitative indicators, dovetailing easily with the policy by numbers approach that we have suggested has become globally dominant over the past two decades. These assume that access alone is enough to produce educational justice. In this way, they work with a very weak definition of the concept of justice.

Justice is a highly complex idea which does not admit any universal definition. While, as an ideal, it may be universally applicable and aspired to, its expressions vary across different cultural and national traditions. Indeed, its meaning is historically constituted and is a site of conflicting and divergent political endeavours. It does not refer to a single set of primary or basic goods, conceivable across all moral and material domains. Having said this, it needs to be acknowledged, however, that injustice does have a material reality that is readily recognized by those who experience it. Those who are hungry or poor, or homeless, do not need abstract philosophical discussions in order to realize that they are subjected to marginalization, discrimination and oppression. The idea of injustice thus points to something real and tangible, and represents a moral blight on communities that do not attempt to do their best to mitigate its worst effects.

In the political realm, however, social justice is an essentially contested notion, and the search for its realization arises from the meeting of a particular kind of authority with political aspirations and activism located in particular historical circumstances. In the past few decades, for example, policy thinking around the notion of social justice in most western countries has revolved around three distinct philosophical traditions: liberal-humanism, market-individualism and social democratic. A liberal-humanist notion of social justice, associated most notably with the ideas of John Rawls (1972), conceptualizes social justice in terms of fairness, implying principles of individual freedom, as well as the idea that the state has a major responsibility in creating policies and programmes directed towards removing barriers arising from unequal power relations that prevent access, equity and participation.

Market-individualism, on the other hand, invokes not so much the idea of fairness as what people deserve (Nozick 1974). It suggests that the state has no right to distribute the private goods that people have produced through their own efforts. Highlighting the importance of the market in economic and social exchange, this tradition of thinking rejects redistributive notions, and suggests that it is unjust for the state to transfer property owned by individuals without their consent. Social democratic notions of justice (Walzer 1983), in contrast, reject both liberal-humanism and market-individualism, and stress the importance of social relationships and the needs people have within a community. The social democratic conception views 'need' as a primary rather than a residual category. In this way, its interpretation of needs is different from charity-based arguments about the 'needy', which are perfectly compatible with both the fairness and desert principles.

It is important to note, then, that market-individualism and social democracy rest on very different understandings of the nature of the relationship between justice and the market. In the former, the market is seen as crucial in facilitating social exchange and the exercise of individual choice, while the social democratic view suggests that the idea of justice is not entirely compatible with markets unless they are controlled (regulated) in a sufficiently rigorous manner. The former view is based on an assumption about 'property rights' that individuals possess and are able to exchange in the market. In contrast, the social democratic perspective emphasizes 'person rights', involving equal treatment of citizens, freedom of expression and movement, equal access to participation in decision-making, and reciprocity in relations of power and authority. The achievement of person rights within the social democratic definition requires that the state intervene in and against the market to ensure an acceptable level of equality/inequality thought necessary to protect person rights.

A comparative analysis of educational justice shows how different countries have emphasized different aspects of these traditions. In Scandinavian countries, for example, social democratic principles, until recently at least, have been dominant, and exercised in terms of Keynesian principles. The state has sought to provide equality of educational opportunities for all through various redistributive programmes. In the post-colonial developing world, the project of nation-building has necessarily required a commitment to the principles of social democracy, designed to increase levels of literacy and educational participation. The United States, in contrast, has leaned more toward market-individualism, encapsulated in education most notably in policies of choice and accountability, especially since the so-called Reagan economic revolution, and the hegemony of neoliberalism.

Since the late 1980s market-individualism has become increasingly hegemonic in educational policy development around the world. This seemingly global convergence toward neoliberal thinking in education has occurred within a broader discourse about the changing nature of the global economy, which is characterized as 'knowledge-based' and which is assumed to require greater levels of education and training than ever before. In this way, the idea of educational justice based on market-individualism is consistent with a focus in educational policies on access to educational provisions. Since the purposes of education are now increasingly conceived in human capital terms, encouraging individuals, organizations and even nations to consider investment in education largely in economic terms, access has been thought to benefit both individuals, who can sell their skills in the market, and corporations, who need those skills in a knowledge-based economy. Moreover, since access can be measured in participation and retention rates and so on, the broader cultural and political issues of educational justice are sidelined. The characteristics of new public management of individual choice, quasi-markets and system accountability are thus able to claim a commitment to educational justice without having to deal with the criticism that market-individualism reproduces and perhaps even extends patterns of educational inequalities.

We have argued that globalization has transformed the ways in which educational policies, often couched in a language of reform, have been developed and enacted. But we have also maintained that the effects of globalization on different groups and communities have varied greatly, creating considerable disparities around the world, with some communities benefiting enormously from globalization, while others have encountered major disruptions to their economic and cultural lives. The discursive terrain within which educational priorities are now set is increasingly informed by a range of neoliberal precepts that have undermined, in various ways, stronger social democratic claims to educational justice.

At the same time, moreover, globalization has weakened the authority of the state in promoting stronger redistributive policies and programmes. Traditional ways of thinking about justice in education assumed a strong role for the state in bringing about greater equality of access, opportunities and outcomes. It was the state to which the claims for greater redistribution of resources were addressed. And it was the state that was expected to develop programmes designed to ensure conditions that reflected desert or fairness principles. In an era of globalization, however, the state's policy choices have become somewhat restricted, with an increasing preference for a minimalist state, concerned to promote the instrumental values of competition, economic efficiency and choice, underpinned by an individualistic rather than collectivist philosophy. National policy mechanisms have become increasingly interconnected. A new logic of networks has demanded state restructuring. Yet not all countries have restructured the state in the same way, highlighting the importance of looking at issues of education justice from international perspectives, in terms that are not only comparative but also relational.

The state is, however, not the only site of struggle over social justice. Contemporary social movements, often working at the global level, have underscored a new politics of difference around issues not only of class, but also of gender, ethnicity, race, disability, sexuality and religion, as well as their complex articulations with each other. As Nancy Fraser (1997) has pointed out, the struggle for recognition is fast becoming the paradigmatic form of political conflict, and therefore heterogeneity and pluralism must now become the norms against which the demands for justice are articulated. In this way, group identity has supplanted class conflict as the chief medium of political mobilization. Of course, material injustices have not disappeared, but are now linked to the demands for recognition of difference, and for representation in the institutions of local and national, as well as global, decision-making.

What this suggests is that the distributive paradigm, as Young (1990) calls it, that informed the three major traditions of thinking about social justice is no longer sufficient to capture the complexities of global interconnectivity and interdependence on the one hand and of contemporary identity politics on the other. The distributive paradigm was concerned with the morally proper distribution of benefits and burdens among all members of a society. While this logic clearly applies to the distribution of material goods such as wealth and income, it is inadequate for moral concerns such as respect, recognition, rights, opportunities and power, because injustice can also be rooted in social patterns of representation, interpretation and communication. In this way, while concerns of distribution upon which most equity policies in education are couched in terms of access are important, so too are issues of identity, difference and cultural recognition and exploitation.

These issues are highly relevant to the concerns of educational justice because it is in education that students learn to develop their sense of self-worth and acceptable modes of social communication. Of course, these cultural facts are interpreted differently in different communities, and therefore require an understanding not only of difference, but also of relationalities that link considerations of justice in one place to others. The emphasis on relationalities points to the importance of cosmopolitan sensibilities needed to negotiate differences that are now resulting from the increased volume and intensity of cultural interactions produced by the global flows of people, ideas and technologies. This has led to demands for a new ethics of globalization (Singer 2002), in which claims to educational justice are addressed not only to nation-states, but also to an emerging global community. In this community, issues of identity and culture play a central role, requiring a robust set of political principles for an interdependent world (Parekh 2008). It is upon these principles that a new policy framework for educational equity might be developed.

8 Mobility and policy dilemmas

Introduction

We have noted throughout this book that the concept of globalization is associated with increasing levels of mobility, not only of capital and finance, images, information and ideologies, but also of people. Never before in history have there been more people moving across national boundaries. People are moving for a whole host of reasons: for migration; as refugees; for trade and business; for employment opportunities; as tourists; to attend international conventions and conference; and for education. There are more international migrants – both documented and undocumented – than ever before, even more than after the Second World War when a large number of displaced people sought residence and safer havens around the world. Despite declining instances of major wars, political conflict and famines, there are now more people registered as refugees with the United Nations than at any other time in history (Marfleet 2005). With the globalization of economic activity and trade, business executives are constantly on the move, as are those workers employed by transnational corporations. Many people no longer hesitate, as they once did, to take employment opportunities abroad. Waters (1995: 154) has noted that international tourism, measured in terms of arrivals from another country, expanded 17-fold between 1950 and 1990; these numbers are likely to have doubled since then. International conferences and conventions have become commonplace, despite enhanced possibilities of communication online. And the number of international students is now more than 2.2 million, up from just 300,000 in 1970, and is expected to more than double by 2020 (Open Doors 2007).

This unprecedented level of people mobility has major implications for the ways in which global economic and political systems work. But, in a manner that is equally significant, the movement of people is transforming our social institutions, cultural practices and even our sense of identity and belongingness. Global mobility has transformed our cities, creating urban conglomerates at the intersection of global flows of finance and capital (Sassen 1991). It is in these global cities that most international migrants settle. These shifts have raised major issues of security, sustainability and adaptation to the processes of globalization. They have also made cities more culturally diverse, where people live across multiple time horizons, creating conditions not only for risk and vulnerability, but also for opportunities. As the sociologist John Urry (2000) has pointed out, these changes have led to multiple new cross-national, cross-cultural flows and networks that define the global world of the 21st century: 'the diverse mobilities of peoples, objects, images, information and wastes; and ... the complex interdependencies between, and social consequences of, these diverse mobilities' (ibid.: 1). Another theorist, Nicholas Papastergiadis (2000), suggests these transformations require new ways of thinking about movement, and new ways of accounting for migration, for the traditional push-pull and structural theories; of distinctions between economic and forced migration; and of representations based on classic South–North flows, which are no longer adequate.

In this chapter we explore the various ways in which the global mobility of people is transforming not only the demographic composition of our communities, but also the ways in which we live our lives and the challenges we face. We will consider how individuals and institutions have taken advantage of the opportunities created by increasing levels of mobility, and how states have developed public policies designed to manage the cultural shifts associated with globalization. We will examine how greater mobility of people has education policy implications; how education policy has interpreted cultural diversity and responded to its challenges; how higher education systems in particular have sought to benefit from the desire of people to become transnationally mobile; how the changing demography of campuses in particular and global dynamics more generally have led to demands for the internationalization of education; how, in a related fashion, English has become a global language. The social consequences of increased mobility have not of course been even across all communities. The mobility of skilled people from developing to developed countries, for example, has reinforced global inequalities, expressed most clearly in the idea of a 'brain drain'. In the final part of this chapter we will examine the concept of 'brain drain' and suggest why, in policy terms, it needs to be rethought in an era of globalization.

Policy responses to cultural diversity

Cultural diversity has always characterized human societies. But in a globalizing society issues of diversity have become more complex. We have become increasingly aware of our interconnectivity and interdependence, and yet confront conditions in which differences are exploited, as communities increasingly define their identities against the encroaching forces of globalization and against each other. Touraine (2000) argues that although at one level we desire diversity and mobility, we feel nonetheless that our cultural distinctiveness is increasingly under attack by homogenized mass culture. Never before in human history have the issues of identity politics and intercultural relations been as important in policy debates as they are today.

Most nation-states now confront a dilemma of how to develop public policies which acknowledge the importance of cultural diversity and at the same time acknowledge that in a globalizing world our problems and their solutions are interconnected and transcend national boundaries, but to recognize that we inevitably interpret the world from a particular position, and that most of us wish to remain attached to cultural norms we find comfortable. If this is so, a new policy understanding of cultural identity and intercultural relations is needed, that is, 'a new analytical optic which makes visible the increasing intensity and scope of circular flows of persons, goods, information and symbols' (Cagler 2001: 607) on the one hand, and which addresses our anxieties about these flows on the other.

These questions are of course not entirely new. Nation-states have struggled for a long time with issues of how best to interpret diversity and to construct simultaneously a moral universe in which policies operate with a relatively stable understanding of interculturality that works across the binary of global and local attachments. Over the past three decades, and more specifically in the post-9/11 era, these questions have clearly become more complicated and urgent. New patterns of mobility have contributed to a sense of urgency, as have the anxieties about security. In such a context, traditional institutions appear to have also lost their capacity to cope with the new modalities of cultural difference and social complexity. As we move rapidly from imagining nation-states as being constituted by unitary cultures to spaces that are characterized by significant levels of cultural diversity and exchange, public policy struggles to define ways of both celebrating these new conditions and keeping them in check.

From the public policy point of view, it has been through the discourse of multiculturalism that many countries have sought to deal with these issues. Multiculturalism suggests that all citizens, no matter what their cultural background, should be able to contribute to a nation's cultural and economic development; and that it is the role of the state and its institutions, such as schools and universities, to create conditions necessary for all citizens to be able to utilize their skills and talents, and thus be able to contribute to national development. The policy discourse of multiculturalism, developed during the 1970s, has not been without its problems, however. It is just as well to remember that in countries like Canada, Australia and the UK, multiculturalism emerged as a compromise formation designed to pacify increasingly volatile ethnic communities and their supporters on the one hand and to allay the fears of the dominant cultural groups, alarmed by the changing demography of their cities, on the other. It turned out partly to be a strategy for managing inter-group relations and accommodating the interests of the ethnic middle class (Rizvi 1985). At the same time, multiculturalism provided ethnic communities with symbolic resources around which they could organize themselves politically, utilizing a politics of difference (Young 1990).

As a policy construct, the idea of multiculturalism remains highly contested. This should not surprise anyone because, like other politically contested ideas such as equality, democracy and autonomy, it is a term that does not admit any clear-cut definition. There are a number of competing discourses of multiculturalism. Each definition seeks a new accommodation between competing values, and is resisted by dominant groups unprepared to give up their power and privileges on the one hand, and by the minority communities suspicious of compromise rhetoric on the other. The debates surrounding the educational implications of cultural diversity are located within this contested political terrain, either as part of a social movement, as is the case in the United States, or as a state-sponsored policy, as has been the case in Australia and Canada.

Despite opposition to its various formulations, multiculturalism has proved, yet, to be a fairly flexible and dynamic concept, able to accommodate changing economic, political and cultural conditions. For example, multiculturalism has been able to work simultaneously with a politics of redistribution, embodied in its emphasis on access and equity, and a politics of recognition, expressed in its support for the right of migrant communities to maintain their cultural traditions. It has even been able to work with the neoliberal discourses of economic efficiency and market rationalism. It is assumed, for instance, that skills of intercultural communication are essential for global trade in services in particular. The idea of 'productive diversity' (Cope and Kalantzis 2002), for example, seeks to promote this understanding, linking to the requirements of the knowledge economy.

Flexible though the notion of multiculturalism clearly has been, we want to argue that it has remained trapped within a set of nation-centric assumptions. It continues to address issues of cultural diversity within a national framework. It thus appears divorced from the processes of cultural globalization that are increasingly affecting the ways in which many people think about their identity, their sense of belonging and the cultural spaces they inhabit. If multiculturalism is to survive as a useful policy concept, it cannot remain tied exclusively to the agenda for managing inter-ethnic relations within the nation-state. For it to be useful in dealing with the transnational and transcultural spaces that have become central to our understanding of cosmopolitan futures, multiculturalism needs to interpret the local and the national within the wider global context. It has to deal, for example, with the diasporic spaces that enable many people to now belong simultaneously to more than one country, and to interpret their sense of identity with respect to economic, social and political relations that span national boundaries (Cohen and Kennedy 2007).

Globalization has encouraged new 'deterritorialized' ways of thinking about cultural identities (Tomlinson 2000), defined in terms of a set of closed cultural boundaries expressed in language, arts and cultural traditions, bracketed as homogenized entities frozen outside history and contemporary interactive cultural relations, located within particular national spaces. Within a nation, the relationship between ethnic communities and their originating cultures can no longer be treated as a clear-cut one. In the global context, the interaction between the cultural identities of individuals and their originating homes is much more complex than that captured by notions of nostalgia, of collective memory and of desire for singular attachment (Ahmed *et al.* 2003).

Far too often, multiculturalism embraces a notion of culture that is inherently naturalistic and anthropological, conceptualized as a 'way of life'. Not surprisingly, therefore, in public policies this focus on 'way of life' is reduced to cultural forms made most visible in language, habits and customs, and iconic objects. This reduction both appeals, and lends itself, to cultural essentialism. By ignoring and obscuring its historical and political construction, multiculturalism thus reifies culture and accords it an autonomous status. This essentialism implies that society is fundamentally constituted by an uninterrupted accord between diverse cultural traditions and that, as a consensual social site, it can accommodate differences in an impartial manner. However, as a number of critics (for example Papastergiadis 2000) have pointed out, this pluralism ignores the workings of power and privilege. It presupposes harmony and agreement as natural states within which differences can coexist without disturbing the prevailing structural norms.

The main problem with this view of intercultural relations is that it interprets difference in terms of negotiations among culturally diverse groups against a backdrop of presumed homogeneity. In doing this, it does not acknowledge that identities are forged in histories based on differentially constituted relations of power; that is, knowledges, subjectivities and social practices, including practices of cultural negotiation, are established within asymmetrical and often incommensurate cultural spaces. This is even more evident in the global context than in a national one. Identity is thus a dynamic relational concept, established by symbolic markings in relation to others. It is therefore a construct, maintained and developed in response to changing social and material conditions. It does not therefore so much frame intercultural relations, but is framed by them.

This brief discussion reveals the complexities inherent in theorizing the relationship between identity and cultural difference. As Jamaican-born English cultural theorist Stuart Hall has argued, identity needs to be understood in terms of a politics of location, positionality and enunciation – not so much as a process of discovery of lost 'roots', but as a construction of a 'new' or 'emergent' form of understanding of ourselves, linked to both contemporary social relations and prevailing relations of power. While most of us clearly want to honour many of the overt aspects of our traditions and history, Hall (1996: 15) suggests that we also need to understand the languages, which we have not been taught to speak. We need to understand and revalue the traditions and inheritances of cultural expressions in new and creative ways because the context of interculturality in which they are expressed is continually changing.

If this is so, societies must accept their cultural condition to be a necessarily complex and 'hybrid' one – and not as something that can be neatly packaged as a collection of ethnicities, for purposes either of administrative convenience or of hegemonic control. The idea of hybridity, with its connotations of mixture and fusion, applies unequivocally to this context, as a space in which we must learn to manage cultural uncertainties as we imagine and project both the national and the global condition. If hybridity is a basic characteristic of cultural globalization, we cannot know cultures in their pristine and authentic form. Instead, our focus must shift to the ways in which cultural forms become separated from existing practices and recombine with new forms, in new practices in their local contexts set against global forces. In a world in which flows of information, media symbols and images, and political and cultural ideas are constant and relentless, new cultural formations are deeply affected. In a world increasingly constituted by flows of finance, technology and people, through tourism, education and migration, hybridization has become a condition of social existence and not something that can be regarded as exceptional.

Policymakers, then, need to reconsider the ways in which the idea of intercultural relations ought to be interpreted and worked with. Such relations are now best explored as complex and inherently unstable products of a range of historical narratives and the contemporary experiences of the cultural economies of globalization. Such cultural economies are increasingly restructuring our established ways of looking and working across cultures, even if some policymakers and institutions appear reluctant to recognize this. And such is the pace of cultural change that the politics of looking and working across cultural differences involves inherent fluidity, indeterminacy and open-endedness. Many educators have of course long understood this, as they work with the complexities of identity that defy the packaging of people into neat and convenient stereotypes, especially now in the age of globalization.

Recent theorists of globalization of culture use the notion of 'deterritorialization' (Tomlinson 2000) to suggest that localities where we live our everyday lives have become implicated in broader global relations. Néstor García Canclini (1998), for example, refers to 'the loss of the "natural" relation of culture to geographical and social territories'. Similarly, Tomlinson suggests a 'weakening or dissolution of the connection between everyday lived culture and territorial location'. Tomlinson argues that increased global mobilities are deterritorializing forces that have the effect of reshaping both the material conditions of people's existence and their perspectives on the world. He insists that this has led to 'the gradual and constant alterations in the cognitive maps of people, in their loyalties and in their frames of social and cultural reference' (Tomlinson 2000: 34). Global mobilities have enabled people to express cultural diversity as dynamic and creative, but they have also led to the homogenization of cultural practices and contributed to some people becoming dislodged from their communities, removed from their social links and obligations. Either way, Tomlinson argues that deterritorialization has been a powerful transformative agency in an era in which borders and boundaries are quickly eroding and becoming more porous.

If this is so, should we not assume that the world will gradually become standardized through technological, cultural and commercial synchronitization? Emanating perhaps from the United States? Our view is, that to assume that cultural globalization is simply another form of Americanization or Westernization is to misread the complex processes involved. It is to assume, for example, that the West, however it is now characterized, remains unaffected by the processes of economic, political and cultural globalization. If our argument has any merit, the local is always transformed as a result of engagement with others, but this transformation is never uniform across cultural sites; globalization produces new hybrid formations that are highly context-specific and localized. As Pieterse (2005: 87) puts it, the cultural uniformity and standardization argument:

> overlooks the counter-currents – the impact that the non-Western cultures have been making on the Western cultural practices. It downplays the ambivalence of the globalizing momentum and ignores the role of local reception of Western cultures, for example, the indigenization of Western elements.

It overlooks the fact that different parts of the same community may relate differently to the same social processes.

If the response to global pressures is characterized by much variability, it is hard to ignore the conclusion that interculturality is always political; and it underlines the processes of fuzziness, cut-and-mix and criss-cross and crossovers of cultural identity, which have often been referred to as the processes of cultural hybridization. But hybridization is never neutral; it involves a politics in which issues of economic and cultural power are central. As Shohat and Stam (1994) have argued, 'A celebration of syncretism and hybridity *per se*, if not articulated with the issues of hegemony and neo-colonial power relations, always runs the risk of appearing to sanctify the *fait accompli* of colonial violence.' As a theoretical idea, hybridity is indeed a useful antidote to cultural essentialism, but cannot in itself provide the answers to the difficult questions of how hybridity takes place, the form it takes in a particular context, the consequences it has for particular sections of the community, and when and how particular hybrid formations are progressive or regressive.

These political questions of hybridity need to be placed within the broader politics of how globalization is helping to reshape people's sense of themselves and others. As we have suggested, through accumulation strategies, mobility and modern mass media, people are no longer linked just to one place, but through their transnational connections and imagination may identify with a number of locations. Globalization has engendered complex, shifting and fragmented subjectivities that are at once local, yet also global. This demands new kinds of social organization that are deterritorialized, flexible and mobile. At the same time, globalization has resulted in the proliferation of new commodity markets which promote new lifestyles and create consumers whose cultural identities are defined by their association with products rather than with their obligations to particular communities.

A new education policy agenda needs to take account of these changing conditions. But here too we confront a number of dilemmas. While we might support initiatives that recognize shifting and hybrid cultural practices, we cannot afford to simply valorize difference and hybridity, allowing such practices to be shaped by transnational cultural markets, media and capital. In recent years neoliberal states have indeed celebrated the emergence of global markets in the production, consumption and distribution of cultural diversity, consistent with the imperatives of what has been referred to as 'globalization from above'. But nor has the state been able to overlook the realities of other practices of globalization, 'globalization from below', which involve the criss-crossing transnational circuits of communication, the contested practices of place-making, the resistance of power differentials and the making of new identities with their corresponding fields of difference.

Academic mobility

Nowhere have the issues of cultural diversity been more seriously addressed than in universities. They have become centres of struggle over identity and cultural meaning, as they deal with issues arising from the changing demography on their campuses. They have also had to meet the challenges of globalization and the knowledge economy, and prepare students for workplaces that are increasingly transnational and transcultural. At the same time, they have viewed the global mobility of people as a new opportunity. Over the past two decades, higher education systems around the world have thus worked vigorously to develop policies that promote academic mobility, with the support of both governments and international organizations.

Of course, there has always been international mobility of students and researchers in search of new knowledge and training, where this is not available within the nation. Higher education was only available to very talented students in countries of the South if they went abroad. The countries of the North, on the other hand, provided scholarships to assist students from poorer countries, as part of programmes of overseas aid and in line with the responsibilities they felt they had to help in the nation-building projects of the newly independent countries of the developing world. An example of such a commitment was the Colombo Plan, developed in the 1950s. Designed primarily as a foreign aid programme, it highlighted the commitment of the developed countries within the British Commonwealth to ameliorate economic distress in Asia and help create local elites needed to develop the social, administrative and economic infrastructure of the developing countries in Asia (Oakman 2005). It was also linked to the strategic interests of the developed countries within the broader politics of the Cold War. Within this geopolitical context a large number of students were educated in the former USSR, while programmes like the Colombo Plan provided financial aid to students in developing countries around the world to attend First World universities.

However, the educational rationale underlying international education was largely concerned with the development of skills, attitudes and knowledge so that, upon their return, graduates could make a robust contribution to national development. The purposes of international education were thus defined in terms of the need to increase intercultural knowledge and to enhance the level of international cooperation. In this way equal weight was given to the economic, political and cultural purposes of education. Even as late as the 1980s, IGOs such as the OECD and UNESCO sought to define the complex idea of internationalization by seeking to reconcile its commercial and economic concerns with issues of cultural diversity and interpersonal dimensions of global relations (Marginson and McBurnie 2004). It was suggested that internationalization was important to the development of universities because changes represented by globalization demanded it. For individuals, on the other hand, international education was motivated not only by emerging labour market opportunities, but also by considerations of personal and social development.

Over the past two decades there has emerged, however, a contrasting discourse of academic mobility, which involves viewing international education more as a matter of global trade than as overseas aid. The discourse of internationalization of education has thus shifted, with the introduction of a set of market principles to guide its practices. Education is now increasingly viewed as 'an export industry', driven by a growing demand for international education, most notably in the fast-developing economies of Asia. This has enabled countries such as the UK and Australia to set themselves up as major suppliers. According to Marginson and McBurnie (2004), the growing demand for international education is simultaneously 'a cause, consequence and symptom of globalization'. It responds to the need of industries at the cutting edge of the knowledge economy, such as ICT, financial management, science and engineering, in which the demand for globally mobile labour is growing at a rapid rate. Since most governments are unable to meet this need through public funds, a global market in education has emerged. Those developed countries that have strong traditions of higher education have been a major beneficiary of this development. In the developed countries, universities have seen student moblity as a major source of revenue to replace the declining levels of public funds. Indeed, universities in Australia and the UK have now become highly dependent on income generated from international students, and have developed complex marketing structures to sustain this source of revenue. Countries such as Singapore, Malaysia, India and Japan are now seeking to follow their example, and have developed a range of policy initiatives to enter this lucrative market.

Data on student flows in and out of the Asia-Pacific countries for education shows spectacular patterns of growth (Marginson 2006). Universities in the

USA, Australia and the UK are the main providers of education for globally mobile students, while India and China are emerging as main source countries from where students go abroad for their higher education. Indeed, the English-speaking countries are the beneficiaries of almost 80 per cent of the world's globally mobile students (Guruz 2008). In contrast, very few Australian, American and British students enrol in universities in the developing world. The flow is thus largely one-directional (Marginson 2006), confirming a pattern in the global knowledge distribution that appears to have a language: English.

The reasons for student demand for international education in the Asia-Pacific region vary considerably, and include lack of opportunities for higher education in their own countries; particular national policies, such as affirmative action policies in Malaysia, which favour Bumiputras and force many ethnic Chinese students to seek higher education abroad (Rizvi 2000); and perceptions concerning the changing patterns of opportunities within the globally changing labour market. It is assumed, for example, that those with good English and international experience have a better chance of getting well-paying jobs, especially in transnational corporations. There is also a growing interest in cosmopolitan experiences, together with a sense that in a globally networked world, those with intercultural skills and an international outlook are better equipped to benefit from the global knowledge-based economy. And finally, strong economic growth in both China and India over the past decades has created a strong middle class for whom international education has become a status marker and an object of desire.

Around such sentiments, there has emerged a powerful new discourse of internationalization which seeks to redefine the ways in which universities need to engage with the 'imperatives' of globalization. This discourse points to the commercial opportunities offered by the increasing movement of people, capital and ideas. It encourages a new kind of knowledge about international relations and programmes based on a neoliberal imaginary of the global economy, which is assumed to be knowledge-based and requires increased levels of intercultural communication. Alongside, a new administrative technology of global marketing of education and recruitment has emerged (Sidhu 2005). As with other industries, this technology has its own rules of operation based on expertise that incorporates knowledge of market segments and specificities, as well as promotional language about the distinctive benefits of internationalization. Within universities that attract a large of number of international students, it involves the creation of highly specialized structures and functions responsible for international operations; for example, well developed advertising and marketing programmes conducted not only through the media, but also through educational expos and market-orientated conferences at which education is bought and sold.

In promoting these discourses and practices, governments and IGOs play an important role. To manage global flows of students, many governments have developed policies for regulating cross-border mobility of students, and have established programmes designed to encourage international linkages, cooperation and trade. In the so-called exporter nations such as Australia and the UK, the main policy objective has been to sustain the flow of income derived from international student fees, through not only targeted advertising, but also a national system of quality assurance, and even developing immigration programmes designed to favour international graduates in particular fields of labour shortage. In contrast, the so-called importer countries have developed policies that have involved monitoring cross-border trade in education, in an attempt to protect consumers of international education. There has emerged also a complex web of bilateral and multilateral regional arrangements between countries that encourage academic mobility. An example of such an arrangement is the Bologna Process, which involves a commitment by ministers responsible for higher education from European countries, which now number 46, to reform their higher education systems in order to 'harmonize' their structures in an effort to both encourage and facilitate academic mobility.

Despite these arrangements, international trade in education continues to be surrounded by a great deal of policy confusion, concerning not only issues of capacity, volume, commitment, balance, orientation and quality of international programmes, but also issues relating to the rules by which educational trade should be conducted. At the global level, many governments have insisted on the need of an international agreement governing commercially-driven academic mobility. It is upon this insistence that the General Agreement on Trade in Services (GATS) within the World Trade Organization (WTO) is based. GATS is designed to specify a range of conditions under which global trade in education is to be pursued. These conditions include such matters as transparency of rules; liberalization of markets; elimination of practices acting as barriers to trade and student mobility; and the development of rules for resolving disputes. Now while in one sense these rules appear perfectly sensible, from another perspective they serve a more ideological function, of institutionalizing a particular way of looking at international education, defined in terms of the efficiency of global markets in education rather than in terms of international education's more general political, social and cultural purposes.

The main assumption underlying GATS is that education is a commodified service, in which trade is not only possible but desirable. In terms of this neoliberal imaginary, it is assumed that trade in education should not be subject to national restrictions. Jane Knight (2002) has called this phenomenon 'trade creep' in higher education, driven by an increased emphasis on the market economy and the liberalization of rules governing trade in both goods and services. Of course, in an era of globalization, this emphasis is enmeshed with other market-orientated trends in higher education. Knight (ibid.) suggests that:

> These trends include the growing number of private for-profit entities providing higher education opportunities domestically and internationally; the use

> of information and communications technologies (ICTs) for domestic and cross-border delivery of programs; the increasing costs and tuition fees faced by students at public and private institutions; and the need for public institutions to seek alternate sources of funding, which sometime means engaging in for-profit activities or seeking private sector sources of financial support. (p7)

These trends appear well entrenched in higher education systems in most of the Asian-Pacific countries, raising issues of social efficiency, such as modes of funding and student support, regulation of private and public cross-border providers, recognition and transferability of credits and quality assurance, ahead of some of the traditional concerns of education such as access and equity. This policy shift has a number of important implications for education in the developing countries.

The heavily commercial character of international education, for example, serves to reproduce global inequalities in education. Under earlier programmes of international education such as the Colombo Plan, universities in the developed countries provided access to a large number of students from poorer, less developed countries. But in a market regime, the number of financially sponsored students has dwindled markedly, further widening the skills gap between the industrialized and industrializing countries and poorer countries, whose economic prospects have declined further. This again exemplifies the globally uneven and asymmetrical nature of student flows within the global market of international education. Marginson (2006) has noted the magnetic attraction of American higher education, and has argued that the UK, Australia, Canada and New Zealand sit 'in the American slipstream, operating on a more entrepreneurial basis than American institutions. They gain the referred power as lesser English-language providers and sites for migration, often in a transitional stage in passage to the USA.'

This presents a major dilemma for universities in the countries of the South of how to deal with this global phenomenon of Western dominance, how to diversify their own student base and provide opportunities to those of their talented students who are marginalized by commercialization, and what remedial actions to take to stop the economic and social haemorrhaging caused by the new global geometry of power, manifest in the dominant version of the internationalization of higher education.

Internationalization of curriculum

This emphasis on global mobility of students is part of a broader policy discourse in education that has emerged around the world. This discourse highlights the importance of internationalizing the curriculum as a way of engaging with the complex processes of globalization. The idea of the 'internationalization of curriculum' has become something of a slogan within modern corporatized educational systems. One does not have to look far to find it in the mission statements of most leading universities, from Austria to

Australia, from the United States to the United Arab Emirates, as well as in the policy advice of most IGOs. As Olson *et al.* (2006) for the American Council on Education, for example, suggest, in the global context it is now necessary to renovate the curriculum, making it more responsive to the compelling requirements of globalization. Curriculum must now be characterized by its international content, its engagement with the global circuits of knowledge and communication.

What this suggests is that internationalization is relevant not only to those students who are globally mobile, but to everyone. In a global economy, cultural understanding and 'an international outlook' are important for all, crucial among students and academics alike. This is so because internationalized curricula are based on the values of innovation, flexibility, client-centredness and enterprise culture on the one hand and intercultural understanding and sensitivity on the other. This rhetoric is particularly strident among regional and intergovernmental organizations such as UNESCO, the OECD and the European Union (EU). The EU, for example, has long highlighted measures to support student mobility and cooperation between member states and others. The Union's ERASMUS, SOCRATES and LEONARDO programmes are based on the principles of internationalization, as a way of not only supporting structural cooperation but also promoting curriculum development and the creation of networks and credit transfer arrangements. In order to internationalize its curriculum, suggests UNESCO (2002), the university must:

> express its knowledge work in a new and changed environment. If the university is to serve well both scholarship and national needs, if it is to prepare graduates for this new era, the university is obligated to modernize and to contribute to the global exchange of knowledge through the movement of people, information, and ideas.

Now while the appeal of the idea of internationalization of curriculum appears ubiquitous, its policy effects are less clear. It is not always clear what it means and how it might represent a new way of prioritizing and organizing learning. Most of its definitions lack specificity. So, for example, they do not specify how the notion of an 'international orientation' might be interpreted, and how the efficacy and relevance of international content might be judged. An inventory of initiatives undertaken to internationalize curriculum appears to suggest that most initiatives fall under three interrelated categories: facilitating study abroad and educational exchange to broaden and enrich students' cultural experiences; learning about other languages and cultures as a way of developing their skills of intercultural communication; and preparing graduates to work in the global knowledge economy. Each of these measures is supposed to contribute to the realization of the others.

Administratively, study abroad programs represent a most pragmatic, quick and achievable way of internationalizing the curriculum. They do not require any significant structural changes to the existing curriculum, and can always be 'added on' as options provided to students within an existing programme. Because of their high visibility, moreover, institutions can claim success, even if the benefits of study abroad programmes cannot be easily demonstrated. A second way educational systems have sought to internationalize the curriculum is by encouraging the teaching of languages and cultures other than one's own. The contention here is that learning about other cultures broadens students' experiences, and is also a means through which intercultural exchange and understanding can be promoted. If the global mobility of people has made most communities diverse and if the global flow of ideas and media has made cultural insularity and isolation impossible, then, it is suggested, university curriculum cannot afford to ignore these cultural realities.

And finally the development of skills of intercultural competence is considered key to internationalizing the curriculum, especially in professional disciplines such as Economics and Business Studies. This focus is based on a particular interpretation of the requirements of the global economy. In a knowledge-based and service-orientated economy, it is argued, knowing facts and theories is less important than an understanding of the world of cultural and social relations and the networks through which knowledge is converted into innovation and commercially viable products. This has led to an emphasis on developing in students a 'global competence' that enables them to become globally mobile and work in a range of different cultural contexts. It has also underscored the need to develop qualifications less geared towards the demands of the national labour market and more towards international requirements, suggesting curricular frameworks that are globally networked and fully utilize the possibilities of new information and communication technologies.

Initiatives around study abroad, intercultural understanding and global competence clearly hold out considerable potential for internationalizing the curriculum, even if they are difficult to implement in a coherent and systematic institution-wide fashion. They represent attempts to prepare students for a world in which the nature of work and labour processes and cultural exchange are constantly changing, as a result not only of shifts in the global knowledge economy and social relations, but also of rapid advances in information technologies. Preparing students to negotiate these changes is clearly worthwhile. However, promising though these initiatives are, their potential cannot be fully realized without conceptual thinking that is more systematic, addressing a range of issues both practical and theoretical about the broader curriculum architecture within which the ideas of study abroad, cultural exchange and global competence might be located.

The proposition that study abroad programmes promote a more cosmopolitan outlook among students, leading them to become culturally sensitive is, for example, often asserted but seldom demonstrated. The research on the outcomes of study abroad programmes is at best limited. Much of it relates to questions of access to these programmes and to the administrative arrangements involved in their implementation. Very little of it examines the assumptions underlying study abroad programmes. Much of it assumes that they are intrinsically good, and that global mobility will necessarily produce a cosmopolitan outlook in everyone alike, regardless of their gender, race and socio-economic background, or their prior learning. There is very little examination of study abroad experiences as a curriculum issue. Nor is there any assessment of the conditions necessary for ensuring their curricular success, beyond their value as educational tourism.

Beyond issues of administration, there are more serious issues surrounding study abroad programmes, relating not only to questions of access and educational experience, but also to issues concerning the development of transnational networks and the global politics of cultural knowledge and communication. Here, questions of which students go on study abroad programmes, and where, are crucial. Evidence suggests that much of the study abroad traffic is within the developed world (Clyne and Rizvi 1998), and that the universities in the countries of the North generally fail to develop effective sustainable exchange arrangements with universities in the developing world. This does little to help students explore broader issues of global inequalities. Despite much talk about global interconnectivity and interdependence, international contact remains within globally differentiated cultural communities – the west versus the rest. Insofar as mobility is considered a major characteristic of the current phase of globalization, the circulation of students through study abroad programmes appears to reproduce asymmetrical power relations within the world community.

It is within the context of these power relations that the objectives of learning about other cultures and developing intercultural communication skills are located. These objectives are based on the recognition that under contemporary conditions of mass migration and other forms of mobility, both of people and ideas, all communities are exposed to the growing flows of cultural meanings and knowledge emanating from other societies. Advances in information and communication technologies have made it almost impossible for people to remain isolated, and we 'now have the means to access rapidly far greater quantities of cultural meanings of every kind than ever before and from a multiplicity of sources' (Cohen and Kennedy 2007: 27). We live in a world in which our consumerist tastes converge and our cultural traditions come into contact with others, but in ways that are not always easy to reconcile. This demands an approach to the curriculum that helps students to develop skills of intercultural communication, dialogue and negotiation through learning about other cultures.

Now while this goal is indeed important, the social imaginary within which it is located is at best limited. To begin with, it interprets the need to learn about other cultures largely in instrumental economic terms. Cultural meanings are thus reduced to the benefits that students are able to accrue within the global marketplace. In the process, it converts students into economic units, with the implication that only those aspects of other cultures that are commercially productive are worthy of attention. This approach to internationalization has become commonplace in business schools around the world. But the consequences of this approach are that only the superficial aspects of a cultural tradition are learnt, making much learning appear patronizing, especially to marginalized groups and nations. A further risk associated with this view is the temptation to assume an inherently naturalistic and reified view of culture.

If knowledge of, and ability to interact productively with, people from quite different cultural backgrounds, both within one's own society and across the globe, are desirable educational goals, cultural traditions need to be viewed as dynamic and creative, and cultural relations as always contingent and historically specific. The focus must be on learning not so much about cultural traditions, but about the modalities of cultural interactions, how these are produced across differing political and economic interests, and how these have differential consequences for different individuals and communities. The notion of 'the requirements of the global economy' itself needs to be deconstructed, as do the ideological assumptions about the nature of individuals and societies that are implied by the idea of 'global competence'. Crucially important here are the questions of competence 'for what ends', 'to do what', 'in whose interests', 'with what consequences' and 'what cultural knowledge is most worthwhile'.

Globalization of English

The issues of global academic mobility and research collaborations are inextricably linked to the globalization of English. According to a UNESCO report (2002), no discussion of internationalization of curriculum is possible without examining the role that the English language now plays in economic, political and cultural exchanges. It notes that, facing the challenges of globalization, education systems around the world are paying 'special attention to foreign languages, first and foremost it is English' (ibid.: 47–48). The report goes on to say that the choice of language in education policy is 'largely driven by the demands of the international labour market, in particular in the field of ICTs and science'. In this way, the rationale for the English language in education policies is framed almost exclusively in terms of system efficiency and the requirements of the market. This is so because English has not only become the most common medium for communication in a global world, but it is also assumed to provide job opportunities, access to higher education and a broader flow of information in business negotiations. It has become the primary medium for communication in science and technology.

In Cohen and Kennedy's (2007: 88) view, the use of English as a world language 'has fostered the emergence of a world society'. English has often been called an international lingua franca. This rise accompanies Anglo-American hegemony, with the USA dominating mass media and advertising, shaping consumer tastes and lifestyle aspirations of people, especially the young, around the world. As the global economy has grown, so has its reliance on English as a world language. Between 80 and 90 per cent of the world's academic papers are written in English. Cohen and Kennedy (ibid.) have shown that while the number of people speaking English as their first language rose from 377 million in 1990 to 400 million in 2004, the number of people who spoke English as their second language rose in the same period to 600 million, and that number is likely to double by 2050. More people will still speak Chinese and Hindi, but the use of English is likely to grow at a much faster rate, and it is likely to remain the most dominant language in the foreseeable future.

Educational systems around the world have taken note of these trends, and have shaped their policies to reflect the global dominance of English. In the countries of the South Pacific, for example, English is the predominant official medium of instruction, even if few people use it at home. In Polynesia, although a native language is the medium of instruction in primary education, English is generally introduced as a subject early, often in the first or second year of primary school. In most of Melanesia, English is the sole recognized medium of instruction, and in Fiji, Fijian and Hindi are mediums of instruction for the first three years, but are subsequently entirely replaced by English (Lynch and Mugler 2004). This trend is becoming almost universal, with systems around the world making English as a second language compulsory at an increasingly early stage. In Korea, the age at which English is introduced has recently been reduced from 12 to 9 years of age. Similarly in China, in 2001, the age at which English is offered as a second language was lowered from 11 to 9 years old (Kaplan and Baldauf 2003: 37). In Malaysia, all maths and science are taught in English.

It is not only the national systems of education that have promoted English; international organizations have also been active. At a meeting in 2004, the Asia-Pacific Economic Cooperation (APEC) Ministers of Education developed a formal agreement about English in which they encouraged officially offering the teaching of English as a foreign language starting from the first to fifth grades. They also emphasized the need to enhance the training programmes for English teachers in elementary schools, together with revision of curricula, and teaching materials to be more communicative in approach. They suggested reducing elementary school class sizes to no more than 35 students and connecting all elementary schools to the Internet by providing computers in all classrooms. These policy goals were directly linked to that of improving levels of English, which it was assumed would help in meeting the challenges of the new era of information technology and the knowledge economy.

There is thus a clear policy trend toward lowering the age of English instruction around the world, as well as an increase in those courses for which English is the medium of instruction, particularly in science, mathematics, technology, finance and business. This trend is accompanied by the development of a huge private industry in the teaching of English, with the emergence of a parallel education system that offers English as an after-school enrichment activity. Some of these private schools are tiny one-person enterprises, while others like Sylvan Learning Centres represent a large multinational corporation. Universities in English-speaking countries, as well as organizations such as the British Council, have also benefited financially from the rise of English as a world language, both recruiting international students eager to learn English and often also setting up offshore operations, even campuses. This desire to learn English, especially in fast-developing countries such as Korea, is based on a conviction that English is necessary for success in the global economy, and that the ability to use English effectively ensures a market advantage.

The local effects of this relentless drive towards English are hard to assess. There is no indication that the global rise of English has led to any significant decline in the use of local languages. On the contrary, there is some evidence to suggest that the world is increasingly becoming multilingual, that students can readily learn two or more languages and find it easy to switch usage, and that multilingualism might even help them to acquire cognitive flexibility. Indeed, as Crystal (1997) has argued, the desire for a globally common language and the desire to preserve local languages, and by extension cultural identities, are not mutually exclusive. He points also to the emergence of a variety of 'New Englishes', as English dialects are transformed by localized uses. A language, it needs to be recognized, is a dynamic phenomenon that changes through interaction with other linguistic traditions, producing new hybridized forms. At the same time, 'global English' also appears to be emerging. This is the product of a range of factors, including the global dominance of American popular culture, new patterns of communication across national boundaries, the use of English in academic and business discourses, efforts to standardize English through various testing regimes such as the International English Language Testing System (IELTS), and of course language used by the new technologies.

It also needs to be recognized that as a contemporary phenomenon, the global rise of English has been driven by British imperialism and the ascension of the US economy following the Second World War. While it is true that forms of English have become multiple and hybridized, it is also true that English is an instrument of global hegemony. This is clearly evident in the fact that while the rest of the world is becoming multilingual, this trend is resisted in English-speaking countries, where a decline in second language learning has been noted. If access to English education is a condition of success in the global economy, it can also be a source that perpetuates or exacerbates the economic divide within and across nations. We might ponder, therefore, a range of questions raised by Alistair Pennycook (2001):

> ... we need always to consider the larger context of what we are doing, the cultural, political, social and economic implications of language programs. What might language development in English mean for other languages? What might

> it mean for the representation of culture? What forms of culture and knowledge may it privilege and what may it deny? What world is opened up by an education through English? How might English be a language that allows us to be more rather than just to have more? (p22)

Brain drain

In this chapter we have noted how increasing levels of global mobility of people have presented policymakers with a range of opportunities and challenges. One of these challenges relates to the consequences of mobility of highly skilled workers across national boundaries. National governments in developing countries have a deep anxiety about the loss to the more developed countries of their talented workers, in whom they have invested heavily through education. Some of these governments have been forced to develop specific policies and programmes to encourage the return of emigrants. Of course, this anxiety is not new, and issues around which it revolves date back to the 1950s when the concept 'brain drain' was first coined. But in the era of globalization these issues now present themselves in new forms. In a global economy, people understandably aspire to live and work in places which can provide them with greater financial and other rewards.

This creates a range of dilemmas for policymakers in developed and developing countries alike. The developed countries seek to attract skilled immigrants, on the one hand, but insist on preventing the unfettered movement of people such as refugees on the other. Equally, while some developing countries have become increasingly reliant for their economic sustainability on remittances sent home by emigrants, they find that this cannot be a long-term solution to their social and economic development. They are attracted to the so-called 'diaspora option' (Meyer and Brown 2003), which seeks to create networks which enable skilled emigrants to still remain effectively and productively connected to their country of origin. But this new network logic seems trapped within an asymmetrical world economic order, in which the mobility of people is limited to those who possess expertise needed in the global economy.

The rate of skilled migration from developing to developed countries has increased significantly under the conditions of globalization. International organizations such as the World Bank, the United Nations Development Program (UNDP), the International Labour Organization (ILO) and the Organization for Economic Cooperation and Development (OECD) have noted this trend with alarm. A report of the World Bank, *Constructing Knowledge Societies: New Challenges for Tertiary Education* (2002), for example, has expressed concern at the rapidly increasingly rates of emigration of knowledge workers from the developing countries, depriving these nations of the conditions necessary to sustain their universities. The report suggests the emergence of a global 'knowledge divide' which will inevitably delay economic growth in developing countries. According to a study by the International Monetary Fund (Carrington and

Detragiache 1998), the annual rate of skilled emigration, defined as people with university degrees, from Africa over the past decade is over 30 per cent. Sizable 'brain drain' from Mexico, Iran, Korea, the Philippines and Taiwan has also been reported. The levels of 'brain drain' from India and China to OECD countries via international education have slowed over the past decade, but remain significant.

The debate among development and migration economists over the impact of this 'brain drain' on economic growth is intense. Various economic models have been developed to examine the relations between education, emigration and national productivity. Since education is widely regarded as a major determinant of long-term economic growth, it has long been argued that the migration of people with high levels of human capital is detrimental to the country of emigration. The negative impact of 'brain drain' on developing countries has been stressed in the so-called New Growth literature (for example Miyagiwa 1991), which emphasizes the cumulative effects of skilled migration on productivity. According to Wong and Yip (1999), the 'brain drain' not only affects the growth rate of a developing country, but also has a negative impact on infrastructure, education and income distribution of an economy.

In contrast, some researchers challenge this view, suggesting that 'brain drain' may in fact be good for the developing economies. Mountford (1997), for example, argues that the 'brain drain' may in fact increase average productivity and equality in the source economy. He has asserted that temporary emigration in particular may in fact permanently increase the average level of productivity of an economy. Another economic model suggests that 'optimal brain drain' can be shown to increase a developing country's average productivity, especially if the worker returns after gaining expertise and skills in a more advanced economy (Johnson and Regets 1998). Research has also indicated that when skilled emigrants send part of their earnings abroad back to their country of origin, the remittances have 'GDP multiplier effects' that increase national income (Taylor 2006).

Just as the issues relating to the economic impact of 'brain drain' are hotly debated, so is the question of how policymakers should respond. One option has been to recognize that nothing much can be done about it, and that in the end the global labour market will prevail. However, most developing countries have been more proactive in attempts to reverse the 'brain drain' with a range of measures, including restrictive policies aimed at delaying emigration through various taxation regimes. Various systems of incentives that encourage international students to return home, sometimes to lucrative positions in their own areas of expertise, have been developed. Another strategy has involved bilateral and multilateral arrangements under which wealthy countries pledge not to recruit skilled people from developing nations. Other agreements require international students to work for a certain period of time in their home country before they can apply to emigrate. Another increasingly popular option involves the construction of 'diaspora networks' that enable emigrants to make a contribution to economic and social development at home, no matter where they live.

This diaspora option (Meyer and Brown 2003) is based on a particular understanding of the relationship between social identities and the nation-state under the conditions of globalization. The 'turbulence' of mobility, Papastergiadis (2000) argues, has had a range of unpredictable consequences both for individuals and for nation-states. The commitment of people to the development of their countries of origin has become destabilized, and can no longer be taken for granted. If we resist the temptation to theorize globalization in an abstract manner, it does not merely refer to the construction of a global economic space but also to the restructuring and extension of networks of money, technologies, people and ideas and of their articulations with real spaces at different scales. The movement of people leads to the emergence of transnational diasporic networks that are spatially and temporally specific, and involve socially constructed relations of power and meaning. We can no longer ignore how social identities are linked to transnational communication circuits, and if this is so, people are able to think about being affiliated with more than one place at the same time. The assumption that there is a one-to-one relation between territoriality and citizenship can no longer be sustained. Movements of people cannot, moreover, be assumed to involve a zero-sum game, because nation-states have never been completely homogeneous entities, and are being reshaped by global processes; the loss of expertise in one country does not necessarily mean its gain in another.

Against this analysis, the concept of 'brain drain' is highly problematic. The issue is no longer where people are physically located, but what contribution they are able to make to the social, cultural and economic development of the (multiple) countries with which they identify. Global mobility of skilled people is now both a consequence and a necessary stimulus to sustain the processes of economic and cultural globalization. The increasingly globalized knowledge economy demands circulation of knowledge workers and brokers (Cao 1996). This is as important for the developed countries as it is for the developing economies. If this is so, it is suggested by a number of policy scholars such as Meyer and Brown (2003) that for the developing countries to benefit from the knowledge economy, the physical location of people is immaterial so long as the developing economies are able to draw upon their expertise, regardless of where they live. More important is the need to create links through which skilled emigrants could remain effectively and productively connected to their country of origin.

Of course, in many ways the diaspora option is not new. Relationships between expatriates and their countries of origin have often existed in the past. In recent years, many of these links have been formalized into such networks as Arab Scientists and Technologists Abroad (ASTA) and the Association of Latin American Scientists (ALAS). Many of the members of such networks prefer to speak not of 'brain drain' but of 'brain circulation', underlining the importance they attach to the role of vibrant, virtual and global networks of professionals in imagining and pursuing national development, consistent with the imperatives of a global knowledge economy. Important as these developments are, however, a range of problems is associated with such networks. As Teferra (2004) has pointed out, brain circulation is still characterized by its sporadic, exceptional and limited nature. Most of these networks have short lifespans, and fail to become systematic, dense and productive. Among those of the networks who have not had extensive opportunities to travel and live abroad, there remains a great deal of resentment towards those who have; and the attitude of emigrants towards their own country of origin often appears arrogant and patronizing.

Beyond these social and technical problems, there is a more fundamental issue: that the space within which brain circulation takes place is not a neutral one, but is characterized by uneven distributions of opportunities and asymmetrical flows of power. The notion of brain circulation rests on an assumption that the new knowledge economy is potentially less exploitative of developing countries than was the old economy. While it is true that the globally integrated knowledge economy requires the development of greater transnational collaboration, and mobility among skilled workers, it is still based on modes of capital ownership and production that are inherently unequal. The substitution of the concept of 'brain drain' with that of 'brain circulation' does not solve this problem. However, what it does demonstrate is that under the conditions of globalization, the notion of 'brain drain' needs to be reconceptualized in more contemporary terms, because issues of mobility now present themselves in markedly different ways. Mobility has the potential to reshape social identities, and requires new ways of thinking about relations between globally mobile people and their social obligations to the nation-state.

Conclusion

In this chapter we have shown how globalization has given rise to increasing levels of mobility, not only of capital and finance, images, information and ideologies, but also of people. For education policymakers this has presented both opportunities and challenges. It has led them to consider how global resources can be used to expand educational opportunities, and how the cosmopolitan possibilities of education might be realized. But the global mobility of people has also created a range of policy dilemmas: how to deal with the cultural diversity that mobility has enhanced; how to encourage academic flows without exploiting them; how to internationalize the curriculum; how to develop language policies that are respectful of all linguistic and cultural traditions; and how to support international mobility of skilled people without leaving poorer countries bereft of the talent and expertise they need to ensure sustainable development. Sadly, many of the policy solutions to these dilemmas remain trapped within the neoliberal social imaginary that has either reproduced or even extended existing patterns of global inequalities and eliminated any potential that education might have for socially just social transformation. In the concluding chapter we will examine some of the ways in which various communities and social movements are resisting this imaginary in order to forge alternatives to hegemonic neoliberal globalization.

9 Imagining other globalizations

Introduction

We have demonstrated throughout this book that a particular social imaginary of globalization, namely neoliberalism, has underpinned education policy shifts around the world over the last two decades. It is this imaginary that has been at the base of a global trend toward policy convergence in education. This has been evident in both policy means and policy ends, but always in ways that are mediated by politics, history and culture at national and local levels. Policy processes, we have argued, work differently across the Global North/Global South divide, in vernacular ways at local and national levels. We have suggested, however, that these processes are located within a global architecture of political relations that not only involves national governments, but also IGOs, transnational corporations and NGOs. Policies are developed, enacted and evaluated in various global networks from where their authority is now partly derived. In this sense, neoliberal policy preferences in education are articulated at the intersection of local, national, regional and global spaces.

Underpinning the neoliberal view of education is a particular conception of the individual, which education is expected to help produce. Nikolas Rose (1999: 160–161) has brilliantly captured this conception in relation to the new or emergent education policy paradigm:

> Education is no longer confined to 'schooling', with its specialized institutional sites and discrete biographical locus. The disciplinary individualization and normalization of the school sought to install, once and for all, the capacities and competencies for social citizenship. But a new set of educational obligations are emerging that are not confined in space and time in the same ways. The new citizen is required to engage in a ceaseless work of training and retraining, skilling and reskilling, enhancement of credentials and preparation for a life of incessant job seeking: life is to become a continuous economic capitalization of the self.

It is the self-responsibilizing, self-capitalizing individual that is the desired product of neoliberal education policy reforms. The notion of a self-governing individual also underpins Foucault's (1991) conception of governmentality, an effect of government and governance. This emphasis on self-capitalizing required across the entire life-cycle replaces the older, more liberal humanist and social democratic constructions of education which were underpinned by education's multiple purposes. The best economic outcomes for a nation are now deemed to flow from the production of individuals pursuing their self-interest. This is a conception of human beings as at base individual economic beings, an account that fails to recognize the collective social and cultural aspects of human behaviour. This has led to a greater focus on the market as the site where education policy is best negotiated. The state's role in policy development has been reduced to ensuring that markets work efficiently and enhance the choices of 'citizen-consumers'.

However, as we have argued, this perspective on education has had major social consequences, benefiting some individuals and communities while further marginalizing the poor and the socially disadvantaged. This is so because the neoliberal social imaginary upon which this policy framework generally is based, has rejected the need for redistributive policies, extensive social protection and measures to ensure equality of educational opportunity. Until the Thatcher and Reagan regimes in the1980s, the Keynesian settlement in most liberal democracies had meant that education was a principal means for ensuring social justice, meritocracy and social cohesion. In that settlement the state, through public policy, intervened against the market in providing 'social protection' for vulnerable citizens and equality of opportunity for all. Neoliberalism views education differently, placing a greater focus on market efficiency and individual liberty. The values of community and social justice are now replaced by the principles of the market economy and citizen-consumer choice, not only in the west but elsewhere as well. Even in China and Vietnam, where Communist Parties rule, the idea of a 'socialist market economy' has become dominant, framed by a vernacular version of neoliberalism.

In Chapter 4 we argued that all public policies embody the values of efficiency, equity, community, liberty and security, but that the way in which these values are assembled and allocated varies across time and across national policy regimes. Much depends not only on how these values are politically mediated by particular national traditions, but also on how they are discursively formed within particular social imaginaries. As we have demonstrated throughout this book, in the contemporary world the dominant social imaginary has been neoliberalism, even as its hegemony is being challenged by the global financial crisis. In a country like India, for example, education policy was until recently informed by a mix of Gandhian post-colonial sentiments and initiatives designed to modernize and industrialize the nation, in a strictly planned manner with Soviet-style five-year plans (Pathak 2006). Education policy was thus located within a national imaginary about India's economic and social development. In more recent decades India too has embraced a neoliberal imaginary, with the values of market efficiency becoming dominant as issues of equity and community have been sidelined. A commitment to the notion of equity has not been entirely abandoned, but its meaning has been re-articulated as simply access to society's institutions, the responsibility for which lies largely with individuals themselves.

Stephen Klees (2008: 1) has documented a range of policy initiatives in education consistent with the neoliberal focus 'on the efficiency of a free-market system and the associated role of the public sector' supported by the World Bank and other international organizations. These initiatives include: cost-recovery and user pays principles; the introduction of school fees even at primary schools; an emphasis on primary education on the assumption that economic returns are greater there than from investment in secondary and tertiary education; putting a budget cap on public funding of education; encouragement of privatization policies and voucher schemes; the introduction of performance management and budgeting schemes; output-based calculations for providing support to education; merit pay for teachers and educational administrators; greater freedom of choice for parents; standardized tests to facilitate this choice within and across national systems; various other performance contracting schemes; and decentralization of education delivery against a set of nationally agreed goals and curriculum expectations.

Almost all of these policy initiatives rest on market efficiency. Significantly, around the world, education has become central to the production of the requisite human capital needed to achieve the maximum competitiveness within the global economy for individuals and nations alike. The dominant values underpinning education policy have been individualistic and economistic in character. Governments, international organizations and transnational corporations have promoted this view of education, using a symbolic and magisterial rhetoric that suggests that there is no alternative to neoliberal market principles. Ideological notions such as 'global imperatives' and 'demands of the global economy', which discursively position contemporary rationales for education policy, are based on this neoliberal imaginary of globalization. There is, however, nothing inevitable about this imaginary of globalization 'from above', especially when its negative social consequences are becoming all too clear. Neoliberalism has clearly benefited some individuals and communities, where others have been left struggling in its wake. Since the financial crisis beginning in late 2007, first in the United States and then across the entire globe, its contradictions have become abundantly clear. As we have noted throughout this book, it has created a global architecture of economic and political relations that is not only largely undemocratic, but which has also polarized global wealth. It has enabled transnational corporations to acquire unprecedented, and arguably unregulated, amounts of power, and has also reduced collective opposition such as that of the trade union movement.

As Buckman (2004: 28) points out, 'globalization from above' has created a 'casino economy' in which 'there are few barriers to unhindered global transfer of money', disproportionately affecting poorer countries, which were not set up to be able to handle huge inflows of money. It is now becoming abundantly clear how the relatively unfettered global circulation of finance has created enormous problems of governance. It has enabled corrupt politicians in the Global South to take advantage of the new opportunities created by large capital inflows, while it has enhanced the capacity of transnational corporations to operate across borders without many restrictions. Although TNCs have been able to bring new technology, new employment and foreign exchange to the developing countries, they have also 'crowded out' existing business in many countries and at the same time have brought little technology transfer and know-how. Predictably, their ever-increasing economic clout has given them growing policy influence that they have not been reluctant to wield. They have been able to steer policy priorities, not only of national governments but also of key international financial institutions, namely the International Monetary Fund, the World Bank and the World Trade Organization. Each of these institutions has thus pursued a similar set of policy objectives based on the principles of a market economy and free trade.

The effects of these objectives on poorer countries in particular have been evident for quite some time, but over the past decade various scholars and social movements have recognized that the neoliberal imaginary of globalization is in the long run economically, politically and environmentally unsustainable – economically because of the social inequalities and economic instability it produces, politically because of its undemocratic character, and environmentally because it assumes that the world's exploitable resources are inexhaustible. They have suggested various alternatives, some designed to 'tame' the excesses of neoliberal globalization while others are based on a radically different conception of the ways in which human societies might relate to each other. In this concluding chapter we will briefly describe some of these alternatives, characterized as 'globalization from below' – involving responses and resistance to 'globalization from above'. It should be noted, however, that those struggling politically for 'globalization from below' do not deny that the new information and communication technologies have altered our sense of time and space, but insist that globalization can be imagined differently, in ways which are more socially progressive, which do not destroy individual and community lives but put the values of community and social justice ahead of market efficiency and individual self-interest. These social movements view human beings as more than just economic beings concerned only with their own interests.

Taming globalization

Critics of the global political and economic systems, as they have emerged over the past two decades, occupy a wide spectrum of positions. Towards the end of the 1990s a number of theorists and political leaders acknowledged that neoliberalism undermined community life, created conditions that perpetuated social inequalities, and increased the possibilities of social instability. Even the investor and currency speculator George Soros (2008), who has benefited greatly from financial flows across national boundaries and the globalization of the economy, warned that market fundamentalism had the potential of 'undoing' capitalism itself. He argued that the current system of financial speculation undermined healthy economic development. As a fallabilist in the tradition of Karl Popper (1949), Soros denies the assumption that markets always correct themselves without any government intervention in financial affairs, and insists that for capitalism to work for everyone it requires an appropriate mix of social and educational policies designed to promote and sustain 'open societies'. A contradiction, however, seems to lie at the heart of Soros's politics, for on the one hand he has been an active participant in the global currency flows, while on the other he has invested heavily in social and educational projects throughout the world, most notably in former Soviet states.

A similar contradiction characterizes the work of the economist Jeffery Sachs. As one of the leading architects of the Millennium Development Goals, Sachs became famous in the mid-1980s when as an economic advisor to the Bolivian government he proposed a plan, later known as 'shock therapy', to drastically cut inflation by liberalizing the Bolivian market, ending government subsidies, eliminating quotas and linking the Bolivian economy to the US dollar. In more recent years Sachs has addressed issues of economic development, health policy, environmental sustainability and, in particular, poverty alleviation within the developing world. In his book *The End of Poverty*, Sachs (2005) argues that African countries are not poor because their governance is poor, but that their governance is poor because of high levels of poverty. He believes that extreme global poverty can be alleviated with relatively modest increases in carefully targeted aid from richer countries. Sachs suggests, for example, that improved supply of seeds, irrigation and fertilizer could lead to greater crop yields, thus significantly increasing the income of subsistence farmers and thereby reducing poverty.

While he has been a consistent critic of the IMF and its policies, as well as international bankers, for what he sees as their ineffective investment strategies, Sachs has been reluctant to view the structure of the capitalist global economy itself as a major cause of extreme poverty and social inequalities. In this way, both his analysis of the problems and his proposals to solve them remain trapped within the neoliberal imaginary. As Holmstrom and Smith (2000) point out, Sachs appears to assume that low levels of investment and poor strategic investment decisions are the only problems facing poorer countries, and that abandoning state planning, freeing up prices, promoting private competition with state-owned industry and selling off state industry as fast as possible, would inevitably create conditions for economic prosperity. In her book *The Shock Doctrine: the Rise of Disaster Capitalism*, Naomi Klein (2007) contests the narrative Sachs presents of the Bolivian 'success' resulting from his 'shock therapy'. She argues that neoliberal reforms pushed by Sachs were neither democratically agreed upon nor achieved without violent state repression, and left the majority of Bolivians in far worse circumstances. What is clear is that Sachs's policy proposals seem to rely upon the very principles of the global economy that arguably exacerbated the problems of global inequalities in the first place.

In a manner not dissimilar to Sachs, Joseph Stiglitz (2002) has documented many of the discontents of globalization. Like Sachs, he too puts much of the blame for growing levels of social inequalities in the developing world on the IMF and the structural adjustment schemes it promoted in the 1980s and 1990s. For Stiglitz, globalization has the potential to bring enormous benefits to both the developing and the developed countries. Stiglitz (2007: 4) argues that 'the problem is not with globalization itself but in the way in which globalization has been managed'. His theoretical argument rests on the belief that markets are never complete or perfect, and that if this is so, the invisible hand of the so-called free markets cannot be expected to work perfectly either, especially in the developing countries, where the information needed to make sound economic decisions is often both lacking and mediated by corrupt politicians. He maintains that IMF policies have been disastrous because they have ignored the implications of incomplete information, inadequate markets and unworkable institutions that often exist, especially in developing countries. The IMF, Stiglitz suggests, has often called for policies in the developing countries that conform to the abstract principles of neoliberal economics, but do not always make sense in the specific material conditions that prevail there. In this way, he believes markets need to be steered if they are to produce beneficial social outcomes.

For Stiglitz (2007), this implies the need to democratize globalization. He maintains that neoliberal globalization has produced a 'democratic deficit' created by the fact that the international organizations which have been entrusted to write the rules for managing the global economy mostly reflect the interests of the rich within the advanced industrial countries. It is possible, he argues, for governments to temper the excesses of the global economy by developing more democratic political institutions, both within and across nation-states. At the global level, he insists, the IMF, the World Bank and the World Trade Organization have to be reformed to make them more representative, with increased transparency and openness. The developing countries need to be given a greater voice and the ability to participate meaningfully in decision-making, with an effective system of accountability and enforcement of the international rule of law. At the national level, Stiglitz believes that governments have a major role to play in shaping market behaviour, with well-chosen policy interventions. In a Keynesian tradition, he insists that governments can fight recessions by using expansionary monetary and fiscal policies to create demand for goods and services. They can regulate banks and other financial institutions to prevent exploitative practices, and use tax policy to steer investment into more productive industries, so that they can mature to the point at which they can survive foreign competition. And governments can use a variety of policy instruments ranging from job creation to human resource development to welfare assistance.

In his effort to tame the excesses of globalization, Stiglitz does not however abandon the underpinning neoliberal emphasis on the individual. He does not suggest going back to Keynesian economics entirely. In this way, his views are consistent with theorists like Giddens (1998) who propose a 'third way', a term used to describe a variety of political approaches to governance that embrace a mix of market and state interventionist philosophies. Both Stiglitz and Giddens support the notion of public-private partnerships, and their world view thus represents a centrist or centre-left synthesis of capitalism and socialism, or of market liberalism and democratic socialism. But while Stiglitz mostly speaks of a new global economic and political architecture, the idea of a 'third way' involves a mixture of Fabian Socialism, Keynesian economics, Franklin D. Roosevelt's New Deal and even Harold Macmillan's One Nation Conservatism. It retains some of the principles of market-individualism but gives equal weight to the values of social cohesion and community building. It suggests a particular way national governments might work with both the opportunities and the challenges of globalization by engaging with the global economy, but retaining a sense of national identity and its distinctive interests. In a third way approach, social and educational policies are not simply derived from economic policies but play an equally important role in the development of society that is both economically productive and socially inclusive.

The most notable political figure to have embraced a third way was Tony Blair in the United Kingdom. But the Clinton administration in the United States also accepted it as a way of transcending the binary between market liberalism and democratic socialism, and also containing some of the excesses of the market. The current Australian Prime Minister, Kevin Rudd, in the wake of the global financial crisis, has clearly articulated a third way position as well, which he refers to as 'social democratic'. Rudd (2009: 25) has noted, 'social democrats maintain robust support for the market economy but posit that markets can only work in a mixed economy, with a role for the state as regulator and as a funder and provider of public goods'. Both Clinton and Blair saw a role for the state in social investment, but when under political pressure, left markets to run rampant. At the same time, they stressed technological development, education and competitive mechanisms to pursue economic progress and governmental objectives. In their own way, each sought to protect the modern welfare state through reforms that preserved its economic integrity. However, economic and social inequalities continued to grow within the USA and the UK under third way regimes, not least because they represented a nation-centric approach in an era in which major economic exchange largely took place in a globalizing space.

Both Blair and Clinton promoted free trade and the globalization of economic activity, little realizing how these undermined national policy initiatives. It was under their regimes that the global financial system that has given rise to the current global financial crisis was established, and was given unprecedented latitude to make money. The principles of 'trickle down' economics they often decried to their political constituencies were actually left intact. The large public investments they made in education were geared to support privatization regimes, which were often accompanied by structures of educational accountability designed more to enable individuals to make school choices and reassure the markets, than to develop critical cosmopolitan individuals and self-governing communities with a commitment to equality of educational opportunity.

What is clear, then, is that these efforts to tame globalization do not sufficiently address the contradictions of neoliberal globalization. This is so because while they do not deny the importance of state policy interventions, they remain trapped within the neoliberal social imaginary. They recognize that the state has an important role to play in the development of social and educational policies, but view these policies largely in terms of the contribution they (and the self-capitalizing, entrepreneurial individuals they produce) are able to make to enhance the competitiveness of nations (and individuals) within the global economy. They view strong state structures more in terms of ensuring successful participation of individuals and communities in open markets, than in terms of the development of democratic institutions and practices. Even their support of equity and social cohesion policies is designed more to ensure the social conditions necessary for capital accumulation, than to create communities marked by their commitment to social justice. They are committed to negotiating regimes of international *free trade* more favourable to them than to the principles of *fair trade* that might benefit the developing countries. It is the realization of these contradictions that has led various radical scholars and social movements to insist that the main problem with neoliberal globalization is not only its excesses, but the core ideas embedded within its imaginary. What is needed, they argue, are more radical alternatives which conceptualize human beings as social beings with collective and common good concerns, to a discussion of which we now turn.

Radical alternatives

Over the past decade there has emerged a strong anti-globalization movement that contests the basic tenets of neoliberalism. At the same time, however, anti-globalization does not represent a coherent worked-out alternative, but a diversity of views focusing variously on political, economic, environmental and cultural consequences of 'globalization from above'. As a movement, anti-globalization is a collection of many different associations and individuals, some of whom belong to non-government organizations (NGOs) working outside the state, while others are members of alternative political parties, such as the Greens, who work within the state system. As a social movement, anti-globalization activists see themselves initially in terms of a politics of resistance, and only then as policy actors. Various gatherings of anti-globalization activists at events such as the meetings of the World Trade Organization (WTO) and G7 are designed largely as a site for protest against the rules of neoliberal economic and political globalization. The meetings of WTO in Seattle in 1999 and Cancún in 2003 were targeted for protest, for example, because it was there that the emerging rules of global trade were being negotiated. In contrast, the hugely popular World Social Forum (WSF) and regional social forums bring together activists to discuss and formulate policy alternatives and strategize ways of protesting free-market economic and political orthodoxies. Some of these activists work for NGOs, which operate in highly localized settings to challenge not only neoliberal state policies but also the exploitative practices of transnational corporations.

Insofar as much of its work occurs outside the state policy arena, the anti-globalization movement attaches considerable importance to information sharing. Organizations such as Ralph Nader's Public Citizen in the USA, the UK-based New Economic Foundation, the Malaysia-based Third World Network, the Thailand-based Focus on the Global South, and the New York-based Foundation of Ethics and Meaning have created excellent interactive websites and publish outstanding policy reports. The World Social Forum, created in 2001 partly in response to the highly successful World Economic Forum held in Davos every year to promote neoliberal thinking, views itself as:

> ... an open meeting place where social movements, networks, NGOs and other civil society organizations opposed to neoliberalism and a world dominated by capital or by any form of imperialism come together to pursue their thinking, to debate ideas democratically, to formulate proposals, share their experiences freely and network for effective action.

Included among the policy positions articulated at the WSF are the convictions that neoliberalism has created a one-size-fits-all recipe for international economic management that is brazenly free-market; that it has led to a global democratic deficit; that its growth-at-all-costs orientation is environmentally unsustainable; and that it has the potential to destroy long-cherished cultural traditions.

Anti-globalization activists associated with the WSF have paid particular attention to the emerging rules of global trade. They have denied the very possibility of free trade, and have argued instead for trade rules that are fairer to the developing communities in particular. Oxfam, a British NGO, argues that the way international trade is currently conducted is highly biased against poor countries, but that managed well it can help alleviate global poverty. It argues, for example, that if Africa, South Asia and Latin America were each to increase their share of world exports by just one per cent, extreme poverty could be eliminated for some 128 million people. Its Fair Trade campaign launched in 2002 advocated lifting of trade barriers against products of developing countries by industrialized societies. The main policy tools of the advocates of Fair Trade is the end of what they refer to as 'rich-country protectionism', in the form of subsidies and import restrictions, and other bilateral and multilateral agreements disadvantageous to poorer countries. Equally, it is argued that developing countries be allowed to use tariffs to protect their local agricultural industries. In this way, many anti-globalization activists are not opposed to global trade, but rather insist on rules that protect labour rights and environmental conditions. Greenpeace, for example, advocates trade agreements to achieve environmental ends.

The main political targets of Fair Trade advocates are the World Trade Organization and the World Bank. It is argued by the European Greens, for example, that the WTO negotiations are marked by lack of transparency, openness and consultation, and that the WTO's influence has already spread too far and has often worked against the principles of human rights, labour standards, cultural diversity and the environment. The World Development Movement goes as far as to suggest that all of the WTO's General Agreement on Trade in Services (GATS) negotiations should be stopped, while grave concerns remain about the impact of GATS on the poor. In respect of the World Bank there is an almost universal belief that current Third World debt levels are unsustainable, and that some portion of this debt, if not all, should be cancelled. The advocates of Fair Trade also express concern over the lack of control of capital flows, especially as these are exploited by transnational corporations (TNCs). Instead, they support the introduction of the Tobin Tax on speculative foreign exchange transactions, which have been a major source of the current global financial crisis. The Tobin Tax is named after Keynesian economist James Tobin, who proposed this tax as a means of discouraging short-term speculative global capital movements, and as a way of raising money that could be invested in the poorest countries.

One of the main problems with these policy proposals, however, has to do with their reliance on the potential of global trade in alleviating poverty and promoting global justice. It is not at all clear that the benefits of freeing up global trade would be equally distributed. Further, as Buckman (2004: 181) points out, these policy proposals appeal 'to values of international fairness based upon agreed upon global rules', but this is predicated on a legalistic assumption that 'all nations are equal in the eyes of international globalization laws'. Furthermore, the terms of international trade rules are too often determined by power relationships, and it is the powerful that have the greatest interest in maintaining these relationships of inequalities in trade.

This is a point that has been powerfully made by Walden Bello (2002), who argues that nothing short of what he refers to as 'deglobalization' is needed. He suggests that the organizations promoting neoliberal economic globalization – the World Bank, the IMF, the WTO and the Group of Seven – have no real interest in transforming the world's financial and trade rules. Various proposals for reform such as those put forward by the Commission on Global Governance and the US Congress's Meltzer Commission proposals have merely tinkered with marginal policy changes. The world, he insists, needs a radical shift towards a decentralized, pluralistic system of economic governance, allowing countries to follow development strategies appropriate to their needs and circumstances. This 'deglobalization' means radically reducing the powers and roles of the existing TNC-driven WTO and Bretton Woods institutions, as well as the formation of new institutions helping to devolve the greater part of production, trade and economic decision-making to national and local levels. It is interesting that Barack Obama and Gordon Brown, in the wake of the global financial crisis, have both called for the creation of a new, post-Bretton Woods global system of financial regulation to reflect the global character of the economy today.

Bello's policy proposals are in line with another element within the broader anti-globalization movement: localization. The idea of localization has been powerfully advocated by a whole range of scholars and environmentalists who argue that globalization has already gone too far and can no longer be tamed, and that therefore a new approach to economic, cultural and environmental sustainability is needed. In his highly influential book *Going Local*, Shuman (1998) describes the aim of localization as one that:

> … does not mean walling off the outside world. It means nurturing locally owned businesses which use local resources sustainably, employ local workers at decent wages and serve primarily local customers. It means becoming more self-sufficient and less dependent on imports. Control moves from the boardrooms of distant corporations and back to community where it belongs.

According to another localization theorist, Colin Hines (2000: 29), there is an alternative to corporate neoliberal globalization, but localization policies 'must be seen as a plausible way to reverse the instability and insecurity that trade liberalization has wrought upon the world'. He insists on the need to reclaim control over local economies, to make them as diverse as possible and to rebuild stability into community life. This does not mean a return to overpowering state control, but a policy framework that enables people and businesses to develop patterns of social exchange that are immediate and reciprocal.

This implies the development of a new overarching economic and political architecture that enables local initiatives to flourish, not only with respect to commerce and trade but also in relation to cultural, social and educational policies. Hines (2000) argues that local control does not guarantee democracy, equality, environmental protection and so on, but makes it more likely. He lists six main potential advantages of localization: maximum devolution of political power and democratic accountability; local control of the economy; protection of the environment; the improvement of social and environmental conditions; a positive role for local competition; and the development of trade and aid rules for self-reliance. Hines (ibid.: 37) recognizes that his is a call for a new imaginary of social life, and that it requires a fundamental 'mind-wrench', but he insists that human society is fast running out of options and that neoliberal globalization may have run its course. As environmental problems associated with global production and movement of goods become ever more evident, as communities become more fragmented and dysfunctional, and as the current neoliberal world economic management system breaks down, localization now becomes at least thinkable, demanding a new set of rules for the development of human society.

As appealing as some of these sentiments seem, the localization agenda is also beset with a number of contradictions. For example, it appeals to universal values of empowerment, democracy and self-sufficiency, but always within a context of local control. What it does not do is to recognize the importance of inter-community relations, which in an era of globalization potentially stretch across the entire world. The idea of localization invariably refers to specific geographically bounded communities, but there are now competing definitions of community, along with a whole host of identity categories. The advocates of localization insist that they are not against internationalization but opposed to economic globalization, yet do not specify how this distinction might work with respect to particular policy positions. Their ideas also appear to lack a theory of the state: that is, some notion of exactly how the state at the national level might relate to local initiatives and safeguard people against local economic control becoming a recipe for exploitation. To dismantle globalization, furthermore, localization theorists appear to rely on a huge amount of international cooperation that the world has never witnessed before. In the end, various elements of the anti-globalization movement engage in a fair amount of utopian thinking about the desirability of local policy control, without addressing the need for a more general policy architecture that specifies rules for the conduct of the global networks within which public policy (including education policy) is now developed and enacted.

Reimagining globalization

To a considerable extent, the globalization genie has been let out of the bottle; there is thus no turning back to some imagined past when social relations were highly localized. There is no return from the communication and information technologies that have transformed the nature of work, production processes and economic activity. A return to localized modes of production may be possible on the edges, but is not likely on a mass scale. Global movements of people have created diasporic networks that have redefined people's identities and senses of belonging; it is hard to imagine how they could return to purely local affiliations. Globalization has changed the ways people and communities now relate to each other. They (the more privileged) have developed cosmopolitan tastes for goods and services and for travel. Cultural diversity has now become a permanent feature of global cities in particular. Globalization has also created new practices of governance, new possibilities of international cooperation, without which it is impossible to solve global environmental problems such as climate change and the distribution of water across local communities and national borders. Nor is it entirely desirable to abandon those aspects of globalization that have greatly benefited individuals and communities. While many economic nationalists, religious fundamentalists and radical environmentalists have rightly stressed various destructive effects of contemporary neoliberal globalization, they have overlooked that it has sometimes also helped to improve the material conditions of people, to reinvigorate rather than undermine cultural heritages, and has offered potential solutions to our collective environmental problems.

Throughout this book we have argued that the problem is not with globalization itself, but with the particular manner in which global interconnectivity has been interpreted, through the conceptual prism of a neoliberal social imaginary. We have shown how this imaginary has become globally hegemonic, leading to a range of economic policies that have benefited some communities while destroying others. Neoliberal globalization has created new forms of social stratification, and on the whole has tended to widen gaps in social chances. These injustices are not, as Scholte (2000: 234) has argued, 'inherent to globalization, but have mainly flowed from neoliberal approaches to the new geography'. Central to neoliberalism has been its market fundamentalism, the assumption that markets provide the best policy mechanism for organizing societies, and that their development best flows from an emphasis on the values of individual freedom and self-interest and market freedom and efficiency. Recent policy reforms in education around the world have mostly assumed the validity of this assumption. Educational policy objectives have thus become closely tied to economic goals, as the production of individuals with the knowledge, skills and dispositions that can help them enhance their own and national competitiveness within the global economy. In this way, educational values are no longer considered in their own terms, but have become *derivative* of neoliberal economic thinking.

Yet in recent years, the contradictions of this economic orthodoxy have become abundantly clear. The transnational corporations and banks that once rejected any role for the state are now begging it to rescue them from their own excesses. They have begged for large sums of public money to keep intact the financial system upon which they rely. The governments that once rejected any significant role in regulating their behaviour are now struggling to figure out how to hold them accountable for the use of public money and to consider the features of a global system of re-regulation. To prevent a global recession they are no longer reluctant to inject money into public projects and social benefits, designed to ensure that the whole global economic edifice of neoliberalism does not collapse entirely. John Maynard Keynes, so it seems, is back in favour. Indeed, the Australian Prime Minister Kevin Rudd has gone as far as to declare the death of neoliberalism (2009: 25): 'the great neoliberal experiment of the past thirty years has failed'. Explicitly, Rudd (ibid.) has observed:

> With the demise of neo-liberalism, the role of the state has once more been recognized as fundamental. The state has been the primary actor in responding to three clear areas of the current crisis: in rescuing the private financial system

> from collapse; in producing direct stimulus to the real economy because of the collapse in private demand; and in the design of a national and global regulatory regime in which government has ultimate responsibility to determine and enforce the rules of the system.

Not only do left-leaning leaders such as Barack Obama and Gordon Brown seem to agree with Rudd's observations, but so do conservatives such as Nicolas Sarkozy and Angela Merkel who, with the Group of 20, are struggling to develop a new set of regulatory rules for the global economy in which state regulation is no longer a dirty word.

It is premature to assume the death of neoliberalism, however. While in macro-economic policy some of its key tenets are being rethought, the reach of its social imaginary runs deep. Over the past two decades the neoliberal social imaginary, as we have argued, has transformed thinking in almost all policy arenas, including education. For example, neoliberalism has steered education policy priorities towards a particular curriculum architecture with an emphasis on the skills and dispositions needed for participation in the global knowledge economy, modes of governance that have highlighted the principles of privatization and choice, and an audit culture that stresses performance contracts and various national and international regimes of testing and accountability, which have thinned out the purposes, pedagogies and potential of education.

These policy priorities were largely derived and justified in terms of neoliberal economic thinking, but even as the flaws in this mode of thinking become apparent, governments seem unprepared to reconsider the education policies that are derived from it. Indeed, the neoliberal social imaginary remains intact in education policy, with continuing emphasis on national curriculum and testing regimes as well as on the ideology of school choice and the production of entrepreneurial individuals. What seems clear is that this neoliberal social imaginary continues to hold us captive, well after its key assumptions have been rejected and been seen to have precipitated the global financial crisis, which is having negative real economy effects worldwide, with consequences for public policy. The capacity of national governments to fund education will be challenged because of the economic stimulus packages that have been instigated to ensure continuing consumer spending and inhibit economic slowdown and the money expended on stabilizing banks and other financial institutions.

Yet, just as it is important to rethink economic policy, so must we reconsider social and education policies that look beyond the dictates of neoliberal globalization, and reimagine another globalization that does not reject the facts of global interconnectivity and interdependence, but seeks to interpret them differently, so as to consider the important role education must play in creating a more environmentally and economically secure, socially just and democratic global future. In working towards such a future it is not simply possible to rely upon governments or the wisdom that resides with local communities, but we must rely on a new global network of networks. In the current financial crisis, attempts are being made to redirect and regulate the markets that have caused so much distress; however, these reforms do not challenge the deeper social order, and they are located within the existing framework of capitalist production and bureaucratic governance. In contrast, radical alternatives, while they challenge the underlying neoliberal social imaginary, are based on communitarian logic, which neither recognizes the facts of global interconnectivity nor allows the possibility of another form of globalization, delivering greater security, justice and democracy. They risk the dangers of romantic localism that can easily degenerate into inward-looking reactionary politics, such as that associated with various forms of fundamentalism.

Public policies, as we have argued in chapter 4, always involve concern for human security. In recent years, however, this concern has become narrowly defined as physical security from the acts of terrorism. But security is about much more than simply physical security (Peters 2005). In a globally interconnected world, environmental security, for example, requires policies to reduce ecological destruction, but these policies cannot succeed if they are simply local or national, no matter how well-intentioned. Problems of ecological degradation and global warming are global, and require solutions that involve a robust system of international relations. Similarly, interstate conflict cannot be resolved bilaterally, and requires an agency such as the United Nations, albeit in a form that is much more effective. Similarly, economic security of people cannot be assured without a fundamental restructuring of the global economic system. The neoliberal economic order, with its emphasis on lightly regulated production, finance and trade, has imposed heavy social costs on many communities. Policy reforms are now needed to ensure that there is not only greater regulation, but also policies that are people-orientated, involving socially useful programmes and jobs that meet certain environmental and labour standards, and that protect cultural traditions and yet at the same time promote social cohesion, opportunity and more equality.

The value of equity has also always been important to public policy, but in recent decades a very weak concept of equity has been promoted, often becoming secondary to the requirements of human resource development for participation in the global economy. So, for example, the importance of gender equality in the Global South has been recognized, but not because it is morally just, but because it is assumed it will produce greater economic productivity. A form of globalization that is more gender-sensitive is clearly needed (Unterhalter 2007), in which women have an equal chance of providing political and policy leadership. Under neoliberal policies, social inequalities both within and across nations have increased. This cannot and will not be tolerated by those who are left behind; redistributive policies are therefore needed to address the growing divide across the Global North and Global South. Reforms are also needed to eliminate the neoliberal policy structures that have resulted in the marginalization and subordination of people of colour, rural populations, children and the elderly. A globally humane future is impossible without the social cohesion and security that can only be produced by a greater focus on social inequalities and a commitment to more equality, nationally and globally.

The values of security, equality and social cohesion through public policy cannot, however, be realized without a new kind of politics – and the governance structures through which policies are developed, enacted and evaluated. Nothing short of the democratization of globalization is needed. Despite its rhetoric of individual freedom, neoliberal globalization has created conditions in which political power has become concentrated in the hands of a few rich countries, major transnational corporations and international organizations such as the OECD and the WTO. Power needs to be devolved, so that nations and local communities can become genuinely involved in decision-making processes. While national, regional and transnational agencies have a significant role to play in the governance of global relations, ultimate political authority needs to be as close to local government as possible, with mechanisms for popular consultations on global policies. At the same time, efforts need to be made to ensure greater transparency of policy processes at all levels, as well as local representation on global agencies such as the World Bank. What is clear is that a democratic global civil space is needed to ensure that substantially greater resources flow to civil social development, and that there is at least some measure of popular control over such social development.

A number of theorists and activists have shown how these ideas are not entirely fanciful, but can be realized. Held and McGrew (2002), for example, have argued convincingly in favour of a case for a cosmopolitan social democracy. They have suggested that such a project can revive some of the traditional values of social democracy and be (ibid.: 131):

> … conceived as a basis for uniting around the promotion of the impartial administration of law at the international level; greater transparency, accountability and democracy in global governance; a deeper commitment to social justice in the pursuit of a more equitable distribution of the world's resources and human security; the protection and reinvention of community at diverse levels (from the local to the global); and the regulation of the global economy through the public management of financial and trade flows, the provision of global public goods, and the engagement of leading stakeholders in corporate governance.

Effectively, Held and McGrew insist that it is possible to reimagine the nature of political community in an era of globalization, so that it is more and not less democratic, where civic spaces exist for popular participation in policy-making. This, they argue, requires us to reconsider some of the key terms of political association such as legitimacy, sovereignty, identity and citizenship (Archibugi and Held 1995). Democracy, they maintain, can be reconceptualized to include subnational, national and transnational levels of political organization; and they also maintain that conditions now exist that can make cosmopolitan social democracy not only perfectly plausible, but even necessary.

Democratic accountability is a fundamental requirement of cosmopolitan democracy. A whole range of localities are now experimenting with its possibilities, notably in Porto Alegre, Brazil, where a process of democratic deliberation and decision-making was developed in the 1990s to ensure what has been referred to as 'participatory budgeting'. This meant encouraging ordinary residents to decide how to allocate the municipal or public budget, to present their demands and priorities for improvement, and to more generally influence the determination of programmes through discussions and negotiations. This form of democratic accountability involved election of budget delegates to represent different communities, as well as facilitation and technical assistance by public employees, local and higher-level assemblies to deliberate and vote on spending priorities, and allowing general participation in the evaluation of programmes. The evidence so far suggests many promising outcomes, including more equitable public spending, increased satisfaction of basic needs, greater government transparency and accountability, and increased levels of participation, especially by the marginalized or poorer residents of Porto Alegre. Similar experiments have been tried in India and South Africa, and within the Zapatista movement among the people of Chiapas in Mexico, which has been fighting to ensure protection of their traditional cultural, political and economic rights, especially in the face of predatory globalization.

Each of these experiments in democracy illustrates the importance of education policy, not only with respect to issues of access and opportunity, allocation of resources and structures of accountability, but also in relation to the role that democratic learning must play in developing a new social imaginary that challenges the neoliberal construction of globalization. The citizenship functions of formal education, then, need to be located within local, national and global considerations of the work of citizens today and extended well beyond constructions of citizens as merely consumers of policy. Porto Alegre, for example, is not only a democratic forum but also a site of education in critical participatory citizenship. This gives a broader, democratic meaning to Bernstein's (2001a) talk of the 'totally pedagogised society', currently framed by the neoliberal imaginary. If the neoliberal social imaginary of globalization is to be challenged, new ways of thinking about global interconnectivity and interdependence are necessary.

If global poverty is to be ameliorated, as the welfare economist Amartya Sen has argued, structural rearrangements are not sufficient; the capabilities of people need to be developed. Sen's 'capability approach' stresses the importance of real freedom in an assessment of the ways in which people are able to understand and take advantage of their circumstances, by transforming resources into valuable activities. It emphasizes functional capabilities, 'substantive freedoms' such as the ability to live to an old age, engage in economic transactions or participate in political activities. Sen thus understands global poverty as capability deprivation, and views education as fundamental to the development of capabilities with which to exercise practical choices and to enhance freedom (Walker 2006). There is a rationale for education here as the enhancement of freedom through the universalizing of capability. For Sen, the purposes of economic development ought to be the enhancement of freedom, globally.

The capability approach indicates a promising avenue for exploring an alternative imaginary of globalization, based not on a singular, individualistic and economistic view of human needs, but emphasizing the importance of not only freedom of choice but also individual heterogeneity and the multidimensional nature of welfare and welfare needs. An emphasis on capabilities means that education policies can no longer overlook the importance of learning new ways of engaging with and responding to global interconnectivity and interdependence. This might be referred to as the requirement of 'cosmopolitan learning' (Rizvi 2008) and the production of cosmopolitan citizens focused locally, nationally and globally on achieving the greater collective good.

If the neoliberal imaginary steers us towards a particular formation of subjective awareness, together with a particular ideological interpretation of recent changes in the global economy and culture, it cannot be challenged without a competing imaginary. This competing and new social imaginary will emphasize cosmopolitan learning that does not 'ontologize' market logic and the self-capitalizing individual, but seeks to work with a different moral sense of people's 'situatedness in the world', in ways that are both critical and reflexive. This imaginary would recognize the social and cultural nature of human behaviour and being, as well as concern for the collective common good within an environmentally sustainable politics.

If the current global financial crisis has demonstrated quite starkly the multifarious shortcomings of the neoliberal social imaginary of globalization, constructing a new imaginary needs to be the focus of contemporary political explorations, conversations and theorizing. Even in those countries where the threadbare character of neoliberal globalization has now been acknowledged, there has however been little thought given to new social policies, including education policy frameworks, which need to flow from the failure of neoliberalism. In Australia, for example, where the Prime Minister has been a vehement critic of neoliberalism and its abundant failures, education policy is still conceptualized solely as contributing to economic productivity, with somewhat weaker acknowledgment and recognition of its social justice and social and cultural purposes. Accountability pressures are also still of the narrow kind, with reductive effects on pedagogies and purposes of schooling. The pressing need for a new education policy framework is a challenge to views of education that are narrowly framed.

We need a new imaginary which recognizes that human beings are social and cultural beings as well as economic ones, an imaginary that recognizes the need to think locally, nationally and globally. Such an imaginary suggests the need for the construction of cosmopolitan citizenship that emphasizes collective well-being sutured across local, national and global dimensions. This implies the need to rethink, for example, the idea of accountability, which recognizes in all its complexity the broader and democratically progressive purposes of education. This form of accountability would be not only top-down and vertical in character, but also bottom-up, as well as horizontal, linking schools in reciprocally accountable ways to their communities. A new social imaginary is necessary to frame education policy in the wake of the egregious failures of neoliberalism. Education policy needs to be globalized and deparochialized in new ways. This demands that we rethink the meanings of the values of efficiency, equity, community, liberty and security which have hitherto underpinned all public policies, including education policy, and also rethink their collective articulation and assemblage.

References

Adams, R.-J. (2003) 'Response to "Cautions on OECD's recent educational survey (PISA)"', *Oxford Review of Education*, 29(3): 377–89.

Adie, J. (2008) 'The hegemonic positioning of "Smart State" policy', *Journal of Education Policy*, 23(3): 251–64.

Aguilar, D. (2004), 'Introduction', in D. Aguilar and A. Lacsamana (eds) *Women and Globalization*, New York: Humanity Books.

Ahmed, S., Castaneda, C., Foster, A. and Sheller, M. (eds) (2003) *Uprooting/Regrouping: Questions of Home and Migration*, Oxford: Berg Press.

Alexander, R. (2004) 'Still no pedagogy? Principle, pragmatism and compliance in primary education', *Cambridge Journal of Education*, 34(1): 7–33.

Ali, S. (2006) 'Why does policy fail? Understanding the problems of policy implementation in Pakistan – a neuro-cognitive perspective', *International Studies in Educational Administration*, 34(1): 2–20.

Aly, J. H. (2007a) *Education in Pakistan: A White Paper – a document to debate and finalize the national education policy*. Online. Available at http://www.moe.gov.pk/nepr/PolicyDevStage.asp

Aly, J. H. (2007b) *Education in Pakistan: A White Paper revised – document to debate and finalize the national education policy*. Online. Available at http://www.moe.gov.pk/nepr

Anderson, B. (1991 revised edn) *Imagined Communities: Reflections on the Origin and Spread of Nationalism*, London: Verso.

Anthony, K. D. 'Problems and failures of education in St Lucia: feature address', paper presented at the St Lucia Teachers' Union's annual Teachers' Week Rally, at the Gros Islet Primary School, March 1990, in *The St Lucia Teachers' Union souvenir booklet of teachers' week 1990* (Castries, SLTU).

APEC (2004) 'Strategic plan for English language/foreign language learning', 3rd APEC Education Ministerial Meeting: Sub Theme Paper 1, Santiago, Chile. Online. Available at http://biblioteca.mineduc.cl/documento/English_APEC_strategic_plan_final_21-4-04.pdf

Appadurai, A. (1996) *Modernity at Large: Cultural Dimensions of Globalization*. Minneapolis: The University of Minnesota Press.

Appadurai, A. (2001) 'Grassroots globalization and the research imagination', in A. Appadurai (ed.) *Globalization*, Durham, NC: Duke University Press.

Appadurai, A. (2006) *Fear of Small Numbers: An Essay on the Geography of Anger*. Durham, NC: Duke University Press.

Apple, M. W. (2001) *Educating the 'Right' Way: Markets, Standards, God and Inequality*, New York: RoutledgeFalmer.

Archibugi, D. and Held, D. (1995) *Cosmopolitan Democracy: An Agenda for a New World Order*, Cambridge, UK: Polity Press.

Arnott, M., David, M. and Weiner, G. (1999) *Closing the Gender Gap: Postwar Education and Social Change*, Cambridge, UK: Polity Press.

Auge, M. (1995) *Non-places: Introduction to an Anthropology of Supermodernity*, London: Verso.

Ball, S. (1990) *Politics and Policy Making in Education: Explorations in Policy Sociology*, London: Routledge.

Ball, S. (1994) *Education Reform: A Critical and Poststructuralist Approach*, Buckingham, UK: Open University Press.

Ball, S. (2004) 'Performativities and fabrications in the education economy: towards the performative society', in S. Ball (ed.) *The RoutledgeFalmer Reader in Sociology of Education*, London: RoutledgeFalmer.

Ball, S. (2006) *Education Policy and Social Class: The Selected Works of Stephen J. Ball*, London: Routledge.

Ball, S. (2007) *Education Plc: Understanding Private Sector Participation in Public Sector Education*, London: Routledge.

Ball, S. (2008) *The Education Debate*, Bristol, UK: Policy Press.

Ball, S. and Youdell, D. (2008) *Hidden Privatisation in Public Education*, Brussels: Education International.

Barthes, R. (1979) 'Non multa sed multum', in Y. Lambert (ed.) *Catalogue Raisonné des Oeuvres sur Papier Cy Twombly*, Milan: Multipha, vi: 7–13.

Bate, P. and Robert, G. (2003) 'Where next for policy evaluation? Insights from researching national health service modernisation', *Policy and Politics*, 31: 249–62.

Bauman, Z. (1998) *Globalization: The Human Consequences*, Cambridge, UK: Polity.

Beck, U. (2000) 'The cosmopolitan perspective', *British Journal of Sociology*, 51(1): 79–105.

Becker, G. (1964) *Human Capital: A Theoretical and Empirical Analysis, with Special Reference to Education*, New York: Columbia University Press.

Bell, L. and Stevenson, H. (2006) *Education Policy Processes, Themes and Impact*, London: Routledge.

Bello, W. (2002) *Deglobalization: Ideas for A New World Economy*, London: Zed Press.

Berliner, D. (2007) 'Our impoverished view of educational reform', in A. R. Sadovnik (ed.) *Sociology of Education: A Critical Reader*, New York: Routledge.

Bernstein, B. (1971) 'On the classification and framing of educational knowledge', in M. F. D. Young (ed.) *Knowledge and Control*, London: Collier-Macmillan.

Bernstein, B. (2001a) 'From pedagogies to knowledge', in A. Marais *et al.* (eds) *Towards a Sociology of Pedagogy: The Contribution of Basil Bernstein to Research*, New York: Peter Lang.

Bernstein, B. (2001b) 'Video conference with Basil Bernstein', in A. Marais *et al.* (eds) *Towards a Sociology of Pedagogy: The Contribution of Basil Bernstein to Research*, New York: Peter Lang.

Bernstein, B. (2004) 'Social class and pedagogic practice', in S. Ball (ed.) *The RoutledgeFalmer Reader in the Sociology of Education*, London: RoutledgeFalmer.

Black, P., Harrison, C., Lee, C., Marshall, B. and Wilm, D. (2003) *Assessment for Learning: Putting It into Practice*, Maidenhead, UK: Open University Press.

Blackmore, J. and Thorpe, S. (2003) 'Mediating change: the print media's role in mediating education policy in a period of radical reform in Victoria, Australia', *Journal of Education Policy*, 18(6): 577–95.

Bourdieu, P. (1986) 'The forms of capital', in J. Richardson (ed.) *Handbook of Theory and Research for the Sociology of Education*, Westport, CT: Greenwood.

Bourdieu, P. (1996) *The Rules of Art: Genesis and Structure of the Literary Field*, Cambridge, UK: Polity Press.

Bourdieu, P. (1998a) *Acts of Resistance: Against the New Myths of Our Time*, Cambridge, UK: Polity Press.

Bourdieu, P. (1998b) *Practical Reason: On the Theory of Action*, Stanford, Calif.: Stanford University Press.

Bourdieu, P. (1999) 'The social conditions of the international circulation of ideas', in R. Shusterman (ed.) *Bourdieu: A Critical Reader*, Oxford: Blackwell.

Bourdieu, P. (2004) *Firing Back: Against the Tyranny of the Market 2*, London: Verso.

Bourdieu, P. and Passeron, J. C. (1977) *Reproduction in Education, Society and Culture*, London: Sage.

Bourdieu, P., Accardo, A., Balazs, G., Beaud, S., Bonvon, F., Bourdieu, E., Bourgois, P., Broccolochi, S., Champagne, P., Christin, R., Faguer, J-P., Garcia, S., Lenoir, R., Oeuvard, F., Pialoux, M., Pinto, L., Podalydes, D., Sayad, A., Soulie, C. and Wacquant, L. J. D. (1999) *The Weight of the World: Social Suffering in Contemporary Society*, Cambridge, UK: Polity Press.

Bowles, S. and Gintis, H. (1985) *Democracy and Capitalism: Property, Community and the Contradictions of Modern Social Thought*, London: Routledge.

Boyd, J. P. (ed.) (1950) *The Chapters of Thomas Jefferson*, Princeton, NJ: Princeton University Press.

Boyer, B. and Drache, D. (eds) (1996) *States against Markets: the Limits of Globalization*, New York: Routledge.

Bray, M. (1996) *Education and Political Transition: Themes and Experiences in East Asia*, Hong Kong: Comparative Education Research Centre, The University of Hong Kong.

Brennan, T. (2006) *Wars of Position: The Cultural Politics of Left and Right*, New York: Columbia University Press.

Brenner, N. (2004) *New State Spaces: Urban Governance and the Rescaling of Statehood*, Oxford: Oxford University Press.

Brenner, N., Jessop, B., Jones, M. and Macleod, G. (eds) (2003) *State/Space Reader*, Oxford: Blackwell.

Brighouse, H. (2003) *School Choice and Social Justice*, Oxford: Oxford University Press.

Brown, P., Halsey, A. H., Lauder, H. and Stuart Wells, A. (1997) 'The transformation of education and society: an introduction', in A. H. Halsey *et al.* (eds) *Education: Culture, Economy and Society*, Oxford: Oxford University Press.

Buckman, G. (2004) *Globalization: Tame It or Scrap It?*, London: Zed Books.

Buck-Morss, S. (2006) *Thinking Past Terror: Islamism and Critical Theory on the Left*, updated edn, London: Verso.

Bulbeck, C. (1998) *Re-Orienting Western Feminisms*, Cambridge, UK: Cambridge University Press.

Burawoy, M., Blum, J. A., George, S., Gillie, Z., Gowan, T., Haney, L., Klawiter, M., Lopez, S., Riain, S. and Thayer, M. (2000) *Global Ethnography: Forces, Connections, and Imaginations in a Postmodern World*, Berkeley, CA: University of California Press.

Cagler, A. (2001) 'Constraining metaphors and transnationalization of spaces in Berlin', *Journal of Ethnic and Migration Studies*, 27(4): 601–13.

Calhoun, C. (2001) 'The class consciousness of the frequent travellers: towards a critique of actual existing cosmopolitanisms', in S. Vertovec and R. Cohen (eds) *Conceiving Cosmopolitanism: Theory, Context and Practice*, Oxford: Oxford University Press.

Canclini, N. G. (1998) *Hybrid Cultures: Strategies for Entering and Leaving Modernity*, Minneapolis: University of Minnesota Press.

Candy, P. and Laurent, J. (eds) (1994) *Pioneering Culture: Mechanics' Institutes and Schools of Arts in Australia*, Adelaide: Auslib Press.

Cao, X. (1996) 'Debating brain drain in the context of globalization', *Compare*, 26(3): 269–85.

Carley, M. (1980) *Rational Techniques in Policy Analysis*, Aldershot, UK: Gower.

Carrington, W. and Detragiache, E. (1998) 'How extensive is brain drain?', *Finance Development: A Quarterly Magazine of the IMF*, 36(2): 1–7.

Castells, M. (1996) *The Rise of the Network Society*, Oxford: Blackwell.

Castells, M. (2000) *The Rise of the Network Society*, 2nd edn, Oxford: Blackwell.

Castoriadis, C. (1987) *The Imaginary Institution of Society*; trans. Kathleen Blamey, Cambridge, MA: MIT Press.

Cerny, P. (1990) *The Changing Architecture of Politics: Structure, Agency and the Future of the State*, London: Sage.

Chakrabarti, R. and Peterson, P. (eds) (2009) *School Choice International: Exploring Public–Private Partnerships*, Cambridge, MA: MIT Press.

Cibulka, J. G. (1994) 'Policy analysis and the study of education', *Journal of Education Policy*, 9(506): 105–25.

Clarke, J. and Newman, J. (1997) *The Managerial State: Power, Politics and Ideology in the Remaking of Social Welfare*, London: Sage.

Clarke, J., Gewirtz, S. and McLaughlin, E. (eds) (2000) *New Managerialism, New Welfare?*, London; Thousand Oaks, Calif.: Open University in association with SAGE Publications.

Clyne, F. and Rizvi, F. (1998) 'Outcomes of student exchange', in D. Davis and A. Olsen (eds) *Outcomes of International Education: Research Findings*, Canberra: IDP Education Australia.

Coburn, C. E. and Stein, M. K. (2006) 'Communities of practice theory and the role of teacher professional community in policy implementation', in M. Honig (ed.) *New Directions in Education Policy Implementation: Confronting the Complexity*, New York: State University of New York Press.

Coffield, F. (1999) 'Breaking the consensus: lifelong learning as social control', *British Educational Research Journal*, 24(4): 279–300.

Cohen, R. (1997) *Global Diasporas: An Introduction*, Seattle, WA: University of Washington Press.

Cohen, R. and Kennedy, P. (2000) *Global Sociology*, New York: New York University Press.

Cohen, R. and Kennedy, P. (2007) *Global Sociology*, 2nd edn, New York: New York University Press.

The Commission on Global Governance (1995) *Our Global Neighbourhood*, Oxford: Oxford University Press.

Connell, R. (2007) *Southern Theory: the Global Dynamics of Knowledge in the Social Sciences*, Crows Nest, NSW: Allen and Unwin.

Connell, R., White, V. and Johnston, K. (1991) *'Running Twice as Hard': the Disadvantaged Schools Program in Australia*, Geelong, Vic.: Deakin University Press.

Considine, M. (1994) *Public Policy: A Critical Approach*, Melbourne, Vic.: Macmillan.

Cope, B. and Kalantzis, M. (eds) (2000) *Multiliteracies: Literacy, Learning and the Design of Social Futures*, London: Routledge.

Cope, B. and Kalantzis, M. (2002) *Productive Diversity*, Sydney: Pluto Press.

Crystal, D. (1997) *English as a Global Language*, Cambridge, UK: Cambridge University Press.

Dale, R. (1999) 'Specifying globalization effects on national policy: a focus on the mechanisms', *Journal of Education Policy*, 14(1): 1–17.

Dale, R. (2006) 'Policy relationships between supranational and national scales: imposition/ resistance or parallel universes?', in J. Kallo and R. Rinne (eds) *Supranational Regimes and*

National Education Policies Encountering Challenges, Turku, Finland: Finnish Educational Research Association.

de Certeau, M. (1984) *The Practice of Everyday Life*, Los Angeles: University of California Press.

de Leon, P. and Danielle V. (2007) 'The policy sciences at the crossroad', in F. Fischer, G. J. Miller and M. S. Sidney (eds) *Handbook of Public Policy Analysis: Theory, Politics, and Methods*, Boca Raton, FL: CRC Press.

Delors, J., Mufti, I. A., Amagai, I., Carnerio, R., Chung, F., Geremek, B., Gorham, W., Kornhauser, A., Manley, M., Quero, M. P., Savane, M-A., Singh, K., Stavenhagen, R., Suhr, M. W. and Nanzhao, Z. (1996) *Learning, the Treasure within: Report to UNESCO of the International Commission on Education for the Twenty-first Century*, 2nd edn, Paris: UNESCO Publishing.

Delpit, L. (2006) *Other People's Children: Cultural Conflict in the Classroom*, New York: The New Press.

Department for Education and Skills (2006) *Making Good Progress: How Can We Help Every Pupil to Make Good Progress at School?*, London: DfES.

Dery, D. (1984) *Problem Definition in Policy Analysis*, Kansas, MO: University Press of Kansas.

Desrosieres, A. (1998) *The Politics of Large Numbers: A History of Statistical Reasoning*, Cambridge, MA: Harvard University Press.

Dewey, J. (1916) *Democracy and Education: An Introduction to the Philosophy of Education*, New York: Macmillan.

Dicken, P. (2003) *Global Shift: Reshaping the Global Economic Map in the 21st Century*, New York: Guildford Press.

Dimitriadis, G. and McCarthy, C. (2001) *Reading and Teaching the Postcolonial: From Baldwin to Basquiat and Beyond*, New York: Teachers College Press.

Dollar, D. and Kraay, A. (2005) 'Spreading the wealth', in D. Held and A. McGrew (eds) *The Global Transformations Reader: An Introduction to the Globalization Debate*, Cambridge, UK: Polity Press.

Drucker, P. F. (1999) *Management Challenges for the 21st Century*, New York: Harper-Collins.

du Gay, P. (1996) *Consumption and Identity at Work*, London: Sage.

Durkheim, E. (1972) *Selected Writings*; edited, trans. and with an introduction by Anthony Giddens, Cambridge, UK: Cambridge University Press.

Dye, T. (1992) *Understanding Public Policy*, 7th edn, Englewood Cliffs, NJ: Prentice-Hall.

Easton, D. (1953) *The Political System*, New York: Knopf.

Education Queensland (2000) *New Basics: Theory into Practice*, Brisbane, Qld: The State of Queensland.

Edwards, R. (1997) *Changing Places? Flexibility, Lifelong Learning and a Learning Society*, London: Routledge.

Elmore, R. (1979/1980) 'Backward mapping: implementation research and policy decisions', *Political Science Quarterly*, 94(4): 601–15.

Elmore, R. and McLaughlin, M. (1988) *Steady Work: Policy Practice and the Reform of American Education*, The RAND Corporation, Report for the National Institute of Education, R-3574-NIE/RC.

European Commission (2008) *Active Inclusion*. Online. Available at http://ec.europa.eu/employment_social/spsi/active_inclusion_consultation2_en.htm

Evans, N. (2003) *Making Sense of Lifelong Learning*, London: Routledge.

Fairclough, N. (1992) *Discourse and Social Change*, Cambridge, UK: Polity Press.

Fairclough, N. (2000) *New Labour, New Language*, London: Routledge.

Fairclough, N. (2001) *Language and Power*, Harlow, UK: Longman.

Fairclough, N. (2003) *Analysing Discourse: Textual Analysis for Social Research*, London; New York: Routledge.

Falk, R. (1993) 'The making of global citizens', in J. Brecher, J. B. Childs and J. Cutler (eds) *Global Visions Beyond the New World Order*, Montreal: Black Rose Books.

Faludi, S. (2007) *The Terror Dream: What 9/11 Revealed about America*, London: Atlantic Books.

Ferguson, J. (2006) *Global Shadows: Africa in the Neo-Liberal World Order*, Durham, NC: Duke University Press.

Field, J. (2003) *Social Capital*, London: Routledge.

Field, J. and Leicester, M. (eds) (2000) *Lifelong Learning: Education across the Lifespan*, London; New York: Routledge.

Fisher, J. and Mosquera, G. (2004) 'Introduction', in G. Mosquera and J. Fisher (eds) *Over Here: International Perspectives on Art and Culture*, Cambridge, MA: MIT.

Fitz, J., Davies, B. and Evans, J. (2006) *Educational Policy and Social Reproduction: Class Inscription and Symbolic Control*, London: Routledge.

Foray, D. and Lundvall, B. (1996) 'The knowledge-based economy: from the economics of knowledge to the learning economy', in OECD (ed.) *Employment and Growth in the Knowledge-Based Economy*, Paris: OECD.

Forsey, M., Davies, S. and Walford, G. (eds) (2008) *The Globalization of School Choice?*, Oxford: Symposium Books.

Foucault, M. (1977) *The Archaeology of Knowledge*, London: Tavistock.

Foucault, M. (1980) *Power/Knowledge: Selected Interviews and Other Writings, 1972–1977*; ed. Colin Gordon, trans. Colin Gordon *et al.*, New York: Pantheon Books.

Foucault, M. (1991) 'Governmentality', in G. Burchell, C. Gordon and P. Miller (eds) *The Foucault Effect: Studies in Governmentality*, Chicago: University of Chicago Press.

Fraser, N. (1997) *Justice Interruptus: Critical Reflections on the 'Post-Socialist' Condition*, New York: Routledge.

Freire, P. (1972) *Pedagogy of the Oppressed*, London: Penguin.

Friedman, M. and Friedman, R. (1990) *Free to Choose: A Personal Statement*, New York: Harvest.

Friedman, T. (1999) *The Lexus and the Olive Tree*, New York: Farrar Straus Giroux.

Fukuyama, F. (1992) *The End of History and the Last Man*, New York: Free Press.

Gale, T. (1999) 'Policy trajectories: treading the discursive path of policy analysis', *Discourse: Studies in the Cultural Politics of Education*, 20(3): 393–407.

Gale, T. (2001) 'Critical policy sociology: historiography, archaeology and genealogy as methods of policy analysis', *Journal of Education Policy*, 16(5): 379–93.

Gellner, E. (1983) *Nations and Nationalism*, Oxford: Blackwell.

Gewirtz, S. (2002) *The Managerial School: Post-Welfarism and Social Justice in Education*, London, New York: Routledge.

Gewirtz, S., Dickson, M. and Power, S. (2004) 'Unravelling a "Spun" policy: a case study of the constitutive role of "Spin" in the education policy process', *Journal of Education Policy*, 19(3): 321–42.

Gewirtz, S., Mahony, P., Hextall, I. and Cribb, A. (eds) (2009) *Changing Teacher Professionalism: International Trends, Challenges and Ways Forward*, London: Routledge.

Giddens, A. (1990) *The Consequences of Modernity*, Cambridge, UK: Polity Press.

Giddens, A. (1998) *The Third Way: The Renewal of Social Democracy*, Cambridge, UK: Polity Press.

Gil, D. (1989) *Unravelling Social Policy: Theory, Analysis, and Political Action Towards Social Inequality*, Rochester, VT: Schenkeman Books.

Gillborn, D. and Youdell, D. (2000) *Rationing Education: Policy, Practice, Reform, and Equity*, Buckingham, UK; Philadelphia, PA: Open University Press.

Gilroy, P. (2004) *After Empire Melancholia or Convivial Culture?*, London: Routledge.

Glenn, J. (2007) *Globalization: North-South Perspectives*, London: Routledge.

Gopinath, C. (2008) *Globalization: A Multidimensional System*, Thousand Oaks, CA: Sage.

Gordon, I., Lewis, J. and Young, R. (1977) 'Perspective on policy analysis', *Public Administration Bulletin*, 25: 26–35.

Green, A., Preston, J. and Janmaat, J. G. (2006) *Education, Equality and Social Cohesion: A Comparative Analysis*, Basingstoke, UK: Palgrave.

Gregory, D. (2004) *The Colonial Present*, Oxford: Blackwell.

Grek, S. (2009) 'Governing by numbers: the PISA "effect" in Europe', *Journal of Education Policy*, 24(1): 23–37.

Grek, S., Lawn, M., Lingard, B., Ozga, J., Rinne, R., Segerholm C. and Simola, H. (2009) 'National policy brokering and the construction of the European education space in England, Sweden, Finland and Scotland', *Comparative Education*, 45(1): 5–21.

Gret, M. and Sintomer, Y. (2005) *The Porto Alegre Experiment: Learning Lessons for Better Democracy*, London: Pluto Press.

Gulson, K. and Symes, C. (eds) (2007) *Spatial Theories of Education Policy and Geography Matters*, New York: Routledge.

Guruz, K. (2008) *Higher Education and International Student Mobility in the Global Knowledge Economy*, Albany, NY: State University of New York Press.

Haas, E. (1990) *When Knowledge is Power: Three Models of Change in International Organizations*, Berkeley, CA: University of California Press.

Hacking, I. (1975) *The Emergence of Probability: A Philosophical Study of Early Ideas about Probability, Induction and Statistical Inference*, Cambridge, UK: Cambridge University Press.

Hacking, I. (1990) *The Taming of Chance*, Cambridge, UK: Cambridge University Press.

Hall, S. (1996) 'New ethnicities', in D. Morley and K-H. Chen (eds) *Stuart Hall: Critical Dialogues in Cultural Studies*, London: Routledge.

Hall. S. (2000) 'Conclusion: the multi-cultural question', in B. Hesse (ed.) *Un/settled Multiculturalism*, London: Zed Books.

Hardy, I. and Lingard, B. (2008) 'Teacher professional development as an effect of policy and practice: a Bourdieuian analysis', *Journal of Education Policy*, 23(1): 63–80.

Hartley, D. (2003) 'New economy, new pedagogy', *Oxford Review of Education*, 29(1): 81–94.

Harvey, D. (1989) *The Condition of Postmodernity: An Enquiry into the Conditions of Cultural Change*, Oxford: Blackwell.

Harvey, D. (2005) *A Brief History of Neoliberalism*, Oxford: Oxford University Press.

Hatcher, R. (2000) 'Profit and power: business and education action zones', *Education Review*, 13: 71–77.

Hayes, D., Mills, M., Christie, P. and Lingard, B. (2006) *Teachers and Schooling: Making a Difference*. Sydney: Allen and Unwin.

Head, B. (2008) 'Three lenses of evidence-based policy', *Australian Journal of Public Administration*, 67(1): 1–11.

Held, D. and McGrew, A. (eds) (2000) *The Global Transformation Reader: An Introduction to the Globalization Debate*, 2nd edn, Cambridge, UK: Polity Press.

Held, D. and McGrew, A. (2002) *Globalization/Anti-globalization*, Cambridge: Polity Press.

Held, D. and McGrew, A. (eds) (2005) *The Global Transformation Reader: An Introduction to the Globalization Debate*, 3rd edn, Cambridge, UK: Polity Press.

Henry, M., Lingard, B., Rizvi, F. and Taylor, S. (2001) *The OECD, Globalization and Education Policy*, Oxford: Pergamon Press.

Hines, C. (2000) *Localization: A Global Manifesto*, London: Earthscan Publishers.

Hirst, P. H. and Peters, R. S. (1970) *The Logic of Education*, London: Routledge and Kegan Paul.

Hirst, P. Q. and Thompson, G. (1996) *Globalization in Question: The International Economy and the Possibilities of Governance*, Cambridge, UK: Polity Press.

Hogwood, B. W. and Gunn, L. A. (1984) *Policy Analysis for the Real World*, Oxford: Oxford University Press.

Holmstrom, N. and Smith, R. (2000) 'The necessity of gangster capitalism: primitive accumulation in Russia and China', *Monthly Review*, 51(9).

Honan, E. (2004) '(Im)plausibilities: a rhizo textual analysis of policy texts and teachers' work', *Educational Philosophy and Theory*, 36(3): 267–81.

Honig, M. I. (ed.) (2006) *New Directions in Education Policy Implementation: Confronting Complexity*, Albany, NY: State University of New York Press.

Hudson, J. and Lowe, S. (2004) *Understanding the Policy Process*, Bristol, UK: The Policy Press.

Hursh, D. (2008) *High-stakes Testing and the Decline of Teaching and Learning: The Real Crisis in Education*, Lanham, MD: Rowman and Littlefield Publishers.

Jayasuriya, K. (2001) 'From political to economic constitutionalism', *Constellations*, 8(4): 442–60.

Jessop, B. (1998) 'The narrative of enterprise and the enterprise of narrative: place marketing and the entrepreneurial city', in T. Hall and P. Hubbard (eds) *The Entrepreneurial City: Geographies of Politics, Regime and Representation*, Chichester, UK: John Wiley.

Jessop, B. (2002) *The Future of the Capitalist State*, Cambridge, UK: Polity Press.

Jha, J. and Kelleher, F. 'Boys' underachievement in education: an exploration in selected commonwealth countries', paper presented at Commonwealth of Learning, Triennial Conference of Commonwealth Education Ministers, Capetown, South Africa, December 2006.

Johnson, J. and Regets, M. (1998) 'International mobility of scientists and engineers to the US: brain drain or brain circulation?', *National Science Foundation Issue Brief*, 98–316.

Jones, P. W. (1998) 'Globalisation and internationalism: democratic prospects for world education', *Comparative Education*, 34(2): 143–55.

Jones, P. W. (2007) *World Bank Financing of Education: Lending, Learning and Development*, London; New York: Routledge.

Jones, P. W. and Coleman, D. (2005) *The United Nations and Education: Multilateralism, Development, and Globalisation*, London; New York: RoutledgeFalmer.

Jules, D. (2006) 'Power and educational development: small states and the labour of Sisyphus', in M. O. Afolayan, D. Jules and D. Browne (eds) *Current Discourse on Education in Developing Nations: Essays in Honor of B. Robert Tabachnick and Robert Koehl*, Hauppauge, NY: Nova Science Publishers.

Kallo, J. and Rinne, R. (eds) (2006) *Supranational Regimes and National Education Policies Encountering Challenge*, Turku, Finland: Finnish Educational Research Association.

Kaplan, R. B. and Baldauf, R. B. Jr. (2003) *Language and Language-in-Education Planning in the Pacific Basin*, Dordrecht, NL: Kluwer Academic.

Kennett, P. (ed.) (2008) *Governance, Globalization, and Public Policy*, Cheltenham, UK: Edward Elgar Press.

Kenway, J. (1990) *Gender and Education Policy: A Call for New Directions*, Geelong, Vic.: Deakin University Press.

Kenway, J., Bullen, E., Fahey, J. and Robb, S. (2006) *Haunting the Knowledge Economy*, London: Routledge.

Klees, S. (2008) 'A quarter century of neoliberal thinking in education: misleading analyses and failed policies', *Globalisation, Societies and Education*, 6(4): 311–48.

Klein, N. (2001) *No Logo: No Space, No Choice, No Jobs*, London: Flamingo.

Klein, N. (2007) *The Shock Doctrine: The Rise of Disaster Capitalism*, New York: Allen Lane.

Knight, J. (2002) 'Trade creep: implication of GATS for higher education policy', *International Higher Education*, 28.

Knoepfel, P., Larrue, C., Varone, F. and Hill, M. (2007) *Public Policy Analysis*, Bristol, UK: Policy Press.

Koh, A. (2004) 'Singapore education in "New Times": global/local imperatives', *Discourse: Studies in the Cultural Politics of Education*, 25(3): 335–49.

Koh, A. (2007) 'Deparochializing education: globalization, regionalization, and the formation of an ASEAN education space', *Discourse: Studies in the Cultural Politics of Education*, 28(2): 179–95.

Koh, A. (2008) 'Deparochialising education: re-envisioning education in ASEAN', in B. Lingard, J. Nixon and S. Ranson (eds) *Transforming Learning in Schools and Communities: The Remaking of Education for a Cosmopolitan Society*, London: Continuum.

Krasner, S. (2000) 'Compromising westphalia', in D. Held and A. McGrew (eds) *The Global Transformation Reader: An Introduction to the Globalization Debate*, 2nd edn, Cambridge, UK: Polity Press.

Kronstadt, K. A. (2004) *Education Reform in Pakistan (No. RS22009)*, Washington: Congressional Research Service, The Library of Congress. Online. Available at http://www.fas.org/man/crs/RS22009.pdf

Labaree, D. F. (2003) 'The peculiar problems of preparing educational researchers', *Educational Researcher*, 32(4): 13–22.

Ladson-Billings, G. (2004) 'Just what is critical race theory and what's it doing in a *nice* field like education? in G. Ladson-Billings and D. Gillborn (eds) *The RoutledgeFalmer Reader in Multicultural Education*, London: RoutledgeFalmer.

Ladson-Billings, G. (2006) 'From the achievement gap to the education debt: understanding achievement in U.S. schools', *Educational Researcher*, 35(7): 3–12.

Lane, J. (2000) *New Public Management*, London: Routledge.

Latour, B. (1987) *Science in Action: How to Follow Scientists and Engineers through Society*, Cambridge, MA: Harvard University Press.

Lawn, M. (2006) 'Self governance and the learning spaces of Europe', *Comparative European Politics*, 4: 272–88.

Lawn, M. and Lingard, B. (2002) 'Constructing a European policy space in educational governance: the role of transnational policy actors', *European Educational Research Journal*, 1(2): 290–307.

Lee, K. T. (2002) *Globalization and the Asia-Pacific Economy*, London: Routledge.

Legrain, P. (2002) *Open World: The Truth about Globalization*, London: Abacus.

Levitas, R. (1998) *The Inclusive Society? Social Exclusion and New Labour*, Basingstoke, UK: Macmillan.

Lingard, B. (1995) 'Gendered policy making inside the state', in B. Limerick and B. Lingard (eds) *Gender and Changing Educational Management*, Sydney: Hodder.

Lingard, B. (2000) 'It is and it isn't: vernacular globalization, educational policy and restructuring', in N. Burbules and C. A. Torres (eds) *Globalization and Education*, New York: Routledge.

Lingard, B. (2006) 'Globalisation, the research imagination and deparochialising the study of education', *Globalisation, Societies and Education*, 4(2): 287–302.

Lingard, B. (2007) 'Pedagogies of indifference', *International Journal of Inclusive Education*, 11: 245–66.

Lingard, B. (2008) 'Pedagogies of indifference: research, policy and practice', in B. Lingard, J. Nixon and S. Ranson (eds) *Transforming Learning in Schools and Communities: The Remaking of Education for a Cosmopolitan Society*, London: Continuum.

Lingard, B. (2009) 'Pedagogising teacher professional identities', in S. Gewirtz, P. Mahony, I. Hextall and A. Cribb (eds) *Changing Teacher Professionalism*, London: Routledge.

Lingard, B. and Douglas, P. (1999) *Men Engaging Feminisms: Profeminism, Backlashes and Schooling*, Buckingham, UK: Open University Press.

Lingard, B. and Rawolle, S. (2004). 'Mediatizing educational policy: the journalistic field, science policy, and cross-field effects', *Journal of Education Policy*, 19(3): 353–72.

Lingard, B. and Jn Pierre, K. D. (2006) 'Strengthening national capital: a postcolonial analysis of lifelong learning policy in St Lucia, Caribbean', *Pedagogy, Culture and Society*, 14(3): 295–314.

Lingard, B. and Mills, M. (2007) 'Pedagogies making a difference: issues of social justice and inclusion', *International Journal of Inclusive Education*, 11(3): 233–44.

Lingard, B. and Ali, S. (2009) 'Contextualising education in Pakistan – a white paper: global/ national articulations in education policy, *Globalisation, Societies and Education*, 7: 3.

Lingard, B. and Rawolle, S. (2009) 'Rescaling and reconstituting education policy: the knowledge economy and the scalar politics of global fields', in M. Simons, M. Olsen and M. Peters (eds) *Re-reading Education Policies: Studying the Policy Agenda of the Twenty-first Century*, Rotterdam: Sense Publishers.

Lingard, B., Porter, P., Bartlett, L. and Knight, J. (1995) 'Federal/state mediations in the Australian national education agenda: from the AEC to the MCEETYA 1987/1993', *Australian Journal of Education*, 39(1): 41–66.

Lingard, B., Ladwig, J., Luke, A., Mills, M., Hayes, D. and Gore, J. (2001) *School Reform Longitudinal Study: Final Report*, Volumes 1 and 2.

Lingard, B., Hayes, D. and Mills, M. (2003) 'Teachers and productive pedagogies: contextualising, conceptualising, utilising', *Pedagogy, Culture and Society*, 11(3): 397–422.

Lingard, B., Hayes, D., Mills, M. and Christie, P. (2003) *Leading Learning: Making Hope Practical in Schools*, Buckingham, UK: Open University Press.

Lingard, B., Rawolle, S. and Taylor, S. (2005) 'Globalizing policy sociology in education: working with Bourdieu', *Journal of Education Policy*, 20(6): 759–77.

Lingard, B., Mills, M. and Hayes, D. (2006) 'Enabling and aligning assessment for learning: some research and policy lessons from Queensland', *International Studies in Sociology of Education*, 16(2): 83–102.

Lingard B., Nixon, J. and Ranson, S. (2008a) 'Remaking education for a globalized world: policy and pedagogic possibilities', in B. Lingard, J. Nixon and S. Ranson (eds) *Transforming Learning in Schools and Communities: The Remaking of Education for a Cosmopolitan Society*, London: Continuum.

Lingard, B., Nixon, J. and Ranson, S. (eds) (2008b) *Transforming Learning in Schools and Communities: The Remaking of Education for a Cosmopolitan Society*, London: Continuum.

Lingard, B., Martino, W. and Mills, M. (2009) *Educating Boys: Beyond Structural Reform*, London: Palgrave.

Lipman, P. (2004) *High Stakes Education: Inequality, Globalization and Urban School Reform*, London: Routledge-Falmer.

Luke, A. (2002) 'Beyond science and ideology critique: developments in critical discourse analysis', *Annual Review of Applied Linguistics*, 22, 96–110.

Luke, A. (2003) 'After the marketplace: Evidence, social science and educational research', *The Australian Educational Researcher*, 30(2): 87–107.

Luke, A. (2006) 'Teaching after the market: from commodity to cosmopolitan', in: L. Weis, C. McCarthy and G. Dimitriades (eds) *Ideology, Curriculum, and the New Sociology of Education: Revisiting the Work of Michael Apple*, New York: Routledge.

Luke, A. and Hogan, D. (2006) 'Redesigning what counts as evidence in educational policy: the Singapore model', in J. Ozga, T. Seddon and T. Popkewitz (eds) *World Yearbook of*

Education 2006: Education Research and Policy: Steering the Knowledge-Based Economy, London: Routledge.

Lynch, J. and Mugler, F. (2004) English in the South Pacific. Online. Available at http://www.vanuatu.usp.ac.fj/paclangunit/English_South_Pacific.htm

Lynn, L. E. (2006) *Public Management: Old and New*, New York: Routledge.

Lyotard, J. (1984) *The Postmodern Condition: A Report on Knowledge*, Minneapolis: University of Minnesota Press.

MacIntyre, A. (1981) *After Virtue: A Study of Moral Theory*, London: Duckworth.

McLaughlin, M. (1987) 'Learning from experience: lessons from policy implementation', *Educational Evaluation and Policy Analysis*, 9(2): 171–78.

McLaughlin, M. K. (1988) 'Good policy: why and how to write a formal development policy', *Currents*, 14(10): 42–7.

McLaughlin, M. W. (2006) 'Implementation research in education: lessons learnt, lingering questions and new opportunities', in M. I. Hoenig (ed.) *New Directions in Education Policy Implementation: Confronting Complexity*, New York: State University of New York Press.

McNeeley, C. and Cha, Y. (1994) 'Worldwide educational convergence through international organizations: avenues for research', *Education Policy Analysis Archive*, 2(14).

McNeil, L. (2000) *Contradictions of School Reform: Educational Costs of Standardized Testing*, New York: Routledge.

Maffesoli, M. (1993) 'Introduction: the social imaginary', *Current Sociology*, 41(2): 1–7.

Maguire, M. and Ball, S. (1994) 'Researching politics and the politics of research: recent qualitative studies in the UK', *International Journal of Qualitative Studies in Education*, 7(3): 269–85.

Mahony, P. and Hextall, I. (2000) *Reconstructing Teaching: Standards, Performance and Accountability*, London: Routledge.

Mahony, P., Hextall, I. and Menter, I. (2004) 'Building dams in Jordan, assessing teachers in England: a case study in edu-business', *Globalisation, Societies and Education*, 2(2): 277–96.

Mann, M. (1997) 'Has globalization ended the rise and rise of the nation-state?', *Review of International Political Economy*, 4(3): 472–96.

Mann, M. (2000) 'Has globalisation ended the rise and rise of the nation state?', in D. Held and A. McGrew (eds) *The Global Transformation Reader*, Cambridge, UK: Polity Press.

Marfleet, P. (2005) *Refugees in a Global Era*, Basingstoke, UK: Palgrave.

Marginson, S. (2003) 'The phenomenal rise of international degrees down under', in *Change*, May–June.

Marginson, S. (2006) 'National and global competition in higher education', in H. Lauder, P. Brown, J. Dillabough and A. H. Halsey (eds) *Education, Globalization and Social Change*, Oxford: Oxford University Press.

Marginson, S. (2008) 'Global field and global imagining: Bourdieu and worldwide higher education', *British Journal of Sociology of Education*, 29(3): 303–15.

Marginson, S. and McBurnie, G. (2004) 'Cross-border post-secondary education in the Asia-Pacific region', in CERI (ed.) *Internationalization and Trade in Higher Education*, Paris: OECD.

Marsh, J. (2007) 'New literacies and old pedagogies: recontextualising rules and practices', *International Journal of Inclusive Education*, 11(3): 267–81.

Martens, K., Balzer, C., Sackmann, R. and Weymann, A. (2004) *Comparing Governance of International Organizations: the EU, the OECD and Educational Policy*, Bremen: Universität Bremen.

Massey, D. (1994) *Space, Place and Gender*, Cambridge, UK: Polity Press.

Massey, D. (2005) *For Space*, London, Thousand Oaks, CA: Sage.

Meyer, J-P. and Brown, M. (2003) 'Scientific diasporas: a new approach to the brain drain', *Management of Social Transformations, Discussion Paper 41*. Online. Available at http://www.unesco.org/most/meyer.htm

Miyagiwa, K. (1991) 'Scale economics in education and the brain drain problem', *International Economic Review*, 32(3): 743–59.

Mok, K. and Tan, J. (2004) *Globalization and Marketizaiton in Education: A Comparative Analysis of Hong Kong and Singapore*, Cheltenham, UK: Edward Elgar Press.

Mountford, A. (1997) 'Can a brain drain be good for growth in the source economy?', *Journal of Developmental Economics*, 53: 287–303.

Mulderrig, J. (2008) 'Using Keywords Analysis in CDA: evolving discourses of the knowledge economy in education', in B. Jessop, N. Fairclough and R. Wodak (eds) *Education and the Knowledge-Based Economy in Europe*, Rotterdam: Sense Publishers.

Mundy, K. (2007) 'Global governance, educational change', *Comparative Education,* 43(3): 339–57.

National Commission on Excellence in Education (1983) *A Nation at Risk: The Imperative for Educational Reform*, Washington, DC: National Commission on Excellence in Education.

Negroponte, N. (1996) *Being Digital*, New York: Vintage Books.

Newmann, F. M. and Associates (1996) *Authentic Achievement: Restructuring Schools for Intellectual Quality*, San Francisco: Jossey-Bass.

Noddings, N. (1995), 'Response to Suppes', in A. Nelman (ed.) *Philosophy of Education 1995*, Urbana, IL: Philosophy of Education Society, University of Illinois at Urbana-Champaign.

Norman, E. (2003) *Making Sense of Lifelong Learning*, London: Routledge.

Norris, P. (2001) *Digital Divide: Civic Engagement, Information Poverty, and the Internet Worldwide*, Cambridge, UK: Cambridge University Press.

Nóvoa, A. and Lawn, M. (2002) 'Introduction: fabricating Europe: the formation of an education space', in A. Nóvoa and M. Lawn (eds) *Fabricating Europe: The Formation of an Education Space*, New York: Springer.

Nóvoa, A. and Yariv-Mashal, T. (2003) 'Comparative research in education: a mode of governance or a historical journey?', *Comparative Education*, 39(4): 423–38.

Nozick, R. (1974) *Anarchy, State and Utopia*, Oxford: Blackwell.

Nunan, D. (2003) 'The impact of English as a global language on educational policies and practices in the Asia-Pacific region', *TESOL Quarterly,* 37(4): 589–613.

Oakman, D. (2005) *Facing Asia: A History of the Colombo Plan*, Canberra: ANU Press.

OECD (1985) *Education and Training after Basic Schooling*, Paris: OECD.

OECD (1995) *Governance in Transition: Public Management Reforms in OECD Countries*, Paris: OECD.

OECD (1996) *The Knowledge Economy*, Paris: OECD.

OECD (1997) *Education at a Glance: OECD Indicators*, Paris: OECD.

OECD (1998) *Annual Report 1997*, Paris: OECD.

OECD (1999) *Measuring Student Knowledge and Skills – A New Framework for Assessment*, Paris: OECD.

OECD (2002) *International Mobility of the Highly Skilled*, Paris: OECD.

Offe, C. (1975) 'The theory of the Capitalist state and the problem of policy formation', in L. N. Lindberg *et al.* (eds) *Stress and Contradiction in Modern Capitalism*, Lexington, KY: D. C. Heath.

Ohmae, K. (1990) *The Borderless World*, London: Collins.

Olson, C., Green, M. and Hill, B. (2006), *A Handbook for Advancing Comprehensive Internationalization: What Institutions Can Do and What Students Should Learn*, Washington, DC: American Council on Education.

Olssen, M., Codd, J. and O'Neill, A. (2004) *Education Policy Globalization, Citizenship and Democracy*, London: Sage.

Open Doors (2007) Online. Available at http://www.opendoorsusa.org

Oxfam (2008) Gender Justice, London: Oxfam, retrieved from http://www.oxfam.org/en/about/issues/gender

Ozga, J. (1987) 'Studying education policy through the lives of policy makers', in S. Walker and L. Barton (eds) *Changing Policies, Changing Teachers: New Directions for Schooling?*, Philadelphia, PA: Open University Press.

Ozga, J. (2000) *Policy Research in Educational Settings: Contested Terrain*, Buckingham, UK: Open University Press.

Ozga, J. and Lingard, B. (2007) 'Globalisation, education policy and politics', in B. Lingard and J. Ozga (eds) *The RoutledgeFalmer Reader in Education Policy and Politics*, London: Routledge.

Ozga, J., Seddon, T. and Popkewitz, T. S. (eds.) (2006) *World Yearbook of Education 2006: Education Research and Policy: Steering the Knowledge-Based Economy*, New York: Routledge.

Paige, R. M. (2003) 'The American case: the University of Minnesota', *Journal of Studies in International Education*, 7(1): 52–63.

Papadopoulos, G. S. (1994) *Education 1960–1990: The OECD Perspective*, Paris: OECD.

Papastergiadis, N. (2000) *The Turbulence of Migration: Globalization, Deterritorialization and Hybridity*, Cambridge, UK: Polity Press.

Parekh, B. (2008) *A New Politics of Identity: Political Principles for an Interdependent World*, London: Palgrave.

Pathak, A. (2006) *Modernity, Globalization and Identity: Towards A Reflexive Quest*, New Delhi: Aakarbooks.

Paul, D. (2005) *Rescaling International Political Economy: Subnational States and the Regulation of the Global Political Economy*, London: Routledge.

Paul, J. (2002) 'University and the knowledge-based economy', in J. Enders and O. Fulton (eds) *Higher Education in a Globalizing World*, Dordrecht, NL: Kluwer Academic Publishers.

Pawson, R. (2006) *Evidence Based Policy: A Realist Perspective*, London: Sage.

Peck, J. and Tickle, A. (2002) 'Neoliberalizing space', *Antipode*, 34(3): 380–404.

Pennycook, A. (2001) *Critical Applied Linguistics: A Critical Introduction*, New York: Lawrence Erlbaum.

Perron, D. (2004) *Globalization and Social Change*, London: Routledge.

Peters, G. and Pierre, J. (2006) *Handbook of Public Policy*, London: Sage.

Peters, M. (2001) 'Education, enterprise culture and the entrepreneurial self: a Foucauldian perspective', *Journal of Educational Enquiry*, 2(2): 58–71.

Peters, M. (2002) 'Education policy research and the global knowledge economy', *Educational Philosophy and Theory*, 34(1): 91–102.

Peters, M. (ed.) (2005) *Education, Globalization and the State in an Age of Terrorism*, Boulder, CO: Paradigm Publishers.

Peters, M. A. and Besley, A. C. (2006) *Building Knowledge Cultures: Education and Development in the Age of Knowledge Capitalism*, New York: Rowman and Littlefield.

Peters, M. and Britez, R. (eds) (2008) *Open Education and Education for Openness*, Rotterdam: Sense Publishers.

Phillips, D. and Ochs, K. (2004) *Educational Policy Borrowing: Historical Perspectives*, Oxford: Symposium Books.

Pieterse, J. N. (2004) *Globalization or Empire?*, London: Routledge.

Pieterse, J. N. (2005) *Globalization and Culture*, New York: Rowman and Littlefield.

Pieterse, J. N. (2007) *Ethnicities and Global Multiculture: Pants for an Octopus*, New York: Rowman and Littlefield.

Popper, K. (1949) *The Open Society and Its Enemies*, London: Routledge and Kegan Paul.

Porter, T. (1995) *Trust in Numbers: The Pursuit of Objectivity in Science and Public Life*, Princeton, NJ: Princeton University Press.

Power, M. (1997) *The Audit Society: Rituals of Verification*, Oxford: Oxford University Press.

Ranson, S. (2003) 'Public accountability in the age of neo-liberal governance', *Journal of Education Policy*, 18(5): 459–80.

Rawls, J. (1972) *A Theory of Justice*, Oxford: Clarendon.

Rawolle, S. (2005) 'Cross-field effects and temporary social fields: a case study of the mediatization of recent Australian knowledge economy policies', *Journal of Education Policy*, 20(6): 705–24.

Rawolle, S. and Lingard, B. (2008) 'The sociology of Pierre Bourdieu and researching education policy', *Journal of Education Policy*, 23(6): 729–41.

Ray, L. (2007) *Globalization and Everyday Life*, London: Routledge.

Rein, M. (1983) *From Policy to Practice*, London: Macmillan.

Rhodes, R. A. W. (1994) 'The hollowing-out of the state: the changing nature of the public services in Britain', *Political Quarterly*, 65(2): 138–51.

Rhodes, R. A. W. (1995) 'The state of public administration: a professional history of the 1980s', *Public Administration*, 73: 1–15.

Rhodes, R. A. W. (1997) *Understanding Governance*, Buckingham, UK: Open University Press.

Rikowski, G. (1998) 'Only charybdis: the learning society through idealism', in S. Ranson (ed.) *Inside the Learning Society*, London and New York: Cassell.

Ritzer, G. (2004) *The McDonaldization of Society: An Investigation into the Changing Character of Contemporary Society*, Newbury Park, CA: Pine Forge Press.

Rizvi, F. (1985) *Multiculturalism as an Educational Policy*, Geelong, Vic.: Deakin University Press.

Rizvi, F. (2000) 'International education and the production of global imagination', in N. Burbules and C. A. Torres (eds) *Globalization and Education: Critical Perspectives*, New York: Routledge.

Rizvi, F. (2004) 'Debating globalization and education after September 11', *Comparative Education*, 40(2): 157–71.

Rizvi, F. (2007) 'Postcolonialism and globalization in education', *Cultural Studies, Critical Methodologies*, 7(3): 256–63.

Rizvi, F. (2008) 'Education and its cosmopolitan possibilities', in B. Lingard, J. Nixon and S. Ranson (eds) *Transforming Learning in Schools and Communities: The Remaking of Education for a Cosmopolitan Society*, London: Continuum.

Rizvi, F. and Kemmis, S. (1987) *Dilemmas of Reform – An Overview of Issues and Achievements of the Participation and Equity Program in Victorian Schools 1984–1986*, Geelong, Vic.: Deakin University Press.

Rizvi, F. and Lingard, B. (2006) 'Globalization and the changing nature of the OECD's educational work', in H. Lauder, P. Brown, J. Dillabough and A. H. Halsey (eds) *Education, Globalization and Social Change*, Oxford: Oxford University Press.

Rizvi, F. and Lingard, B. (2009) 'The OECD and global shifts in education policy', in R. Cowen and A. Kazamias (eds) *International Handbook of Comparative Education*, Dordrecht, NL: Springer.

Robertson, R. (1992) *Globalization: Social Theory and Global Culture*, London: Sage.

Robertson, S., Bonal, X. and Dale, R. (2006a) 'GATS and the education service industry: the politics of scale and global reterritorialization', in H. Lauder, P. Brown, J. Dillabough and A. H. Halsey (eds) *Education, Globalization and Social Change*, Oxford: Oxford University Press.

Robertson, S., Bonal, X. and Dale, R. (eds) (2006b) *WTO/GATS and the Education Service Industry: Global Strategy – Local Responses*, London: Routledge.

Robertson, S., Novelli, M., Dale, R., Tikly, L., Dachi, H. and Altphonce, N. (2007) *Globalisation, Education and Development: Ideas, Actors and Dynamics*, London: DfID.

Robinson, W. I. and Harris, J. (2000) 'Towards a global ruling class? Globalization and the transnational capitalist class', *Science and Society*, 64(1): 11–54.

Rose, N. (1999) *Powers of Freedom Reframing Political Thought*, Cambridge, UK: Cambridge University Press.

Rosenau, J. N. (1997) *Along the Domestic-Foreign Frontier: Exploring Governance in a Turbulent World*, Cambridge, UK: Cambridge University Press.

Rosenau, J. N. (2005) 'Globalization and governance: bleak prospects for sustainability', in A. Pfaller and M. Lerch (eds) *Challenges for Globalization*, Piscataway, NJ: Transaction.

Rosenau, J. N. and Czempiel, E. O. (1992) *Governance without Government: Order and Change in World Politics*, Cambridge, UK: Cambridge University Press.

Rudd, K. (2009) 'The global financial crisis', *The Monthly*, February, 20–29.

Rutkowski, D. (2007) 'Converging us softly: how intergovernmental organizations promote neoliberal education policy', *Critical Studies in Education*, 48(2): 229–47.

Sachs, J. (2005) *The End of Poverty: Economic Possibilities of Our Time*, New York: Penguin.

Said, E. (1983) *The World, the Text and the Critic*, Cambridge, MA: Harvard University Press.

Saltman, K. (2007) *Capitalizing on Disaster: Taking and Breaking of Public Schools*, Boulder, CO: Paradigm Publishers.

Sassen, S. (1991) *The Global City*, Princeton, NJ: Princeton University Press.

Sassen, S. (1998) *Globalization and Its Discontents: Essays in the New Mobility of People and Money*, New York: The New Press.

Schirato, A. and Webb, J. (2003) *Understanding Globalization*, London: Sage.

Scholte, J. A. (2000) *Globalization: A Critical View*, London: St Martin's Press.

Schriewer, J. and Martinez, C. (2004) 'Constructions of internationality in education', in G. Steiner-Khamsi (ed.) *Lessons from Elsewhere: The Politics of Educational Borrowing and Lending*, New York: Teachers College Press.

Scott, J. C. (1998) *Seeing like a State: How Certain Schemes to Improve the Human Condition Have Failed*, New Haven, CT: Yale University Press.

Scottish Executive Education Department (2007) *OECD Review of the Quality and Equity of Education Outcomes in Scotland*, Edinburgh: Scottish Government.

Seddon, T. (1994) *Context and Beyond: Reframing the Theory and Practice of Education*, London: The Falmer Press.

Sen, A. (1999) *Development as Freedom*, Oxford: Oxford University Press.

Sennett, R. (2004) *Respect: The Formation of Character in an Age of Inequality*, London: Penguin.

Shohat, E. and Stam, R. (1994) *Unthinking Eurocentrism: Multiculturalism and the Media*, London: Routledge.

Shuman, M. (1998) *Going Local: Creating Self-Reliant Communities in a Global Age*, New York: Free Press.

Sidhu, R. (2005) *Universities and Globalization: To Market to Market*, Mahwah, NJ: Lawrence Erlbaum.

Simola, H. (2005) 'The Finnish Miracle of PISA: historical and sociological remarks on teaching and teacher education', *Comparative Education*, 41(4), 455–70.

Simons, M., Olsen, M. and Peters, M. (eds) (2009) *Re-reading Education Policies: Studying the Policy Agenda of the Twenty-first Century*, Rotterdam: Sense Publishers.

Singer, P. (2002) *One World: The Ethics of Globalization*, Melbourne: Text Publishing.

Sleeter, C. (2005) *Un-standardizing Curriculum: Multicultural Teaching in the Standards-based Classroom*, New York: Teachers College Press.

Smith, L. Tuhiwai (1999) *Decolonizing Methodologies: Research and Indigenous Peoples*, New York: Zed Books.

Smith, M. P. (2000) *Transnational Urbanism: Locating Globalization*, Oxford, Blackwell Publishers.

Snyder, I. (2008) *The Literacy Wars: Why Teaching Children to Read and Write is a Battleground in Australia*, Sydney: Allen and Unwin.

Soros, G. (1998) *The Crisis of Global Capitalism*, Boston: Little, Brown.

Soros, G. (2008) *The New Paradigm for Financial Markets: The Credit Crisis of 2008 and What It Means*, New York: Public Affairs Books.

Spring, J. (1998) *Education and the Rise of the Global Economy*, Mahwah, NJ: Lawrence Erlbaum Associates.

Steger, M. (2003) *Globalization: A Very Short Introduction*, Oxford: Oxford University Press.

Steger, M. (2008) *The Rise of the Global Imaginary: Political Ideologies from the French Revolution to the Global War on Terror*, Oxford: Oxford University Press.

Steiner-Khamsi, G. (ed.) (2004) *The Global Politics of Educational Borrowing and Lending*, New York: Teachers College Press.

Stiglitz, J. E. (2002) *Globalization and Its Discontent*, New York: Norton.

Stiglitz, J. E. (2007) *Making Globalization Work*, New York: W. W. Norton.

Stone, D. (2001) *Policy Paradox: The Art of Political Decision-making*, New York: Norton.

Strange, S. (1996) *The Retreat of the State: The Diffusion of Power in the World Economy*, Cambridge, UK: Cambridge University Press.

Suppes, P. (1995) 'The aims of education', in A. Nelman (ed.) *Philosophy of Education 1995*, Urbana, IL: Philosophy of Education Society, University of Illinois at Urbana-Champaign.

Taylor, C. (2004) *Modern Social Imaginaries*, Durham, NC: Duke University Press.

Taylor, J. E. 'International migration and economic development', paper presented at the International Symposium on International Migration, Turin, Italy, June 2006.

Taylor, S. (2004) 'Researching educational policy and change in "New Times": using Critical Discourse Analysis', *Journal of Education Policy*, 19(4): 433–51.

Taylor, S., Rizvi, F., Lingard, B. and Henry, M. (1997) *Educational Policy and the Politics of Change*, London: Routledge.

Teferra, D. 'Brain circulation: unparalleled opportunities, underlying challenges and outmoded opportunities', paper presented at Symposium on International Labour and Academic Mobility, World Education Services, Toronto, October 2004.

Therborn, G. (2007) 'After dialectics: radical social theory in a Post-Communist world', *New Left Review*, 43: 63–114.

Thomson. P. 'Towards a just future: schools working in partnership with neighborhoods made poor', paper presented at UNESCO conference on Reforming Learning, Bangkok, Thailand, December 1999.

Thomson, P. (2006) 'Policy scholarship against depoliticisation', in J. Ozga, T. Seddon and T. Popkewitz (eds) *World Yearbook of Education 2006: Education Research and Policy: Steering the Knowledge-Based Economy*, London: Routledge.

Thrift, N. (2005) *Knowing Capitalism*, London: Sage.

Tikly, L. (2001) 'Globalisation and education in the Post-colonial world: towards a conceptual framework', *Comparative Education*, 37(2): 151–71.

Tollefson, J. W. (1991) *Planning Language, Planning Inequality: Language Policy in the Community*, New York: Longman.

Tomlinson, J. (2000) *Globalization and Culture*, Chicago: Chicago University Press.

Touraine, A. (2000) *Can We Live Together? Equality and Difference*; trans. David Macey, Cambridge, UK: Polity Press.

Tozer, S., Violas, P. and Senese, G. (2002) *School and Society: Historical and Contemporary Perspectives*, 4th edn, Boston, MA: McGraw Hill.

Trifonas, P. P. (2003) 'Introduction: pedagogies of difference: locating otherness', in P. P. Trifonas (ed.) *Pedagogies of Difference: Rethinking Education for Social Change*, New York: Routledge.

Trowler, P. (2003) *Education Policy*, 2nd edn, London: Routledge.

UNDP (1999) *United Nations Development Program 1999 Report: Globalization with a Human Face*, Oxford: Oxford University Press.

UNESCO (2002) *Building the Capacities of Curriculum Specialists for Educational Reform: Final Report of the Regional Seminar*, Vientiane, Laos PDR, 9–13 September 2002.

UNESCO (2006) *Towards Knowledge Societies – First UNESCO World Report*, Paris: UNESCO.

United Nations Statistical Division (2004) 'Statistics and indicators on women and men'. Online. Available at http://unstats.un.org/unsd/demographic/products/indwm/wwpub2000overview.htm

Unterhalter, E. (2007) *Gender, Schooling and Global Social Justice*, London: Routledge.

Urry, J. (2000) *Sociology Beyond Societies: Mobilities for the Twenty-first Century*, London: Routledge.

Urry, J. (2002) 'Mobility and proximity', *Sociology*, 36(2): 255–74.

van Dijk, J. (2005) *The Deepening Divide: Inequality in the Information Society*, Thousand Oaks, CA: Sage.

Vidovich, L. 'A conceptual framework for analysis of education policy and practice', paper presented at the Australian Association for Research in Education Conference, Notre Dame University, Perth, WA, 2001.

Wagner, P. (2007) 'Public policy, social sciences and the state: an historical perspective', in F. Fischer, G. J. Miller and M. S. Sidney (eds) *Handbook of Public Policy Analysis: Theory, Politics, and Methods*, Boca Raton, FL: CRC Press.

Walker, M. (2006) 'Towards a capability-based theory of social justice for education policy making', *Journal of Education Policy*, 21(2): 163–85.

Wallerstein, I. (1974) *The Modern World System: Capitalist Agriculture and the Origins of the European World Economy in the Sixteenth Century*, New York: Academic Press.

Wallerstein, I. (1978) 'World-system analysis: theoretical and interpretive issues', in B. H. Kaplan (ed.) *Social Change in the Capitalist World Economy*, Beverly Hills, CA: Sage.

Walzer, M. (1983) *Spheres of Justice*, Oxford: Blackwell.

Warschauer, M. (2003) *Technology and Social Inclusion: Rethinking the Digital Divide*, Cambridge, MA: MIT Press.

Waters, M. (1995) *Globalization*, London: Routledge.

Weaver-Hightower, M. (2008) 'An ecology metaphor for educational policy analysis: a call to complexity', *Educational Researcher*, 37(3): 153–67.

Weber, M. (1948) *From Max Weber: Essays in Sociology*; trans., edited and with an introduction by Hans H. Gerth and C. Wright Mills, London: Routledge and Kegan Paul.

Weber, M. (1991) *From Max Weber: Essays in Sociology*, London: Routledge.

Wedel, J. R., Shore, C., Feldman, G. and Lathrop, S. (2005) 'Towards an anthropology of public policy', *The Annals of the American Academy of Political and Social Science*, 600: 30–51.

Wei, S-J. and Wu, Y. (2002) *Globalization and Inequality without Differences in Data Definition, Legal System and Other Institutions*, Working paper, Washington, DC: Brookings Institution.

Weimer, D. L. and Vining, A. R. (2004) *Policy Analysis: Concepts and Practice*, 4th edn, Englewood Cliffs, NJ: Prentice Hall.

Weiss, C. (1979) 'The many meanings of research utilization', *Public Administration Review*, 39(5), 426–31.

Whitehead, A. N. (1929; 1985 paperback) *The Aims of Education and Other Essays*, New York: Free Press.

Whitty, G. (2006) 'Education(al) research and education policy making: is conflict inevitable?', *British Educational Research Journal*, 32(2): 159–76.

Whitty, G., Power, S. and Halpin, D. (1998) *Devolution and Choice in Education: The School, the State and the Market*, Melbourne: ACER Press.

Williams, R. (1977) *Marxism and Literature*, London: Penguin.

Williams, R. (1983) *Towards 2000*, Harmondsworth, UK: Penguin.

Williams, R. (1989) *Resources of Hope*, London: Verso.

Williamson, J. (1990) 'What Washington means by policy reform', in J. Williamson (ed.) *Latin American Adjustment: How Much Has Happened?*, Washington DC: Institute for International Economics.

Williamson, J. (2000) 'What should the World Bank think about the Washington Consensus?', *The World Bank Research Observer*, 15(2): 251–64.

Wolfe, M. (2005) 'Are global poverty and inequality getting worse?', in D. Held and A. McGrew (eds) *The Global Transformation Reader: An Introduction to the Globalization Debate*, 3rd edn, Cambridge, UK: Polity Press.

Wong, K. and Yip, C. K. (1999) 'Education, economic growth, and brain drain', *Journal of Economic Dynamics and Control*, 23(5–6): 699–726.

Wood, E. M. (2003) *Empire of Capital*, London: Verso.

World Bank (2002) *Constructing Knowledge Societies: New Challenges for Tertiary Education*, Washington, DC: World Bank Group.

World Development Report (2009) Washington, DC: World Bank, retrieved from http://siteresources.worldbank.org/INTWDR2009/Resources/Outline.pdf

Yang, R. (2006) 'Education policy research in the People's Republic of China', in J. Ozga, T. Seddon and T. Popkewitz (eds) *World Yearbook of Education 2006: Education Research and Policy: Steering the Knowledge-Based Economy*, London: Routledge.

Yeatman, A. (1990) *Bureaucrats, Technocrats, Femocrats: Essays on the Contemporary Australian State*, Sydney: Allen and Unwin.

Yeatman, A. (ed.) (1998a) *Activism and the Policy Process*, Sydney: Allen and Unwin.

Yeatman, A. (1998b) 'Trends and opportunities in the public sector: a critical assessment', *Australian Journal of Public Administration*, 57(4): 138–47.

Yeaxlee, B. (1929) *Lifelong Learning*, London: Cassell.

Young, I. M. (1990) *Justice and the Politics of Difference*, Princeton, NJ: Princeton University Press.

Young, M. (1996) *The Curriculum of the Future – From the 'New Sociology of Education' to a Critical Theory of Learning*, London: Falmer.

Young, R. C. (2003) *Postcolonialism: A Very Short Introduction*, Oxford: Oxford University Press.

Index